AN'

OF THE

NEW ENGLAND INDIANS

WITH NOTES
ON THE ANCIENT CULTURES OF THE
ADJACENT TERRITORY

BY

CHARLES C. WILLOUGHBY
DIRECTOR EMERITUS OF THE PEABODY MUSEUM

FULLY ILLUSTRATED

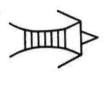

CAMBRIDGE, MASSACHUSETTS, U.S.A.
PUBLISHED BY THE PEABODY MUSEUM OF
AMERICAN ARCHAEOLOGY AND ETHNOLOGY
HARVARD UNIVERSITY
1935

THE COSMOS PRESS, CAMBRIDGE, MASS.

CONTENTS

DEDICATORY

THIS book is gratefully dedicated to the Council of the Peabody Museum of Harvard University and other friends, whose interest has made its publication possible and whose helpful encouragement and assistance have added much to its value.

CHARLES C. WILLOUGHBY

ACKNOWLEDGMENTS

I N the preparation of this volume cordial coöperation has been shown by many museums and individuals and grateful acknowledgment is hereby extended to them. Without their aid it would have been possible to present but a small portion of the material brought together in these pages. The author is under special obligations to the officers of the following institutions: U. S. National Museum, Washington; American Museum of Natural History, N. Y.; Museum of the American Indian, Heye Foundation, N.Y .; Peabody Museum, Cambridge; Peabody Museum, Salem; Peabody Museum, New Haven; Andover Archaeological Museum, Phillips Academy; Amherst College Museum; King Philip Museum, Bristol, R. I.; Slater Museum, Norwich, Conn.; Connecticut Historical Society, Hartford; Rhode Island Historical Society, Providence; Maine Historical Society, Portland; Mattatuck Historical Society, Waterbury, Conn.; Worcester Historical Society; Old Dartmouth Historical Society, New Bedford; Manchester, N. H., Historical Society; Kennebec Historical Society, Augusta, Me.; Framingham Historical Society; Society for the Preservation of New England Antiquities, Boston; Memorial Hall, Deerfield; Pilgrim Hall, Plymouth; Springfield Natural History Society; Holyoke Natural History Society. Among the owners of private collections who have placed their material at his disposal special thanks are due to Mr. Norris L. Bull of Hartford whose Connecticut collection is unsurpassed; also to Dr. E. E. Tyzzer of Wakefield, Mr. C. C. Ferguson of Millbury, Mrs. Adams Tolman of Concord, Mass., and Mr. W. J. Howes of Holyoke. In the text are mentioned other individuals who have loaned specimens or assisted in various ways.

ANTIQUITIES
OF THE NEW ENGLAND INDIANS

INTRODUCTION

INTEREST in the native people of our country has shown a commendable increase during the last few decades and many volumes upon the subject have appeared which are accessible to the general public. These deal largely, however, with Indians of the central and western portions of the United States. People in general have a very meager knowledge of the tribes encountered by the colonists in those portions of the country first settled by the English, of which New England forms an important part. This is largely owing to the fact that most of these groups were dispersed or nearly exterminated during the early Indian wars, and the Christianized descendants of those who survived soon lost most of the remnants of the native culture which they inherited.

The colonists naturally looked upon the Indian as an enemy, and a menace to the peace and welfare of their newly established homes. He was to be exterminated when necessary, and tolerated only when he became Christianized and had lost in a great measure those inherent qualities which at a later day rendered the western tribes of great interest, expecially to students of primitive man.

There were, however, among the early voyagers to these shores, and among the missionaries and colonists of the first half of the seventeenth century, a few writers who left invaluable though fragmentary accounts of their observations on the social organization, family life, agriculture, hunting, fishing, and other customs of our historic New England tribes. From these many fragments, and later comparative studies, one is able to gain a very comprehensive knowledge of the life and habits of this people at the period of their first contact with Europeans. Many extracts from these sources appear in the following pages.

1

The primitive culture encountered by the early colonists had existed in New England for a considerable period. It seems to have been a modified continuance of a somewhat higher culture which developed south of the Great Lakes, and which entered New England before the advent of the Iroquoian migration which nearly isolated the eastern Algonquians from their western kindred. Before the projection of this Iroquoian wedge into the regions bordering Lakes Erie and Ontario and the St. Lawrence River (see figure 3), the eastern outposts of the outer fringe of that group of people whose higher culture we have mentioned, and whose mound building activities centered in Ohio, entered and occupied a large portion of New England. There seems to be little doubt that they belonged to the great Algonquian stock and I have designated their artifacts old Algonquian.

During the eastern expansion of this western group they seem to have gradually driven the older inhabitants of this section before them. There is some evidence of an interchange of certain phases of the cultures of these two groups during the long period of contact previous to the final expulsion of the earlier group from the region south of the St. Lawrence.

The archaeological remains of these principal groups are scattered throughout New England and the adjacent territory. Many burial places have been discovered and the graves opened for the objects they contained. Thousands of stone implements have been unearthed while cultivating land. Old village sites have been located especially near the more important falls and other fishing places, and on fertile intervales. The implements have found their way into private collections, and into the cabinets of local historical societies. Many excellent collections are in our museums.

It is only during the last few years that systematic research has been undertaken into the archaeology of this region by our larger museums and scientific institutions, and by a few individuals of means.

A brief summary of the results of the present writer's studies relating to the successive occupations of New England and adjacent regions by primitive native groups may be useful to the reader preparatory to the perusal of the succeeding pages.

The earliest group to occupy New England of which we have knowledge was apparently composed of a boreal people unacquainted with agriculture. Their southern distribution, worked out

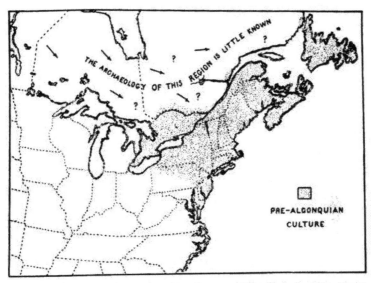

Figure 1. Map showing the pre-Algonquian culture area of New England and the adjacent territory.

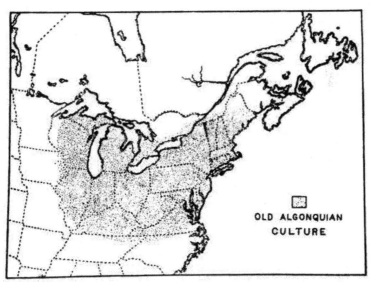

Figure 2. Map showing the old Algonquian culture area of New England and the adjacent territory.

from the occurrence of their stone implements, is shown in figure 1. Their northern habitat cannot be definitely outlined owing to the lack of data from this sparsely settled region, the archaeology of which is little known. Certain phases of their culture, however, may be noted among the Eskimo, and the now extinct Beothuk of Newfoundland. Several hundred graves have been opened in

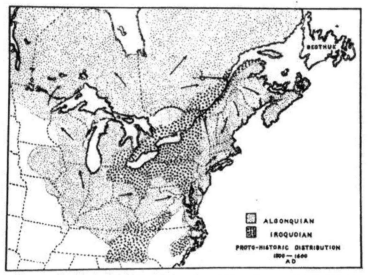

Figure 3. Map showing distribution of Algonquian and Iroquoian groups in New England and the adjacent regions in proto-historic times (1500-1600 A.D.).

New England by the Peabody Museum of Cambridge, and by the Department of Archaeology of Phillips Academy at Andover. They are so old that in nearly every instance the skeleton had completely disintegrated. Only a few small fragments were found in two or three graves. The occupation of New England by this early people must have been an extended one and their entrance into these states very remote.

The second group to enter New England probably came from the west. As we have already noted they seem to have been the outlying tribes of the mound-building people who centered in Ohio but who built no mounds nor stone lined graves east of central New York. They were agriculturists. The general distribution of this group is shown in figure 2. Their graves and artifacts are found throughout New England but more commonly in the western and southern portions. Several burial places have been opened and numerous isolated graves discovered. The artifacts are of a type found throughout the greater part of the northern mound-building area.

In many of the New England graves of this group the skeletons have also disappeared through disintegration but sometimes fragmentary bones are found. Few complete skeletons have been reported.

The third culture group to occupy New England was probably an outgrowth of the second. The material culture of these later Indians underwent a marked modification during the period of their virtual separation by the Iroquois from their western kindred. (See figure 3.) Contact with the Iroquois seems to have been in a measure responsible for this, and in later times intercourse with the many European fishing and trading vessels throughout the greater part of the sixteenth century was a strong factor in the deterioration of certain of their native arts. Nearly all of the skeletal material in our museums from this region belongs to this later group.

The above classification is a broad one and does not take into consideration the many minor local differences familiar to students of our native people. The more important local differences, however, will be noted later in the more detailed accounts of these groups.

THE PRE-ALGONQUIAN GROUP

THE period of time which has elapsed since the region now known as New England first became the dwelling place of man can only be surmised. So far as we can judge by the artifacts which have come down to us, the first inhabitants of this section had already attained a high proficiency in those handicrafts which contribute so materially to the well-being of such tribes as subsist mainly by hunting and fishing.

There is apparently no evidence of a paleolithic people in this section. During the last quarter of the nineteenth century many so-called paleolithic implements were brought to light, but these proved to be unfinished blades or rejects from quarry sites or workshops, such as were produced by all of our tribes down to proto-historic times. Artifacts of stone and other material together with rejects, unfinished implements, and flakes from camp sites may readily be washed from the shores of rivers and redeposited with gravel during spring freshets or floods caused by ice jams or heavy rains. We may expect occasionally to find such objects in the gravel of our eroded river banks, but such finds do not necessarily denote a very remote origin of the objects found.

The weathering of some of the stone implements which have lain for centuries upon the surface of the ground often denotes great age, but no criteria are at hand to enable us to judge even approximately the number of years required to produce such weathering.

The one outstanding discovery bearing upon the antiquity of man in New England was the unearthing of the remains of an ancient Indian fish-weir many feet below the surface while excavating for the Boylston Street subway in Boston in 1913.

As the excavation reached a point a short distance east of the junction of Clarendon and Boylston streets, the workmen discovered a number of decayed pieces of wood at a depth of about thirty feet from the street surface. The attention of the engineers was called to these finds, and as work progressed other pieces were unearthed. They seemed to be portions of stakes, two to three inches in diameter, which had been placed upright at intervals in a line running nearly east and west and which had probably formed parts of an ancient fish-weir. It is probable that only the larger stakes used in the construction of the weir retained their

6

form sufficiently well to be recognized by the workmen. One of the stakes, being unusually well preserved, was very carefully uncovered. The silt which buried its upper portion being removed, a layer of very stiff blue clay was encountered, into which the lower part of the stake had been driven. Thinking that these finds might be the remains of an old Indian weir, the engineer notified the present writer, who, in company with Mr. S. J. Guernsey, carefully examined the ground, removed the stake from its position in the blue clay and transferred it to the Peabody Museum at Cambridge for preservation.

Its lower portion was found to have been driven into the clay stratum to a depth of eighteen inches. The average diameter of the stake was about two and one half inches and the length of the part recovered was forty-six inches. Originally the upper portion was probably longer, for the top seems to have been broken off during the removal of the earth above.

The specimen is illustrated in figure 4. Its lower end had been sharpened, presumably with a stone adze, the marks of which are plainly shown in the largest photograph. Three feet from its lower end the horizontal wattling began, the alternate depressions, caused by the interlaced withes, being clearly defined. Fragments of two of these withes, which were in contact with the stake at this point, were sufficiently well preserved to be removed without injury. The smaller is about three eighths of an inch in diameter and eight inches long; the other is about five eighths of an inch in diameter and thirteen inches long.

Wooden objects that have been submerged in mud or water for a long period become very soft and spongy, which accounts for the distortion of the upper portion of the specimen and for the clear definition of the alternate indentations caused by the pressure of the interlaced withes. It is not improbable that the missing part of the stake, if available, would also show similar marks.

While these specimens have considerable archæological value in themselves, their greatest interest lies in the depth at which they were found. Their position is shown in the diagram, the measurements of which were made and recorded by the engineers in charge of the subway excavations, and may therefore be relied upon.

It is generally known that the Back Bay section of Boston is made land. At the point at Boylston Street where the remains of

7

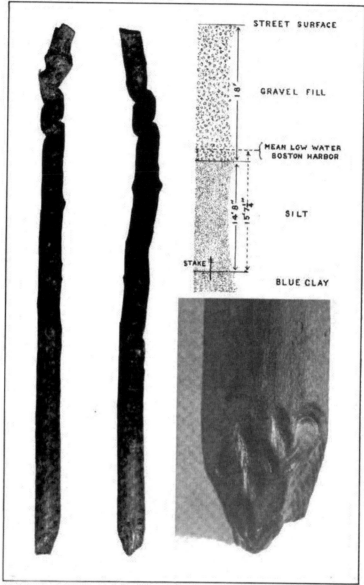

Figure 4. Three views of stake from ancient Indian fish-weir found in place thirty-two feet eight inches below surface while excavating beneath Boylston Street, Boston. The diagram shows its position when discovered in 1913.

the weir were found, the fill had a depth of eighteen feet. This gravel fill rested upon a stratum of silt, fourteen feet eight inches in depth, which had been deposited by the waters of the Charles River and the Back Bay. Beneath this layer of silt was a stratum of very stiff blue clay into which the stake penetrated to a depth of eighteen inches. The top of this clay layer is thirty-two feet eight inches beneath the present surface of Boylston Street, and fifteen feet seven and one fourth inches beneath mean low water of Boston Harbor as recorded in 1913.

The wattlework of the weir began at a point three feet above the lower end of the stake, or eighteen inches above the surface of the blue clay layer; therefore there could not have been more than eighteen inches of silt overlaying the blue clay at the time of the construction of the weir, and the mean low water level of the bay must have been at that period very close to the lower layers of the wattling. Assuming that there has been no change in the sea level during this period of time, we have a subsidence of land at this point of thirteen to fifteen feet since the Indians built the weir.

Dr. Hervey W. Shimer of the Geological Department of the Massachusetts Institute of Technology has made an extended study of the Back Bay region where the remains of this weir were found, the results of which appear in a paper entitled *Post-glacial History of Boston*, published in Volume 53, of the Proceedings of the American Academy of Arts and Sciences, from which the following brief extracts are taken.

That man lived in this Boston region during the warmer climatic period following the retreat of the glaciers is evidenced by the excavation of the remnants of a fish-weir from these older sediments. . . . Some, if not all of the rods penetrated the glacial clay. . . . If we consider the lowest preserved horizontal sticks as originally the lowest and as resting upon the surface when erected, then about thirteen feet of shells and mud had been deposited between the time when man planted the fish-weir and when he blotted out the Bay. If we consider the probability that there was practically no silt present when the weir was erected it would mean the deposition of fourteen feet, eight inches of sediment between that time and the artificial filling of the Bay. . . . How long a time was consumed in the deposition of these thirteen to fifteen feet of silt and shells is largely a matter of conjecture. It has been estimated that the Mississippi River deposits a foot of mud in two hundred years. A similar rate here would have required 2500 to 3000 years for the accumulation of this thickness. The streams of the Boston area would have carried annually much less sediment than the Mississippi. The amount retained in Back Bay, however, would be a balance between the amount of mud delivered into this

inland bay protected by many islands and the strength of the tidal scour. . . .
In the case of the fish-weir the fossil shells indicate that parts of it extended
above the encroaching sediment during the time necessary to deposit three or
four feet of shells and mud, next to suffer a striking climatic change and
finally to deposit another foot or two of sediment. We cannot conceive of
this as taking place in a comparatively few years. . . . To briefly summarize,
— The remnants of the fish-weir excavated on Boylston Street give evidence
of man in the Back Bay region of Boston, probably 2000 to 3000 years ago.
He built this weir during a climatic period as warm as off the Virginia Coast
at present, and upon a sinking coast. Since its erection the region has sunk
sixteen to eighteen feet and suffered a refrigeration to its present climate.

There is another factor which should be considered in relation
to the warmer climatic period during which this weir was apparently erected. Dr. Paul B. Sears, Professor of Botany of the
University of Oklahoma, in a recent article concerning fossil pollen
and other clues from peat layers and other accumulations of old
lake beds, concludes that a warm dry period reached its climax in
northeastern America about 1200 B.C. and that this must have
shifted the most favorable region for growing maize far to the
north and east. This date corresponds approximately with that
given above by Dr. Shimer.

Of the sixty or more species of fossil shells listed by Dr. Shimer
as having been taken from the silt of the Back Bay region and
vicinity, about half are said to be no longer found living north of
Cape Cod, their congenial habitat being the warmer regions
further south.

The encroaching sediment containing these fossil shells buried
the weir to a depth of three to four feet, followed by sediment of a
later, cooler period like the present. We may assume, therefore,
that during this earlier period the climate of southern New
England was warmer than at present and the people who built
the weir must have found their environment more congenial than
that of the later inhabitants.

The culture of our older New England people as shown by the
many artifacts recovered is quite different from that of their successors. They were not agriculturists; they were unacquainted
with the use of tobacco; they made no pottery; both the grooved
and grooveless axe were apparently unknown to them. They used
the Eskimo type of bird spear with side prongs, also the semilunar knife, and many types of slate projectile points now found
only among boreal tribes. In New England they had de-

veloped the stone-bladed adze to a point unknown in other parts of the world.

Judging by their stone implements gathered from ancient graves and found scattered over the fields, the habitat of this ancient people covered the Maritime Provinces, New England, New York, New Jersey, a part of Pennsylvania, eastern Ontario, and the southern part of Quebec. (See figure 1.) It is probable that this old culture extended much farther north, at least to the latitude of Hudson Bay, for the New England monolithic type of semilunar slate knife has been found on the eastern shore of the Bay, and certain forms of New England stone artifacts including the common type of semilunar knife have been in recent use among the Alaskan Eskimo.

If the now extinct Beothuk of Newfoundland, classed by Powell as a separate linguistic stock, were a surviving branch of this old people, as seems probable, a review of some of the more important phases of their culture will be of interest.

Physically the Beothuk[1] were much like their Algonquian neighbors. In the winter the men wore caribou skin coats with the hair innermost and with sleeves reaching to the middle of the arm, and a beaver skin about the neck. Their caps were of sealskin. They wore leggings and moccasins. They also had mantles made of two deer or caribou skins sewed together. The women's dress consisted of deer skins tastily trimmed with martin fur.

Their summer houses, like those of the neighboring Algonquians of the mainland, were conical in form, about ten feet in diameter at the base, made of poles, and covered with bark.

It should be remembered that the northern Algonquians came at no very remote date from the south where the flimsy wigwams of their ancestors served all purposes of a habitation, but in their migrations to a more rigorous climate they did not evolve a more comfortable type of winter dwelling. The winter house of the Beothuk, however, was a most suitable habitation for that season, and great care was taken in its construction.

It was about twenty-two feet in diameter, octagonal in form, with walls about four feet high above the ground on the inner side. The eight corner posts were larger than the others. The upright

[1] J. P. Howley, *The Beothucks or Red Indians*, Cambridge, England, University Press, 1915. In this important work is brought together nearly all that is known historically of this interesting people.

posts forming the wall between the corner posts were flattened upon opposite sides and set close together in the ground and the spaces between them chinked with moss. Earth was banked against the posts on the outer side as high as the eaves. Upon these posts were fixed wall plates which supported the lower ends of the poles forming the rafters of the conical roof, which terminated in a central hole at the apex, of sufficient size for emitting smoke and admitting light, this and the entrance being the only apertures. The roof was covered with a triple layer of birch bark, and between the first and second layer were about six inches of moss. About the hole for the passage of smoke, clay was substituted for moss as a guard against fire.

The interior was divided into alcoves by partitions of lattice work running from the eight corner posts toward the center of the building, leaving a clear space around the fire. This central area seems to have been about ten or twelve feet in diameter, large enough to allow the occupants to lie with their feet to the fire.

In some of the lodges were depressions in the earth about the fire in which the people apparently lay in a semi-sitting posture. In the alcoves the space next the outer wall was filled with neatly dressed skins and other property of the occupants. There were also scaffolds on which were piled a quantity of dried venison, salmon, codfish, and other food. The English who described this habitation were astonished at the neatness which reigned within. The bows, arrows, clubs, stone hatchets (adzes), etc., were all arranged in the neatest order upon the walls, apparently every man's property carefully grouped together.

In a manuscript by Cormack, evidently written after his last expedition in search of the Beothuk, he refers to their custom of adorning the posts or poles outside of their doors, but gives no description of them. He describes the remains of a village he found on this expedition. There were vestiges of eight or ten winter mamateeks (houses) close together, each intended to accommodate six to eighteen or twenty people. There were also the remains of summer lodges. Each of the winter houses had close by a square or oblong mouthed pit dug to the depth of about four feet, some of which were lined with birch bark. These were, of course, for the preservation of supplies. There were also the remains of a sweat-lodge, and a wooden building constructed for drying and smoking venison.

The storehouses were often quite large. William Call saw one in 1810 which was forty to fifty feet long and nearly as wide. In them were stored venison, skins of the caribou, dried salmon, dried lobsters, bladder receptacles filled with oil, and other foods. The walls were made of posts set into the ground in the form of a rectangle. End posts supported the ridgepole and according to Shanawdithit's drawing the gables were quite low.

The form of the birchbark canoe was unique. It was fifteen to twenty-two feet long and three to four feet wide at the middle thwart, with a high pointed bow and stern. From either end the gunwales sloped gradually only to rise again near the middle thwart to about the height of the pointed ends. Near each end were one or two shorter thwarts to add stability. The line of the bottom was straight for most of its length, and was furnished with a small keel, which extended upward to the ends. A cross-section through the center of the canoe was nearly V-shape. Unlike other bark canoes its bottom was not rounded, and when placed without ballast in the water it would not remain upright but lie upon its side. In use it was ballasted with stones, over which sod or moss was laid and upon this the Indians knelt and managed it with paddles. In crossing by carries from lake to lake, the thwarts, or at least the long central one, were temporarily removed so the sides would close together, allowing easy passage through the woods. With these frail craft the Indians made long voyages, visiting Funk Island thirty miles north of Newfoundland to secure the eggs of the great auk which bred in large numbers on this island.

The Beothuk made no pottery. They cooked their food largely in birch bark vessels, which if not placed too near the flames, and kept supplied with sufficient water, made good kettles. A square piece of birch bark properly folded and bound with split roots at the rim to a thin strip of bent wood, makes a seamless, waterproof vessel such as was used by many tribes in the birch bark area.

Whitbourne, who visited Newfoundland early in the seventeenth century, saw in a Beothuk camp at Trinity Bay three large birch bark kettles, each supported over the fire by three stones and in each were boiling twelve fowl, every one as large as a widgeon, and some as large as a duck.[2]

---

[2] Howley, Ibid., p. 21.

The disposition of the dead among the Beothuk varied according to the rank of the deceased, the time of year, and the condition of the ground.

Cormack describes one of the larger grave houses as follows. It resembled a hut

. . . . ten feet by eight or nine, and four or five feet high in the center, floored with squared poles, the roof covered with the rinds of trees, and in every way well secured against the weather and the intrusion of beasts.

Within were the bodies of two grown persons laid at full length, and what seemed to be children. There were also small images of a man and a woman, a bow and quiver of arrows, models of canoes, and several other objects including a pair of fire-making stones. In another mode of sepulcher which he describes the body was wrapped in birch bark and, with the property of the deceased, placed on a scaffold formed of four posts about seven feet high supporting a crib about five and one half feet long and four wide, having a floor of squared beams laid horizontally. In another instance the body was flexed, wrapped in birch bark and enclosed in a box on the ground. This box was made of squared poles laid on each other horizontally and notched at the corners to make them lie close together. It was about four feet by three and two and a half deep, and well lined with birch bark to exclude the weather. The body lay on its right side.

These above-ground structures remind us strongly of the receptacles for the dead built by the Eskimo and some other tribes of western and southern Alaska.

The above writer also tells us that a body was often wrapped in birch bark and placed in some remote spot and covered with stones. Sometimes the body thus wrapped was put a foot or two under the surface, and covered with stones, and in one place where the ground was sandy and soft they appeared to have been buried deeper and no stones placed over the graves.

These people appear to have always shewn great respect for their dead; and the most remarkable remains of them commonly observed by Europeans at the sea-coast, are their burying places. These are at particular chosen spots; and it is well known that they have been in the habit of bringing their dead from a distance to them. With their women they bury only their clothes.[1]

If this people formerly occupied the northeastern corner of the United States, as seems probable, their winter houses were probably

[1] Howley, Ibid., pp. 192-194.

14

less carefully constructed owing to the milder climate, and their clothing much lighter. In the disposal of their dead, inhumation could be followed for a longer period. In some of the old cemeteries in Maine there are indications that communal burials took place probably in the spring, where bodies of those who had died in the winter were buried in a single large excavation, the floor of which was strewn with a thin continuous layer of red ocher.

The Beothuk were very fond of this red pigment which they called odmet. They mixed it with oil or grease.

It appears to have been their universal practice to smear everything they possessed with this pigment. Not only their clothing, implements, ornaments, canoes, bows and arrows, drinking cups, even their own bodies were so treated. Small packages of this material, tied up in birch bark, are found buried with their dead.[4]

There seems to be no evidence that the Micmac of Nova Scotia and northern New Brunswick occupied any portion of Newfoundland previous to the arrival of Europeans in that neighborhood. Many, however, were taken to Newfoundland to serve as hunters for the French and they soon overran a large portion of the western section of the island, and, with the English and French, took a prominent part in the extermination of the peace loving Beothuk. The latter, however, were on friendly terms with the Montagnais of Labrador, and engaged in trade with them across the strait of Belle Isle. It seems probable that the Beothuk occupied parts of New Brunswick and Nova Scotia at a period not very remote, for the Micmac have a tradition of a different people inhabiting their territory whom they drove out and who they believe went over to Newfoundland and settled there.[5]

Many stone implements have been found in Newfoundland. They consist almost wholly of adze blades of various types, chipped knives, scrapers, and projectile points, polished slate points, and a few pear-shaped pendants, types found abundantly in the ancient graves and in the fields throughout New England. Typical Algonquian forms of polished stone artifacts seem to be unknown on the island. In New Brunswick and especially in Nova Scotia all of the above Newfoundland types occur.

While many old burial places undoubtedly exist throughout the provinces, none has been systematically explored, probably owing

[4] Howley, Ibid., p. 262.
[5] Ibid., p. 301.

to the fact that all bones have disappeared through disintegration, and the implements found while cultivating the fields were not recognized as having come from graves. In fields where a considerable number of such implements are turned out by the plow, careful excavations to a depth of at least three feet may reveal numbers of these old graves, especially if traces of red ocher occur on the implements or in the soil. From the farm of William King at the head of Grand Lake, Halifax County, a considerable number have been taken. The site should be carefully explored.

Many of these old cemeteries have been found in New England, especially in Maine where no less than twelve were explored by the Phillips Academy, Andover, under the direction of Dr. Moorehead.[6] These were located at Warren, Blue Hill, Orland, Sullivan Falls, Passadumkeag, Oldtown, and Oakland. In Orland and one or two other of the above towns, more than one burial place was found. In addition to these, numerous other cemeteries have been dug into and destroyed while grading, excavating for buildings, digging gravel, and so forth, and also by collectors, and the contents of the graves more or less scattered. Hallowell, Waterville, Winslow, Damariscotta, Ellsworth Falls, and Mt. Desert Ferry are some of the towns in which they were situated. In Massachusetts several of these old "red paint" cemeteries have been dug out and destroyed. One of the most extensive seems to have been at Marblehead; another was situated on a hill near Fresh Pond, Cambridge. Indications of others have been reported, and isolated graves discovered. Implements belonging to this old culture are found in all our New England states and the adjacent territory as shown on the culture map. (Figure 1.)

The first systematic exploration of these burial places was carried out by the present writer for the Peabody Museum of Cambridge in 1892 at Bucksport and Orland, and at Ellsworth in 1894.[7] A brief résumé of the work follows:

The Cemetery at Bucksport. The peninsula on which the cemetery was located lies about half a mile above the village on the eastern bank of the Penobscot River. Rising from a pebbly beach to a height of fifteen feet is a bluff. A few feet from its edge lies a gravel knoll, the site of the burial place.

[6] W. K. Moorehead, *A Report on the Archaeology of Maine*, Andover Press, 1922.

[7] C. C. Willoughby, *Prehistoric Burial Places in Maine*, Papers of the Peabody Museum, Harvard University, Cambridge 1898, vol. 1, no. 6.

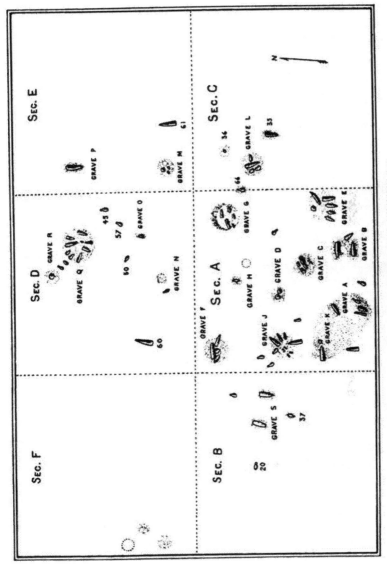

Figure 6. Plan of pre-Algonquian Burial Place, Bucksport, Me.

17

The owner of this land had occasion to remove gravel from its southern slope, and one of the workmen noticed a stone implement embedded in the gravel. Continued excavations revealed other specimens lying in red ocher, and in searching along the road where the gravel had been placed for repairs several more were found. North of the gravel pit a space of about fifteen by fifty feet was subsequently dug over by residents of Bucksport and about forty implements were shown me which came from this area.

Obtaining permission from the owner, Mr. George Blodgett, to explore the site, the ground was staked off as in figure 5 and the work began. Sinking a trench along the southern edge of the undisturbed gravel and working north, a line of ocher was disclosed twenty-four inches from the surface at the southern edge of Section A. The vertical bank of earth was examined with the utmost care to ascertain the outline of the grave, but neither in this nor in any of the other graves could the outline be determined. This was probably due in great measure to the coarseness of the gravel. The graves were also so near to each other as to leave only a small amount of undisturbed earth within the area of the cemetery.

The graves were of great age, so old, indeed, that not a trace of bone was discovered during the exploration. A number of implements were much disintegrated (figure 6, b, g.), owing largely to their having lain in contact with one or more lumps of iron pyrites, which formed the strike-a-light sets or fire-making implements of this people. A detailed account of these sets will be given later.

Practically all of the implements in these graves lay in or near a mass of paint (red oxide of iron), probably from the outcrops of this mineral near the Katahdin Iron Works in central Maine, which seems to have been the source of most of the red paint found in the ancient graves of that state.[8]

It is probable that much of the paint in these graves was enclosed in bags or in birch bark receptacles. These decomposed and the settling of the earth and the percolation of water carried more or less of the pigment beyond its original bounds. Occasionally, however, the bottom of the excavation seems to have been sprinkled with a thin layer of paint. This was especially noticeable in one or two instances where the excavation was large enough to receive two or more bodies.

In the plans of the three cemeteries, the implements are shown

[8] W. K. Moorehead, *A Report on the Archaeology of Maine*, Andover Press, 1922. p. 133.

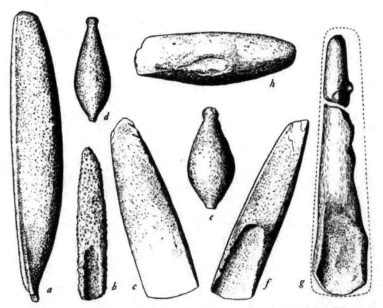

Figure 6. Implements from Grave Q, Section D, Bucksport, Me. Pear-shaped sinkers and adze blades. (1/3.)

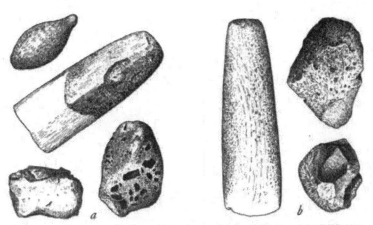

Figure 7. a, Implements from Grave L, Section C. Sinker, adze blade, and fire-making set. b, Implements from Grave C, Section A. Adze blade and fire-making set. Bucksport, Me. (1/3.)

lying in the positions in which they were found. In figure 5, Section D, Grave Q, two quite large stones lay in the grave, and in addition to the implements shown, six pear-shaped sinkers were found outside the central deposit, one of which may have belonged to another grave, as a small amount of red ocher was in contact with it. Most of the cutting implements consisted of adze blades of the usual types. At least some of these were probably hafted when placed with the bodies. Several knives were also found chipped from Kineo felsite.

Occasionally an adze blade was found in or just beneath the sod which probably came from a grave box or scaffold burial, like those previously described as sometimes built by the Beothuk.

Burial Place at Orland. This ancient cemetery was located upon a symmetrical gravel knoll, rising from the shore of a small inlet or bay upon the northern side of Lake Alamoosook, near its outlet. The summit of the knoll is fifteen feet above the surrounding low land. Its oval base has a maximum diameter of about one hundred feet. The knoll and the surrounding land were covered with a thick growth of wood, some of the trees being a foot or more in diameter. Three depressions twenty-seven to thirty-two inches in depth having diameters at the surface of ten to fourteen feet occupied the summit of the knoll. These depressions were called "Indian cellars" by the people of the neighborhood. A superficial examination of these depressions resulted in obtaining several pieces of charcoal and some ashes. Being convinced of the Indian origin of these depressions, a narrow trench was cut along the summit of the knoll and at a depth of fifteen inches were found a mass of red ocher and two implements. (Figure 8, Section D, Grave J.)

This land was owned by Mr. J. Foster Soper of Orland, who not only granted permission to explore the burial place but assisted in many ways.

The trees were removed with the exception of three large oaks and a white birch and the whole area of the knoll was explored excepting beneath these trees, but the graves occurred principally on its summit and western side. No traces of bone were found in any of these graves, neither could the outline of any grave be determined. Various natural causes had completely obliterated all traces of the line of junction between the disturbed and undisturbed gravel. The outlines shown in the vertical sections of the large fire holes could, however, be traced. The implements were found at depths varying from thirteen to thirty-six inches, the average being about twenty-three inches.

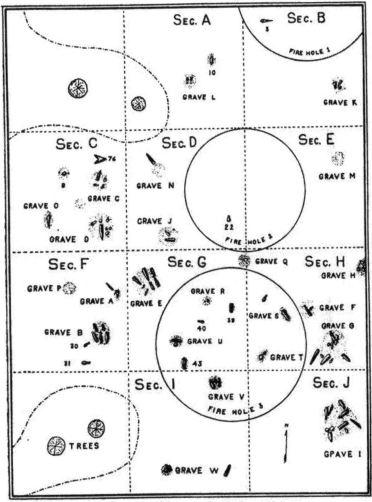

Figure 8. Plan of pre-Algonquian Burial Place, Orland, Me.

As in nearly all of these cemeteries the implements lay in contact with red ocher. The usual large number of adze blades were unearthed. In many instances where more than one of these were placed with the body, both the straight and the curved edged (or gouge form) made up the set of wood-working tools. Three well made chipped knife blades were recovered, one of which is illustrated in figure 9, g. A few smooth, elongated pebbles, possibly for mixing the red pigment with oil were found with the paint. The remains of fourteen fire-making sets occurred in an equal number of graves.

Two small points resembling arrowheads, one of chipped flint and the other of slate, and a beautiful polished slate point about four inches long were recovered. So few of these small points have been taken from the graves that it seems somewhat doubtful if they are arrowpoints. They may be points for toy spears, for a number have been found singly, sometimes with a little ocher, in what seem to be small graves. A few, however, occurred with other implements in graves of adults.

Most of the arrowpoints of this people may well have been made of bone or antler which does not last long when buried in the ground. Two of the finest adze blades from this cemetery are shown in figure 19, e, k. The first was found in grave G, Section H. Its position is shown in the plan a little at the left of the main deposit. The second, k, of this figure, was the only one recovered from Grave N, Section D. Its surface shows the marks of contact with one of the firestones which lay beside it. An interesting combined pick and hoe, one-third natural size, is illustrated in figure 11. This was found just beneath the sod in Section C. It is undoubtedly the implement used in digging some of the graves. When properly hafted it would make a very effective tool for such work.

Burial Place at Ellsworth. This cemetery is in Hancock County, about one mile below the village of Ellsworth, and is situated in a sand and gravel bank terminating in a high bluff which at this point forms the eastern bank of Union River. It was discovered while removing sand and gravel. Each grave had a deposit of red ocher in which the implements were found. The finding of these objects caused much local excitement, and a large area was dug over by citizens and many implements secured. An examination of the bank immediately surrounding the gravel pit revealed indications of undisturbed graves, and preparations were made for its systematic exploration. Mr. J. W. Coombs, the owner of the land,

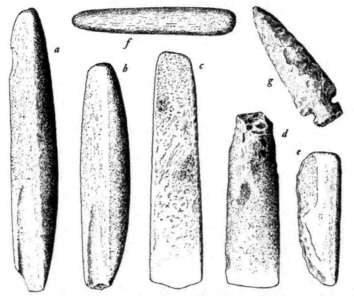

Figure 9. Implements from Grave E, Section G, Orland, Me. a–d, Adze blades; e, chipped pebble; f, pebble showing use as implement; g, chipped knife. (1/3.)

Figure 10. Grave I, Section J, Orland, Me., showing implements in position.

23

very kindly allowed excavations to be carried on, and gave assistance in many ways.

As in each of these cemeteries, the ground to be explored was staked off into sections and each section mapped to scale and numbered as shown in the plan.

Unfortunately, a greater part of this burial place had been destroyed while digging sand and gravel, or by local people in search for implements. Many artifacts were doubtless carted away with the gravel but I was able to secure the following for the Museum through the generosity of Mr. G. S. Cook and Dr. W. M. Haines of Ellsworth and Mr. H. L. Woodcock of Belfast who unearthed them: eighteen adze blades, the workmanship of which was somewhat inferior to those from the graves at Bucksport and Orland; thirteen well made chipped flint knives,

Figure 11. Implement No. 76, Section C, Orland, Me.; probably once hafted and used for digging graves. (1/4.)

examples being illustrated in figure 30, b-e; seventeen finely fashioned slate spear points, four of which are shown in figure 34, g, h, i, and k. The longest of these measured fourteen and one half inches. There were also two hammerstones, evidently parts of the fire-making sets; and one pear-shaped sinker.

The exploration for the Museum was begun in Section 8 and carried northward. (See figure 12.) Fifteen graves in all were uncovered. In only one, however, Grave K, were many implements found. These are shown in figure 13. Red ocher occurred in all the graves and in one, Section 1, M, about three pints were secured of unusually rich dark color.

A part of a fire-making set, and a pear-shaped sinker were the only artifacts found with this large mass of pigment. With the exception of the objects shown in figure 13, the implements obtained during the exploration were seven pear-shaped sinkers, two chipped knives, several much disintegrated fire-making sets,

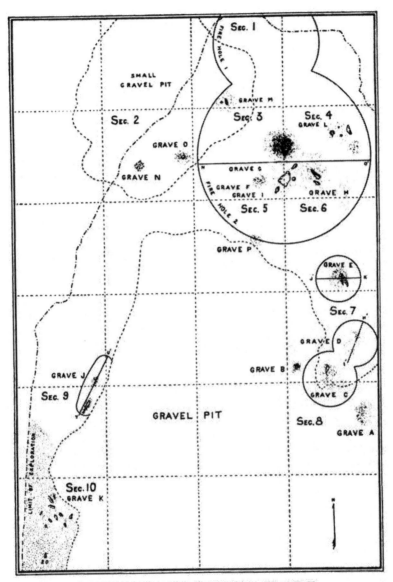

Figure 12. Plan of pre-Algonquian Burial Place, Ellsworth, Me.

one long slate spear point, and a somewhat battered scraper-like implement which seems to have been used on one side for sharpening implements. Upon the opposite side is a crude design in incised lines. This was from Section 4, Grave L, four feet five inches from the surface.

In the northern portion of this burial place was a shallow pit from which gravel had been taken. Within the limits of this pit were three burials, one of which, Grave N, seems to have been intrusive, at least it was very unlike any of the other interments. From four to twelve inches of the upper part of the grave had been removed. The upper remaining portion contained ashes and a small quantity of charcoal mixed with the gravel. The charcoal and ashes were thickest near the center of the grave.

About nineteen inches from the surface and a little to one side of the center were the crumbling fragments of a human occipital bone and twenty-two small beads made of native copper. A number of beads lay in contact with the bone, which may account for its preservation (figure 14). All other parts of the skull and skeleton had disappeared.

About two feet below the original surface were pieces of birch bark, in which the body may have been wrapped. Fragments of this bark, two inches or more in length, were perfectly preserved, and some of them showed contact with fire. No ocher or implements were found with the burial.

Two similar burials were found by Dr. Moorehead in one of these pre-Algonquian cemeteries on the southeast shore of Lake Alamoosook, Orland, on land owned by Thomas and Augustus Mason. They were thought by him to be also intrusive. In each was found at a depth of about twenty-eight inches a layer of charcoal five to six inches thick. In one of these graves was a portion of a human femur, also a number of native copper beads, the tube illustrated in figure 50, k, and fragments of buckskin and birch bark. In the other grave were thirty to forty small native copper beads, the tube shown in figure 50, l, fragments of buckskin, a fine chipped knife of black flint, and two pebbles. In both the graves were a few bits of red pigment, different from the ocher common in the other graves.

The preservation of the few bone fragments in these graves was probably due to the presence of copper. There seems to be little doubt that these apparently intrusive burials were of old Algon-

26

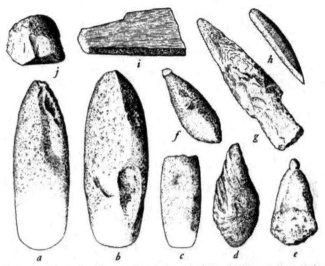

Figure 13. Implements from Grave K. Section 10, Ellsworth, Me. a–c, Adze blades; d–f, sinkers; h, small blade or chisel; g, chipped knife; i, sharpening stone; j, part of a fire-making set. (1/3.)

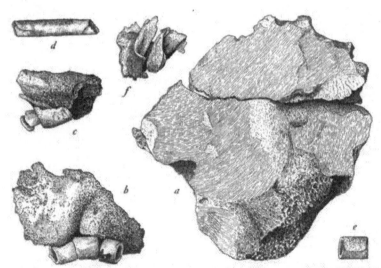

Figure 14. Native Copper Beads and fragments of Occipital Bone. From Grave N, Section 2, Ellsworth, Me. (1/1.)

27

quian origin or may have been the result of contact between the two groups of people. The native copper beads and the shaman tubes seem to point to this conclusion. The burials may have been contemporary with others in these cemeteries or of a later date. The two groups of people were doubtless in contact over a considerable period.

The soil of the burial places at Bucksport and Orland was a coarse gravel while that at Ellsworth was a finer gravel with areas of sand which showed quite distinctly the outlines of the graves, and enabled accurate cross-sections to be made. These show three methods of disposition of the body. The usual method was to dig a basin-shaped hole about five feet in diameter at the top, and

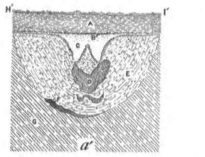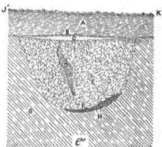

Figure 15. Vertical cross-sections of graves for flexed burials, Ellsworth, Me. a′, Grave D; e′, Grave E. A, Top soil; B, charcoal; C, ashes; D, dark discoloration; E, disturbed gravel within grave; F, red ocher; G, undisturbed gravel; H, stone implement.

approximately three to four feet deep. In this the body was placed in a flexed position, together with a fire-making outfit, a bag or package of red ocher, adzes and other implements. The grave was then filled with earth, and a fire built over it. This fire apparently did not come in contact with the body, otherwise carbonized bone doubtless would be found. Cross-sections of graves D, and E, which are typical, appear in figure 15. The top soil over the ashes showed no sign of having been disturbed.

Figure 16 is a cross-section of what seems to be a communal grave having a diameter of nearly twenty feet where several bodies were deposited, the grave filled with earth, and a great fire kindled over it. A large amount of ashes and charcoal are shown near the center. The purpose for which some of these pits were dug does not seem altogether clear, for several have been found in these cemeteries which show no sign of burials, although charcoal and ashes appear in all of them. Perhaps their use for burials was secondary.

Another type of interment appears in figure 17. Here the body was not flexed, but laid horizontally in a grave twenty-one inches deep in sand. In a few graves a small amount of buff colored powder was found which showed a decided reaction when acid was applied. This was undoubtedly bone dust. It is possible in

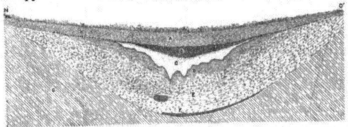

Figure 16. Vertical cross-section through Communal Grave or Fire Hole, 1 Ellsworth, Me. A, Top soil; B, charcoal; C, ashes; D, discoloration caused by lye from ashes; E, disturbed gravel within fire hole; F, red ocher; G, undisturbed gravel. The dark mass to the left of E, contained red ocher and bone dust.

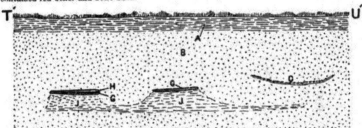

Figure 17. Vertical cross-section through Grave J, for extended burial, Ellsworth, Me. A, Top soil; B, sand; C, ashes and charcoal; G, red ocher; H, slate spear point; J, sand cemented into a compact mass.

all three cemeteries where implements and ocher occurred at a depth not exceeding eighteen or twenty inches that the bodies were not flexed but laid horizontally.

The implements found in these pre-Algonquian graves during the above explorations, and those from the four hundred and forty graves opened during the Andover explorations by Dr. Moorehead, consist mainly of the following type: adze blades, pear-shaped sinkers, fire-making sets, chipped flint knives, long, slender lance heads and projectile points, sharpening stones, a few slate pendants in the form of a whale's tail, and several perforated slate ceremonials commonly called bannerstones. These types are found to a greater or less extent throughout New England and portions of the adjacent territory. The culture to which they belong is very old; the oldest that is known for New England at the present time. It seems to have been fairly homogeneous throughout these states although certain phases of it varied somewhat in different sections.

To the west of New England most of the above types of artifacts occur frequently as surface finds in the dotted area shown in figure 1. Some of these had doubtless been plowed from shallow graves, the skeletons having wholly disintegrated. But few isolated graves have been found and I know of but one cemetery that has been brought to the attention of archæologists. This was situated on the bank of a branch of Rancocus Creek about six miles from the Delaware River in New Jersey. It was explored by Dr. E. W. Hawkes and Mr. Ralph Linton for the Museum of the University of Pennsylvania. A report of the work is published in Volume VI, No. 3, of the Anthropological Publications of that Museum for 1916. Unfortunately the authors of the paper failed to grasp the true significance of their find and much was left unrecorded which if present would add materially to our knowledge of this ancient cemetery. The objects from each individual grave were not recorded separately in the report. This is a serious handicap to the student. The skeletons having disappeared through disintegration the different groups of artifacts were thought by the authors to be deposits connected with some ceremony and not buried with the dead.

The eighteen graves were within an area sixty feet in diameter, the distance between them being approximately six feet. The groups of implements were five to seven feet below the surface lying in white glacial sand above which was yellow sand to a depth of four to six feet, and above all was the usual black top soil. As in several Maine cemeteries fire pits occurred, the largest having colored the white glacial sand to a depth of three feet.

Among the artifacts from the eighteen graves were twenty-one "bannerstones" most of them similar to j, k, l, figure 37. In one grave three were found. The usual grave, however, contained a single bannerstone and a few "ceremonial" objects. Several contained two chipped knives of argillite. One contained among other specimens a beautiful knife of bluish quartzite. From the burials were also taken four adze blades, one being furnished with a tang for securing the lashing.

A beautiful quartz crystal ball, pecked into shape and polished, was found in one grave. There were several hammerstones and small pestles, all natural pebbles, but showing use as implements. Associated with other objects were four fossil brachiopods and several iron concretions. Some of the articles bore traces of red paint which came off in fine scales when exposed to the air. The red color persisted on several specimens, notably the fossils.

The authors apparently found no signs of disturbance of the yellow soil above the deposits. According to Professor A. P. Brown of the University of Pennsylvania, there are indications that the yellow soil above the glacial sand is a wind-borne deposit, hence the probabilities are that the graves were originally much nearer the surface.

An unusual feature in this cemetery was the relatively large number of bannerstones. These are quite common as surface finds in central New Jersey. In New England graves they are rare although many occur on the surface. There were also several thinner crescentic objects without perforations apparently belonging to the same category. These are represented in the Maine graves by more delicate examples apparently used as personal ornaments or talismans. (See figure 38.)

Pre-Algonquian Adze Blades. Scattered quite generally over the culture area shown in figure 1, are a large number of stone implements which were evidently used as adze blades.

The simpler forms of these, having nearly straight cutting edges, have a wide distribution in America and were used in New England also by the Algonquians. They likewise occur in many sections of the world. They are still found hafted in wooden handles among various primitive people. It is in New England, however, that the stone-bladed adze attained its highest development. Nowhere else do they occur in such variety. Special forms were made for different work. The material is usually a compact altered slate of fine grain, although unaltered slates and other varieties of stone are often used in their making.

Probably most of the adze blades illustrated in figures 18-22 are pre-Algonquian and no less than eleven, including the knobbed varieties, i, j, in figure 19, were taken from such graves. The others are surface finds, having doubtless been plowed from shallow

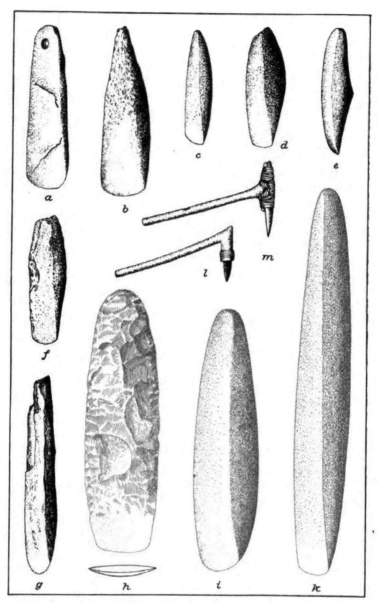

Figure 18. Adze Blades. a, b, d, f, g. From pre-Algonquian graves in Maine: a, b, d, Bucksport; f, Mt. Desert Ferry; g, Ellsworth. h, Jasper blade found with blade d, figure 21, in grave at Wilmington, Mass. c, e, i, k, Surface finds, Massachusetts. l, Probable method of hafting blades b, d, and f. m, Probable method of hafting blades i, and k. e, Peabody Museum of Salem; all others, Peabody Museum of Cambridge. (1/3, except l, m.)

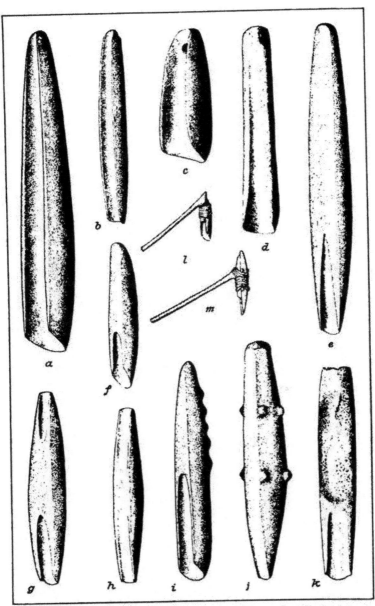

Figure 19. Adze Blades. b, e, i, j, k, From pre-Algonquian graves in Maine: b, Hallowell; e, j, k, Orland; i, Bucksport. Surface finds: d, g, h, Maine; a, c, Massachusetts; f, New Hampshire. l, Probable method of hafting blades a, b, c. m, Probable method of hafting blade j. a, g, Worcester Hist. Soc.; b, Maine Hist. Soc., Portland; h, American Museum, New York; i, after W. B. Smith; j, Andover Archaeological Museum; c, d, e, k, Peabody Museum, Cambridge. (1/3 except l, m.)

33

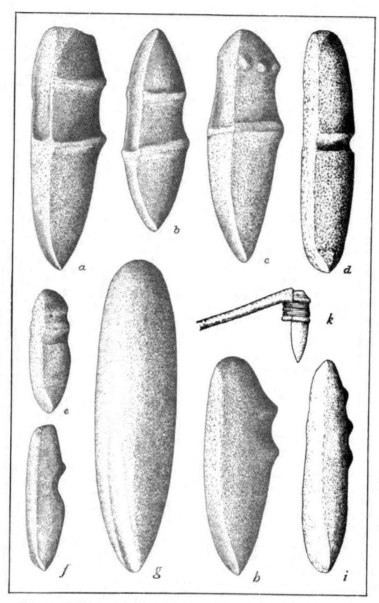

Figure 20. Adze Blades. a–h, Massachusetts: a, Billerica Falls; b, Salem, bank of North River; c, Amherst; d, Nantucket; e, f, Concord; g, Essex Co.; h, West Newbury. i, Eastport, Maine. a, d, e, f, h, Peabody Museum of Cambridge; b, g, Peabody Museum of Salem; c, Andover Archaeological Museum; i, National Museum. k, Probable method of hafting blade a. (1/3, except k.)

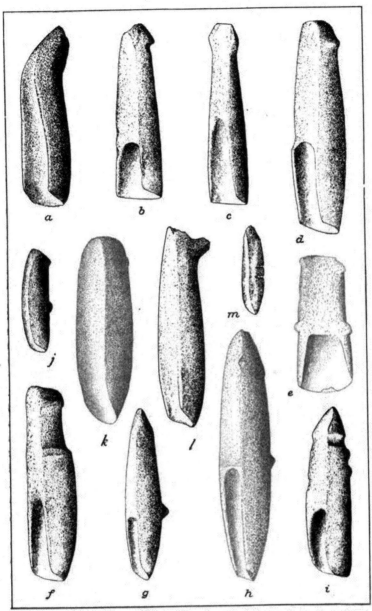

Figure 21. Adze Blades. a, b, d–h, j–m, Massachusetts: a, Wenham; b, Amesbury; d, Wilmington; e, j, Concord; g, Salem; l, Cape Cod; m, Swansea. c, Castine, Me.; i, New Hampshire; a–h, j–m, Peabody Museum of Cambridge. (1/3.)

graves while cultivating the land. Their localities are given in the titles.

The many hundred pre-Algonquian blades from graves in Maine and other sections of New England show a great variety in both form and size. During Dr. Moorehead's extensive explorations for the Andover Museum he found twenty-one blades in one deposit in the cemetery near the outlet of Lake Alamoosook, at Orland.

From sixty or more of these old graves excavated by the present writer in Maine, were obtained seventy-three of these implements. Some graves contained none. In others were found several. The greatest number from any one grave was seven.

Of these seventy-three blades, twenty-one had probably been inserted into a socket in the haft as illustrated in l, of figure 18. Thirty-two had well finished surfaces, and the cutting edges were straight or but slightly curved. These were probably lashed to the haft as in m, of the same figure. Twenty-nine were gouge-shaped with cutting edges showing much greater curvature. Most of these were doubtless hafted in the same manner.

The cutting edges of these implements range from a straight line through various degrees of curvature to a half circle. Those with the greatest curvature like figure 19, a, and c, were probably used among other purposes for excavating charred wood in making wooden bowls and other similar objects. The thin walls near the cutting edge show conclusively that they could not have been employed in heavy work. The larger of these two specimens may have been used without a haft, although probably it was hafted. Originally the blade c, seems to have been much longer but has been shortened by repeated re-grinding. The hole drilled near the top does not perforate the implement. The principal function of these tools was probably wood working. While some forms, figure 18, k, for instance, if attached to the end of a staff, would seem to serve admirably for cutting holes through the ice in winter fishing, I know, however, of no evidence that they were so used.

There seem to be but few references to the use of the stone bladed adze by American tribes, although the older museums have good examples of these implements in their original handles from the Eskimo and a few from the Indians of the Northwest Coast. The superiority of the iron blade to that of stone led to its early introduction. Axes were unknown among the Eskimo until introduced by Europeans, and the earlier trade hatchets obtained by them were nearly all rehafted as adzes. Nelson writes that stone adzes are very skilfully used by the Eskimo for hewing and surfacing logs and planks, although at the present time [1877–1881, they are being displaced by iron and steel tools obtained from white traders. In a *kashim* on the lower Yukon a plank was seen that was made many years ago by use of a stone adz. It was 25 feet long and four or five inches thick. The surface bore so many marks made by the hacking of stone adzes that it looked as if it might have been cut by beavers.[9]

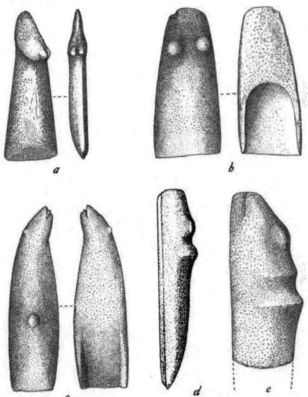

Figure 22. Adze Blades. a, West Upton, Mass., T. C. Lyford Collection, Upton; b, Hancock, N. H.; c, North Andover, Mass., Andover Museum; d, Massachusetts; e, Connecticut, Museum of the American Indian, New York. (1/3.)

Mackenzie found the primitive adze in the Slave and Dogrib region in 1789 and writes

[9] E. W. Nelson, *The Eskimo About Bering Strait*, Eighteenth Report Bureau of Am. Ethnology, p. 91.

Their axes [adzes] are manufactured of a piece of brown or grey stone from six to eight inches long, and two inches thick. The inside is flat, and the outside round and tapering to an edge, an inch wide. They are fastened by the middle with the flat side inwards to a handle two feet long, with a cord of green skin. This is the tool with which they split their wood, and we believe, the only one of its kind among them.[10]

It is interesting to note that this stone adze blade so well described by Mackenzie may be nearly duplicated in almost any New England collection. His description of the method of hafting is interesting. That the stone adze was in use by the Beothuk as late as 1819 seems probable, for one of the men of the party who captured Mary March found in a native house "hatchets" of stone and various other implements and weapons all arranged in the neatest order. As stone axes seem to have been unknown to the Beothuk it is probable that the stone adze was the implement seen. A few stone adzes were in use on the Northwest Coast in Cook's time, but in that region, even at this early period, iron to a great extent had supplanted stone for edged tools.

The following adze blades are from graves which are undoubtedly pre-Algonquian: figure 18, a, b, f, g, h; figure 19, b, e, i, j, k; and figure 21, d. Here we have representatives of most of the types, including those with simple outlines and nearly straight cutting edges; the gouge form; and those with knobs for holding the lashings. The simpler forms are common in most of the old Maine graves. The long grooved variety is rare. The one illustrated in figure 19, b, came from the old cemetery destroyed many years ago on the west bank of the Kennebec at Hallowell, while excavating and grading for an oilcloth factory. It is now in the collection of the Maine Historical Society at Portland. The blades with the short groove, e, k, of this figure were taken from the knoll cemetery at Orland, Maine, in 1892, by the present writer. The specimen with a row of knobs or grooves, i, is from Bucksport, Maine, and is undoubtedly one of several taken from the "Red Paint" cemetery while digging gravel prior to its exploration in 1892. From the old cemetery near the outlet of Lake Alamoosook, Orland, came the interesting knobbed example illustrated in j. It was found during the explorations conducted by Dr. Moorehead. Figure 21, d, was unearthed lying beside the beautiful jasper blade, figure 18, h, two to three feet beneath the surface in a meadow at Wilmington, Massachusetts. This was

[10] A. Mackenzie, *Voyages*, quarto edition, p. 36.

undoubtedly also an ancient grave but was not recognized as such by the finder owing to the complete disintegration of all bones.

Figure 21, d, is of special importance, for with figure 19, i, j, it seems to connect the great variety of blades having knobs or grooves at the back, which occur in such numbers as surface finds, with the pre-Algonquian group of burials.

The great majority of blades from the Maine burial places are without knobs or back grooves. Blades with knobs or grooves are also sometimes found in Nova Scotia, with the more ordinary straight edged and gouge-shaped forms.[11]

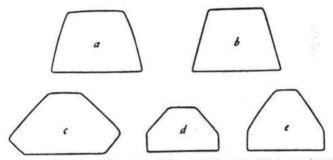

Figure 23. Cross-sections of adze blades with bevelled sides from Maine: a, e, from pre-Algonquian graves at Blue Hill; c, Kennebec Valley; d, Grand Lake. (1/2.)

As one goes southwest, however, they increase in number and are quite common in Massachusetts and other sections of southern New England, where they occur with the more usual forms.

Blades with dorsal grooves are rarely found beyond the borders of New England and the territory immediately adjacent. They occur, however, in the Yukon and Kuskoquim valleys and other parts of Alaska, but most of the other forms illustrated are found over the greater portion of the pre-Algonquian culture area of the Northeast. Excellent examples of the straight and curved edged knobless varieties are found in the Maritime Provinces, Quebec and Ontario. As the region to the northwest of the St. Lawrence and Ottawa rivers becomes better known archaeologically additional specimens will probably come to light.

The larger blades represented in figure 20, are of special interest. It will be noted that they are relatively heavy and that the cutting

11 H. Piers, *Relics of the Stone Age in Nova Scotia*, Proc. and Trans. of the Nova Scotia Inst. of Science, vol. ix, pt. 1, pp. 26–58, plates i–iii.

edge is narrow, also that above the cutting edge the blade widens abruptly as though to withstand a heavy blow. By hafting a blade of this type I found it very effective in cutting across the grain of wood, as a heavy blow could be given without breaking the edge. Two grooves about an inch deep and five or six inches apart were cut across the grain of a log about ten inches in diameter. The wood between the grooves was easily removed with wedges. By repeating the process the requisite number of times the log could be easily cut half through, then turned over and a corresponding V-shaped notch cut on the opposite side. By working in this manner sections for palisades and for other purposes could be quickly produced. The pre-Algonquian people of this section, like the extinct Beothuk of Newfoundland, seem to have been efficient workers in wood.

The large heavy blade, figure 20, g, with a narrow cutting edge, has nearly a circular cross-section. The front or grooved side is but slightly flattened. This is a distinct type and is found principally in eastern Massachusetts. One would naturally infer from the shape of the upper end, which fits the hand well that the implement may have been used without a haft. Other specimens of this type, however, have a more pronounced flattening on the side where the handle is attached and some have a very wide but shallow groove at the back for the lashings. In nearly all New England blades which are without a dorsal groove or knob to assist in holding the lashings the upper half is wedge-shape. The reason for this is obvious, for when lashed to the haft as in figure 18, m, each stroke tends to wedge the blade firmly to the handle. Blades with a cutting edge at either end (figure 19, g, h,) are rare. There is a fine, quite heavy specimen nine inches in length in the Museum at McGill University, Montreal, from Quebec Province which has a straight cutting edge at one end, and a curved or gouge-shape edge at the opposite extremity. These double-edged tools were probably lashed to T-shaped hafts, which would enable either end to be used as desired.

A few exceptional adze blades are illustrated in figure 22. Their upper ends terminate in sculptured heads of animals, which remind one strongly of similar effigies on certain pestles known to be of Algonquian origin. Perhaps these may be Algonquian but they are placed provisionally with the earlier group. If Algonquian, the general type was probably adopted from their predecessors during their long period of contact. More light on the subject, however, is desirable.

Perhaps the most interesting of these five blades, c, from North Andover, is, with the exception of its carved head, much like others represented in figure 21, especially g, and h.

The broken blade, e, was originally much like d. Since it was fractured it has been used as a hammer, its lower face being worn quite smooth. The straight edged example, a, is from West Upton, Massachusetts, and b is from Hancock, New Hampshire. These are surface finds, having probably been plowed from old graves. Adze blades with bevelled sides occur occasionally in different parts of New England. Cross-sections showing various forms are illustrated in figure 23. Two of these blades, a, e, are from pre-Algonquian graves at Blue Hill, Maine.

Pre-Algonquian Sinkers and Fish Lures. Next to adze blades perhaps the most abundant implements from pre-Algonquian graves are the small pear-shaped objects, the more common forms of which are illustrated in figure 24. They occur singly or in groups of two, three, or four, rarely more. They are often accompanied by one or more adze blades, a fire-making set of iron pyrites, and perhaps other implements.

Occasionally one of these is the only object found in a grave excepting red ocher, which is usually present. They are common as surface finds throughout New England, but never so far as I know, have they been found in these states in graves known to be of Algonquian origin. Three were taken by Dr. Moorehead from the lower layer of a shellheap at Sullivan Falls, Maine, and three others now in the Peabody Museum at Salem came from near the bottom of a shellheap on Perkins Island, Ipswich. The above are the only instances known to the writer of these small examples being found in shellheaps, which are principally of Algonquian origin, although their predecessors were doubtless responsible for the accumulation of the lower layers of at least some of these refuse piles.

These objects are made from altered slates, gniess, felsite, sandstone, quartzite, and other stones. In the majority of cases the shape is wholly artificial, but some are made by pecking a groove and knob at one end of a water-worn pebble of the proper size and shape as in figure 24, u, v.

The surface of some is quite smooth but in this region they

are rarely polished. Most of them show more or less distinctively the marks of the pecking tool used in their shaping.

This class of objects has a wide distribution in the United States. They seem to be most abundant in New England, Florida, and California, but they occur in the Middle States, West Virginia, Ohio, Illinois, Iowa, Missouri, Kentucky, Arkansas, Alabama, and probably in other sections. It is in New England, however, that we have the greatest range in size and variety of form, and here perhaps they attained their greatest utilitarian value. In other sections, notably California[12] and Florida[13], great care was often taken in the selection of material and also in the finish of the objects, many of them being very symmetrical and finely polished, an indication to some archæologists that in the southern and western regions they were used as personal ornaments or as talismans rather than for practical purposes. This is borne out to a certain degree by the finding by Mr. Clarence B. Moore in a mound and burial place near Crystal River, Florida, of more than a hundred pendants of this form made of shell, stone, and copper, some of which had evidently been suspended from a belt around the waist of one of the persons buried. It should be remembered, however, that in the less rigorous climate of the South, life became easier, food was more abundant, more time became available for the development of various handicrafts, and common objects of utility were often elaborated for personal adornment and ceremonial use. In New England, the Maritime Provinces, and New York these objects belong to the old pre-Algonquian culture which we have described.

They seem to have passed out of use upon the Algonquian occupation. A few came into the possession of historic Indians who probably picked them up on old burial sites or lake shores.

Some thirty years ago, an intelligent old time Penobscot Indian known as Big Thunder showed the writer one of these objects attached to a line and said that in ancient times it was smeared with "tallow" and used as a decoy and bait for catching large fish. Another similar account was given me by Mr. Langdon Warner of Cambridge, who obtained it from two Ojibwa Indians, Tom Oblossawa and George Cabausa, of Garden River Reservation,

[12] E. W. Gifford and W. E. Schenck, Univ. of California Pub. in Am. Arch. and Eth. vol. xxiii, no. 1, also W. E. Schenck in no. 3 of same volume.

[13] C. B. Moore, *Certain Aboriginal Mounds, Central Florida West Coast*, Journal Acad. Nat. Science of Philadelphia vol. xii, figs. 43–53.

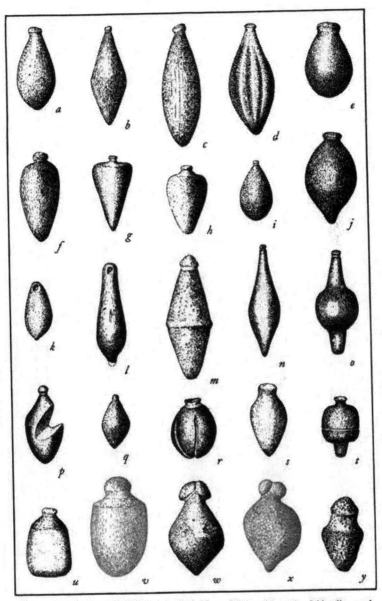

Figure 24. Pendants. Probably used principally as sinkers and lures for fishing lines. c–f, h–j, m, o, r, u–y, Massachusetts: c, x, Belmont; d, v, Concord; e, Ipswich; f, Newburyport; i, Chatham; j, Amesbury; o, Essex Co.; u, Beverly; w, Saugus; y, Swansea. a, b, k, l, n, p, g, Maine: b, q, Mt. Desert Ferry; k, n, Orland; l, Blue Hill; p, Warren. g, Hubbardton, Vermont; s, Rhode Island; t, Manchester, N. H. (1/3.)

43

Lake Huron, about the year 1903. He was told that the pendants were covered with lard and held near the lake bottom for catching pickerel or pike.

However, as there seems to be little archæological evidence that in New England these pendants were used by the later Algonquians the above communications are recorded for what they are worth.

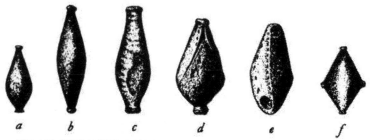

Figure 25. Sinkers for Fishing Lines. From pre-Algonquian graves in Maine: a, b, d, Orland; c, Blue Hill; e, Sullivan Falls; f, Warren. Andover Museum. (1/3.)

The consensus of opinion of the majority of archæologists seems to be that these objects were used as sinkers in fishing.

The odd specimen shown in figure 24, p, from a pre-Algonquian grave in Warren, Maine, may possibly be a combined sinker and

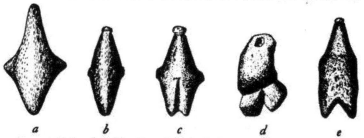

Figure 26. Sinkers for Fishing Lines. b, Wayland, Mass. a, c, d, e, Maine: a, Orland; c, Orland; d, e, Sullivan Falls; c, d, e, from pre-Algonquian graves, Andover explorations. (1/3.)

hook, which if taken into the mouth or swallowed might be more effective as a means of landing the fish than the common type. A similar specimen, from Newfoundland, is figured by Howley.[14]

In figure 26, a, b, c, and figure 25, f, are examples having side projections, which probably served some practical purpose, perhaps

[14] J. P. Howley, *The Beothucks or Red Indians*, plate XXII, fig. 28.

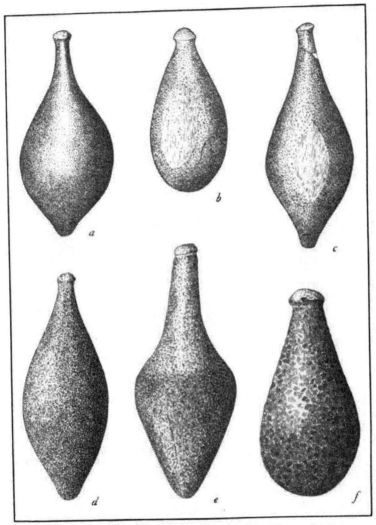

Figure 27. Large Pendants. a, d, e, f, Massachusetts: a, Essex County; d, Gloucester; f, Beverly Cove. b, c, Andover Museum, from pre-Algonquian cemeteries in Orland, Maine. (1/3.)

as a means of more securely fastening bait, or leaders for hooks. Hooks made by setting a sharpened splinter of bone at a proper angle into a wooden shank (figure 121, r) may have been used with some of these sinkers, as it would take considerable weight to sink the larger hooks of this type.

The specimen illustrated in figure 24, r, has four vertical grooves, which may have been intended for holding cords in place. The cords may well have served to secure a fishhook, with leader knotted at the base of the sinker where the lines crossed. At d, is a specimen with six vertical grooves symmetrically placed, which may have served a like purpose.

A specimen with a horizontal groove encircling it is shown at t. This groove may have been intended for a cord, from which two leaders carrying hooks were suspended. For a similar arrangement of lines and hooks on an Eskimo sinker sée Supplement,

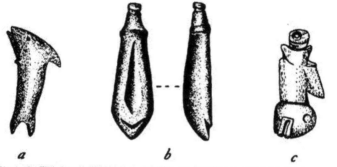

Figure 28. Fish shaped Pendants. a, b, From pre-Algonquian graves in Maine. Andover Archaeological Museum; a, Warren; b, Orland. c, From near Ipswich, Mass. (1/2.)

figure 143, b. The ridge encircling m, of figure 24, may have had a similar function as may also the grooving and notching in the examples in figure 26, c, d, and e.

In figure 25 are illustrated six pendants with a knob or perforation at either end. These are rare in New England. They occur, however, with the single knobbed variety in other sections, notably in Florida and California.

There is little doubt that these are also sinkers for fishing lines, and at the same time, like the other forms, served as lures for attracting fish, the line being attached to the upper end, and a short leader and hook fastened to the lower extremity. In e, the sinker is perforated instead of being knobbed. Several sinkers with hooks and lines attached, which are somewhat analagous to certain New England examples, are illustrated in the Supplement, figure 143, a-d.

A few of the objects shown in figure 24 resemble some of the more carefully made antler or ivory boluses of the Alaskan Eskimo used in bringing down waterfowl. Usually four to eight ivory or antler pendants are each fastened to one end of an equal number of separate cords about thirty inches in length. The opposite ends of these cords are tied together and a bunch of feathers fastened to the knot. In use, the knot is held in the hand and the weighted ends of the cords are swung around the head and thrown into a flying flock, one or more of the gyrating cords often winding itself around the neck or wing of a bird, bringing it to the ground. It seems improbable, however, that they were thus used in New England. If they had been one would expect to find them in bunches of four or five lying together in graves. The number and distribution of these stone pendants in the sixty-six graves opened by the writer at Bucksport, Orland, and Ellsworth do not point to such use. Of the twenty-two graves having one or more of these objects, seventeen contained only one each. In one grave two were found; two graves contained three each; one contained four; and in one were found six scattered over a radius of three feet from the principal deposit of implements. It will, therefore, be seen that only two instances out of twenty-two point to their possible use as bird boluses.

In figure 27 are illustrated six large pendants of the same general form as many of those already described. They are much less widely distributed, however, than the smaller variety, and occur principally in New England, although as time passes others will probably be found in the Maritime Provinces. These objects belong also to the old pre-Algonquian culture, a few having been taken from the graves of this people by Dr. Moorehead during his extensive explorations in Maine, one of which is represented in c, from Grave 31, Hartford's cemetery, Orland; b, is a "stray" from Mason's cemetery also in Orland. The others illustrated are from Massachusetts and are surface finds, having probably been plowed from shallow graves. The localities are as follows: a, Essex County; d, Gloucester; e, Massachusetts; f, Beverly Cove. The best examples are pecked over the entire surface. They are rarely, if ever, polished. It seems quite clear from their form that they were intended for suspension from a single cord. Like the smaller examples they are sometimes made from water-worn ovoid stones, the only modification being a groove pecked near one end.

In the Bates collection from the Maine shellheaps, now in the Peabody Museum at Cambridge, are more than a dozen of these large pendants all of which are of crude workmanship. They have the appearance of having been hastily made from local material. The positions they occupied in these refuse piles are recorded only in seven instances, which are as follows: Taft's Point, West Gouldsboro, three from the bottom of the heap; Golden Cove, Vinalhaven, one from the bottom of the heap, which in places was thirty-eight inches in depth; Turner's Farm, North Haven, two near bottom of heap; Watt's Point, St. George's River, one lying in shells about three inches from the bottom. This heap was two to three feet in depth. We have before referred to three small sinkers being found in the lower layer of a shellheap at Sullivan Falls, Maine, and also three others from near the bottom of a heap on Perkins Island, Massachusetts.

From the foregoing data we learn that some twenty of these pendants, including both small and large types, have been taken from shellheaps, thirteen of which are recorded as having been found at or near the bottom, including six of small and seven of large size, the depths at which the remaining seven were found not being recorded. This seems to show that the pre-Algonquian people were responsible for at least the beginnings of some of the shellheaps of the coastal region of Maine and Massachusetts.

We have tried to show that the smaller examples of the same general form — those up to about three inches in length — were probably used as lures, and as sinkers for fishing lines. If this be true is it not probable that the larger ones of the same general form may have been employed for a somewhat similar purpose? They are apparently confined largely to New England. I know of no record of the use of similar objects among any of our historic tribes. The following paragraph from Brigham's *Hawaiian Stone Implements* is interesting in this connection although it is a far cry from New England to the Hawaiian Islands:

Fishing Stones. — A peculiar method of fishing in vogue among the old Hawaiians consisted in suspending in the water club-shaped pieces of wood smeared with some bate (*palu*) supposed to be attractive to the fish, and then hooking or scooping the assembled prey. Many of these *laau melomelo* are in the Bishop Museum, and many of the formulae for bate used to render the log attractive have been published in an early catalogue of this Museum. Stone was sometimes substituted for wood, although rarely, and the only two that I have seen are shown in Fig. 72. They are well made, doubtless for some person of importance, and have been carefully kept. The longer one measures 9.5 inches and is of very graceful outline. In shape they resemble magnified "amulets" or "plummets" so common on the American continent. Most of the fish caught by means of these *bohaku melomelo* were small shore fish and the process will be described more fully in the chapter on Fisheries.[15]

One of these heavy wooden *laau melomelo* is in the Peabody Museum at Cambridge. It is about two feet in length and three inches in diameter near the lower end which is rounded. It tapers to less than an inch in diameter near its upper extremity which is furnished with a knob for the attachment of a cord. The stone fish lures figured by Brigham are shown for comparison in the Supplement.[16] It will be seen that they are almost identical in size and shape with New England examples.

Fish lures in the form of a fish were used both by the Algonquians and Eskimo. Among the latter they were often made of stone or ivory, and were either attached to a fishing line and carried one or more leaders with hooks, or were fastened to a separate line and used to decoy salmon or other fish within reach of spear or scoop net. Boas says that the incisor of a bear was frequently employed as a lure by the Central Eskimo.

Figure 28 shows three small fish effigies which may have served a similar purpose. The one represented in a, is from a grave at Harts Falls, Georges River, and b is from a grave near the outlet of Lake Alamoosook in Orland. Both belong to the pre-Algonquian group. It will be noted that there is a deep groove along the under side of b. The curious fish-like pendant figure 28, c, is a surface find from near Ipswich.

Another group of effigies which are by no means common is illustrated in figure 29. The fish, c, is from Salem Neck. It is perforated at the tail end and has a well developed dorsal fin. The mouth is indicated by a slight groove. A peculiar feature is the shallow groove analogous to the one in figure 28, b, about half an inch wide along the under side of the body. This does not appear in the drawing. In a, and b, are shown two representations of the whale, with side flippers and horizontal tail. They undoubtedly represent two principal types of this mammal, of which the right whale and the great headed sperm whale are examples. It is doubtful if these effigies should be classed as lures.

[15] W. T. Brigham, Memoirs of the Bernice Pauahi Bishop Museum, vol. i, no. 4, p. 73, fig. 72.
[16] See Supplement, fig. 143, g, h.

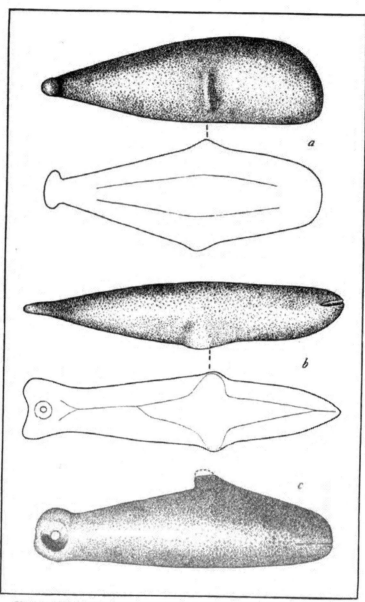

Figure 29. Effigy Pendants. a, Seems to represent a member of the sperm whale family, and b, a member of the right whale group. The former was found near Fall River, Mass., and is in the Andover Museum, the latter is from Seabrook, N. H., and is in the collection of the Amesbury Natural History Society. The fish effigy c, from Salem Neck, is in the Peabody Museum at Cambridge. (1/3.)

Pre-Algonquian Chipped Knives, Polished Slate Points, and Other Tools. Most of the objects figured and described under this heading were taken from the various burial places of this people in Maine. A few came from other sections of New England and are surface finds, having undoubtedly been plowed from similar graves.

Chipped implements in general will be discussed later but there are numerous examples that may be definitely assigned to this pre-Algonquian people that should be mentioned here. A considerable number have been taken from graves. These were undoubtedly knife blades although a few may have been projectile points. An especially fine blade is illustrated in figure 30, a. This is nine and three fourths inches long and is chipped from Mt. Kineo felsite. It was found with two similar ones in a deposit of red ocher near the outlet of Lake Alamoosook at Orland and is now in the Museum at Andover. The remaining examples in this illustration are from graves in the burial places at Bucksport and Ellsworth and are typical of many others from such graves.

The implements illustrated in figure 31 are of special interest. They are chipped from a translucent quartz interspersed with nearly black blotches and shadings of gray, a material apparently foreign to New England and only occurring in these states so far as known in the form of finished blades. The source of this material is apparently in Labrador and possibly also in Newfoundland. In the Peabody Museum at Cambridge are chips and broken implements from workshops across the harbor from Hebron, Labrador, and a few from Okak, some ten miles farther south, both in the Eskimo area. In Newfoundland Dr. Kidder found chips and finished scrapers on a workshop site at Blanc Sablon, Strait of Belle Isle, and a few points have been found at Notre Dame Bay.

Of the six smaller blades in figure 31 the upper one at the right and the two upper ones at the left are from graves in the pre-Algonquian cemetery on the shore of Pemaquid Lake, Damariscotta, Maine. The remaining three are from graves at Orland, Blue Hill, and Oakland, Maine, and are in the Andover collection.

The large leaf-shaped blade is from Rhode Island and the circumstance of its finding is unrecorded. A similar though somewhat smaller blade of this material, also from Rhode Island, is in the museum of the Rhode Island Historical Society. It is probable that all these implements were imported from Labrador in pre-

Algonquian times. Some of them may have been spear points; it seems more probable that they were used as cutting implements.

The beautiful polished slate knives and spear points illustrated in figures 32, 33, and 34, are in keeping with the excellent workmanship shown in most of the stone implements of this ancient

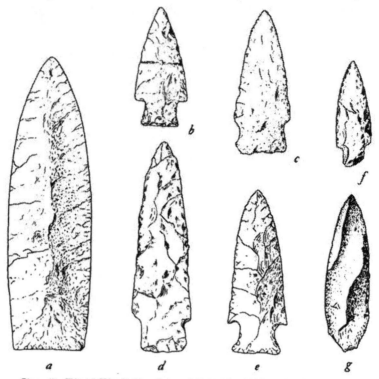

Figure 30. Chipped Flint Knives. From pre-Algonquian graves in Maine: a, from grave near outlet of Lake Alamoosook, Orland; b-e, from graves at Ellsworth; f, g, from graves at Bucksport. a, Andover Museum; b-g, Peabody Museum, Cambridge. (1/3.)

people. The short broad blades, figure 32, are more common in Vermont than in other sections of New England. Although somewhat larger, they are very close duplicates of several Alaskan Eskimo points hafted in foreshafts of wood about a foot in length, which are in the Peabody Museum at Cambridge. The lower end of these foreshafts was set into a socket in the end of the shaft which was usually four to five feet long, and used for lancing the

beluga or white whale. These slate-pointed foreshafts were sometimes detached from the shaft and carried as weapons. Numbers

Figure 31. Knives and Points. Chipped from translucent quartz. The largest is from
Rhode Island, the others from pre-Algonquian graves in Maine. They seem to have been
brought from Labrador where workshops of this material have been found. Andover Museum
and Peabody Museum, Cambridge. (About 2/5.)

of these short broad blades have been found in New England, New York, and Ontario, and Abbott reports one from New Jersey.

Figure 35, a, shows a dagger-like implement of reddish slate from the extensive sites near Amoskeag Falls, at Manchester. I know of but one similar specimen. This is reported by Wintemberg, as "a blade like a bayonet and a handle carved to represent the head of a bird." It was found in Ontario.

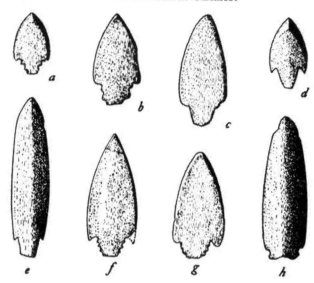

Figure 32. Knives and Points. Made of polished slate. All from Vermont. a, d, e, f, after G. H. Perkins; b, g, h, Slater Museum, Norwich; c, Mattatuck Hist. Soc., Waterbury, Conn. (1/3.)

Two slate knives of unusual form are illustrated in b, and c, of the above figure, each being furnished with a notched tang for the attachment of the handle; b, is from Panther Pond, Sebago Lake region and is figured by Moorehead; c, is from Contoocookville, Merrimack County, New Hampshire. Both are from the surface and may be provisionally classed with the pre-Algonquian group of implements.

The slate knives and projectile points illustrated in figure 33 show a wide range in both size and form. With three exceptions, a, c, and e, they were obtained from graves. The others, without doubt, were washed or plowed from similar graves. The most symmetrical and finely finished example that I have seen is shown

in a. This was picked up on the shore of Lake Alamoosook in
Orland by Mr. Soper, who later assisted the present writer in the

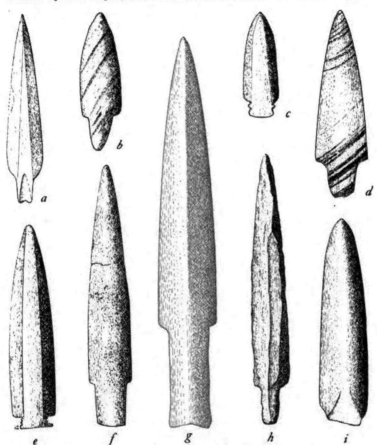

Figure 33. Knives and Points of Slate. b, d, f, g, h, From pre-Algonquian graves in Maine:
b, f, Oakland; d, Orland; g, Harts Falls, Warren; h, Stevens cemetery, Warren. a, c, e, i,
Surface finds: a, Orland; c, Penobscot Valley; e, Sebec Lake; i, Oldtown. b, d, f, g, h, Andover
Archaeological Museum; c, American Museum, New York; i, Worcester Hist. Soc. (1/3.)

exploration of the cemetery on the north shore of this lake. Its
narrow shank indicates that it was used as a projectile point.

Another fine example from Sebec, Maine, is represented in e.
This is somewhat blunted, and one of the tangs at the base is
broken off. Otherwise it is in perfect condition.

An especially interesting specimen is figured in h, as it shows the blocking out of the point by chipping preparatory to the final grinding and polishing. All of these slate points must have passed through this preliminary blocking out process. Comparatively few are made of banded slate. Two of this material are figured in b and d. Their localities are given in the title.

The long slender points of greenish slate, slightly less than one third natural size, illustrated in figure 34 are all from pre-Algonquian graves. The smaller specimens, a-e, are much less common than the longer ones. The smallest example, a, is from twenty-five inches below the surface. It lay in a small mass of red ocher in Section B, of the cemetery at Bucksport (see figure 5, no. 37). It was a very small grave, perhaps that of a child; b, and e, are from the cemetery at Harts Falls, Georges River; c, came from just beneath the sod in the Knoll cemetery at Orland, (figure 8, Sec. B, 3.). The three long points, g, h, i, are from a lot of sixteen taken from graves while removing gravel from the large pit of the cemetery at Ellsworth, and presented to the Peabody Museum at Cambridge by Mr. H. L. Woodcock and his brother of Belfast. Unfortunately we have no further knowledge of the conditions under which they were found.

Only one similar spear was discovered during the subsequent exploration of the remainder of this cemetery by the present writer. This came from Grave J, Section 9, (figure 12) a cross-section of which appears in figure 17. The grave was found while cutting down the wall of sand at the edge of the gravel pit. A layer of red ocher was encountered twenty-one inches from the surface and in it lay the spearpoint. About a foot to the right lay another mass of ocher without implements and still further to the right and on a higher level were ashes and bits of charcoal. The sand beneath the layers of ocher was somewhat discolored and portions of it were cemented into compact masses, evidently by the lime from the disintegrated skeleton. No fragment of bone nor particle of bone dust was found nor could the line of demarcation between the disturbed and undisturbed sand be determined. The body had been deposited in a horizontal position in a grave about two feet deep, red ocher placed near the head and over a part of the body and a spear laid in the grave with the slate point near the head.

The other points represented in figure 34 are from cemeteries

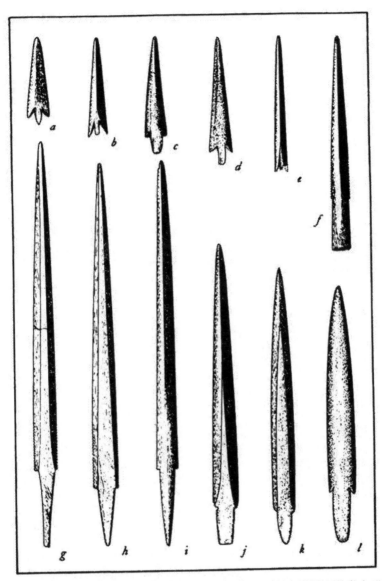

Figure 34. Slate Points. From pre-Algonquian graves in Maine: a, Bucksport; b, d, e, Warren; c, Orland; g, h, i, Ellsworth; f, j, k, l, Blue Hill; d, f, j, k, l, Andover Archaeological Museum; a, c, g, h, i, Peabody Museum, Cambridge. (1/3.)

explored under the auspices of the Archaeological Department of Phillips Academy at Andover by Dr. Moorehead. During these explorations numbers of slender slate points were recovered from burials at Winslow, Georges River, Blue Hill, Orland, and other Maine sites. In one grave at Blue Hill eight were found lying close together, all pointing in the same direction and all of nearly the same size and contour. One of these is shown in j, of the above figure. These were probably without hafts when placed in the grave.

Slate points closely approaching the types we have illustrated are widely distributed. They are found in the Maritime Provinces,

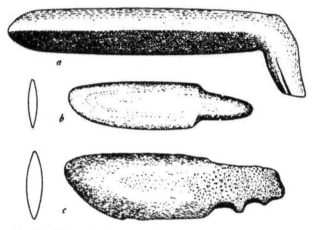

Figure 55. Slate Knives. a, Red slate, Manchester, N. H., Sanford collection; b, green slate, Panther Pond, Sebago Lake region, Me., Andover collection; c, gray slate, Contoocookville, Merrimack Co., N. H., Peabody Museum, Cambridge. (1/3.)

including Newfoundland, also in Quebec, Ontario, New York, and New England, and there is a beautiful specimen in the Peabody Museum at Cambridge from Kadiak Island, Alaska. The longest of these slate points so far recorded, eighteen inches, was found with others in a burial place at Milton, Queens County, Nova Scotia.[17]

I was informed by the late Dr. Frank Russell, that while carrying on ethnological work in the Mackenzie River region in 1892-1894, he had seen the Tinne using spears tipped with similar slate points,

[17] H. Piers, Proc. and Trans. of the Nova Scotia Inst. of Science, vol. ix., pt. 1, p. 34.

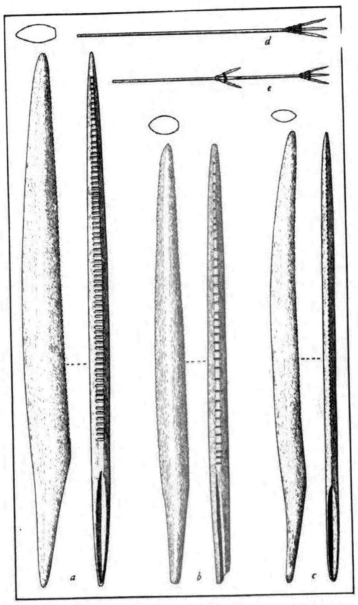

Figure 96. Slate Points for Bird Darts. a, Passadumkeag, Me., Bowdoin College Collection; b, c, from pre-Algonquian grave on ridge, Veazie Dam, near Oldtown, Me., H. A. Harden Collection; d, e, probable methods of hafting. (2/3, except d, e.)

for killing caribou that had been chased through the deep snow by hunters on snowshoes until the animals had become exhausted.

The three slate points for darts used in the capture of large water fowl shown two-thirds their natural size in figure 36 are of unusual interest. In looking over the collections at Bowdoin College many years ago with Professor Lee he called my attention to the point represented in a, and told me that it came from Passadumkeag. I have since learned that a number of graves had been opened in former times on the flat occupied by this village and that red paint and stone artifacts had often been found there.

The two smaller examples, b, c, are also from a pre-Algonquian grave unearthed in a sand-pit at Veazie dam near Oldtown on the Penobscot, by Herbert A. Harnden in 1922. These are in all essential particulars duplicates of points of bone and antler still used throughout the Eskimo area for taking water fowl. The two usual methods of hafting are shown in d, and e. Sometimes the dart is furnished with a long straight point at the end, but also has the three side prongs set well back. If the point does not strike the bird squarely, its neck or wing may become wedged between one of the serrated prongs and the shaft. Such darts are projected by the Eskimo with the aid of a throwing stick. It is probable that in New England similar points were also made of bone and antler which have long since disappeared through disintegration. It is possible that some of the long slate points illustrated in figure 34 may have been used in securing waterfowl.

Pre-Algonquian Ceremonials. Scattered throughout New England are many well made objects, usually of slate, but occasionally of steatite or other varieties of stone, which are commonly called ceremonials or banner stones for want of a more definite designation. They form, perhaps, the most attractive group of artifacts of our area, and the time and patience necessarily given to their making is an indication of the esteem in which they were doubtless held. The distribution of the principal forms illustrated corresponds approximately to that of the women's semilunar slate knives, the gouge-shaped adze blades, and the various types of slate projectile points, objects which may be attributed to that pre-Algonquian culture, the approximate distribution of which has already been shown.

The various New England forms are illustrated in figures 37–42. Examples occur in nearly all of the public and private collections

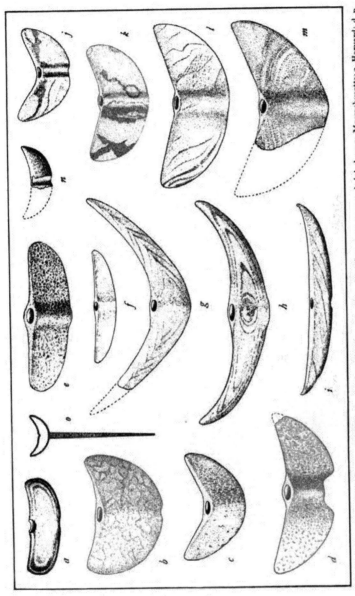

Figure 37. Whale Tail Ceremonial Objects. Made of slate and other attractive stones. a, e, d, j, k, l, m, n, Massachusetts: a, Harvard; d, n, Plymouth Co.; j, Westport; k, Gloucester; l, Concord. b, f, g, Connecticut: b, Portland; g, North Preston. h, Manchester, N. H.; i, Holderness, N. H.: e, near mouth of Otter Creek, Vt.; a, j, l, m, Peabody Museum, Cambridge; d, n, Pilgrim Hall, Plymouth; c, Amherst College Museum; f, National Museum; k, Slater Museum, Norwich; b, g, N. L. Bull Coll.; i, J. B. Sweet Coll.; h, Dr. H. L. Watson Coll. o, Ceremonial staff surmounted by whale tail symbol, Beothuk Indians, Newfoundland. (1/3 except o.)

61

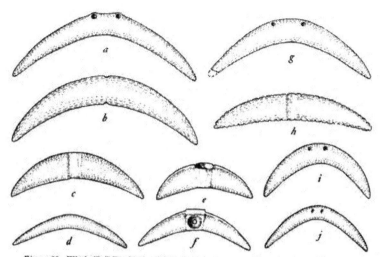

Figure 38. Whale Tail Pendants. Made of slate and apparently worn on the person. c, e, f, i, j. From pre-Algonquian graves in Maine: c, i, j, Orland; e, Georges River; f, Sullivan Falls. Surface finds: a, Bucksport, Me.; d, Orland, Me.; g, Gouldsboro, Me.; b, h, Nashua, N. H. (1/3.)

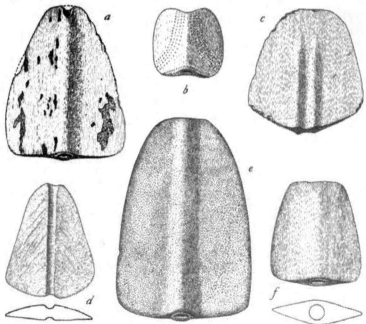

Figure 39. Ceremonial Objects, usually made of slate. a, Danvers, Mass.; b, Franklin, N. H.; c, Oxford, Mass.; d, Roxbury, Conn.; e, f, Massachusetts. (1/3.)

of this region. They seem to have served no practical purpose, but were doubtless used as accompaniments to ceremonial dances or as badges of office, probably for both purposes.

The Beothuk of Newfoundland were probably related to the ancient people who occupied New England before the advent of the Algonquians. One of the last survivors of the Beothuk, an

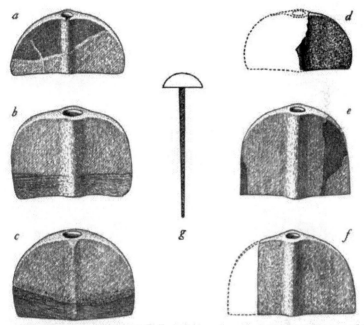

Figure 40. Ceremonial Objects. Made of slate. a, b, c, From pre-Algonquian graves in Maine: a, Emerson cemetery, Orland; b, c, cemetery at Oldtown. Surface finds: d, from vicinity of Norwich, Conn.; e, Wakefield, Mass.; f, Salem, Mass.; g, Ceremonial staff surmounted by a symbol of the moon, Beothuk Indians, Newfoundland. a, b, c, e, Andover Archaeological Museum; f, Peabody Museum, Salem; d, Slater Museum, Norwich. (1/3, except g.)

intelligent young woman of about twenty-two years, whose name was Shanawdithit, was captured in 1823 and lived for several years in families of English settlers. She died in 1829. Soon after her capture she was visited by the Rev. William Wilson in the court house at St. John's, who tells us that when shown a watch and looking-glass she was much interested but

when a black lead pencil was put into her hand and a piece of white paper laid upon the table, she was in raptures. She made a few marks on the paper apparently to try the pencil; then in one flourish she drew a deer perfectly, and what is most surprising, she began at the tip of the tail.[18]

Shortly before her death some five years later this native young artist prepared a set of drawings for W. E. Cormack while residing in his house at St. John's. These are reproduced in Howley's work.

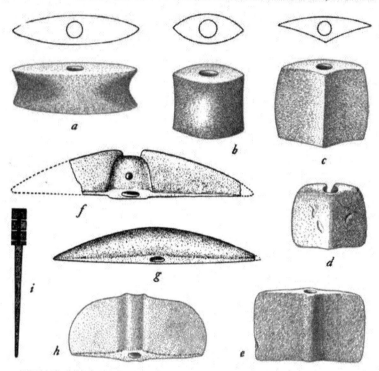

Figure 41. Miscellaneous Ceremonial Objects. a, Derby, Conn.; b, Montville, Conn.; c, Connecticut Valley, Mass.; d, Amherst, Mass.; e, North Stonington, Conn.; f, Cheshire, Conn.; g, Manchester, N. H.; h, pre-Algonquian grave, Passadumkeag River, Me., after W. B. Smith; i, ceremonial staff, Beothuk Indians, Newfoundland. a, Peabody Museum of New Haven; b, N. L. Bull Coll.; c, Amherst College Coll.; d, C. C. Ferguson Coll.; e, Worcester Hist. Soc.; f, Mattatuck Hist. Soc.; g, G. B. Sanford Coll. (1/3, except i.)

Five of them were maps showing scenes which took place on or near the Exploits River and Red Indian Lake between the years 1810 and 1823. The others represent wigwams, store and smoke houses, weapons, utensils, etc., in use by her people. Among them

[18] J. P. Howley, *The Beothucks or Red Indians,* p. 171.

are several staffs the height of a man, each terminating at its upper end with a different symbol. "Totems? or Emblems of Mythology" is the title of the group. Figure 37, o, is a copy of one of these staffs. The legend which accompanies it is as follows, "ow-as-posh-no-un. Emblematic of the whale's tail, considered the greatest prize by the hunter." From Howley's text referring to this group we quote as follows:

No. 2 represents very clearly the crescent shaped tail of a whale, it is called "Owas-bosh-no-un." A note informs us that a whale was considered a great prize, this animal affording them a more abundant supply of food than anything else, hence the Indians worshipped this image of the Whale's tail. Another reference to this occurs amongst some stray notes of Cormack's as follows: "The Bottle Nose Whale which they represented by the fishes tail, frequents, in great numbers the Northern Bays, and creeps in at Clode Sound and other places, and the Red Indians consider it the greatest good luck to kill one. They are 22 and 23 feet long.

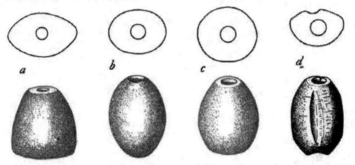

Figure 42. Ceremonial Objects, usually made of Slate. a, b, d, Massachusetts; c, Lake Congamuck, Conn. a, Amherst College Museum; b, Pilgrim Hall, Plymouth; c, N. L. Bull Coll.; d, Peabody Museum, Cambridge. (1/3.)

The late Dr. George Byron Gordon was the first to call attention to the probable identity of the symbol with the slate "ceremonials" of similar shape common in New England and the adjacent territory, and also to its resemblance to the carefully made ivory symbols of the tail of this animal used in the whale ceremony of the Alaskan Eskimo,[19] some of which bore intricate surface patterns of incised circles and curved lines. These ivory symbols are perforated like our eastern specimens and were doubtless likewise carried on the end of a staff.

[19] G. B. Gordon, *The Double Axe and Some Other Symbols.* The Museum Journal (University of Pennsylvania), vol. vii, pp. 46–68.

The whale's tail was a favorite symbol of the Alaskan Eskimo and was often incised upon ivory. Labrets of this form were made of ivory and attractive varieties of stone. Perhaps the most interesting examples are the whale tail breast plates of wood, fifteen to eighteen inches in length, obtained by John Murdoch at Point Barrow in 1881. They were from old cemeteries and were furnished with thongs for attachment to the neck and body of the wearer. The lower edge of each was serrated like the small specimen, figure 38, h, from Nashua. In the center of the Point Barrow specimens was painted a great man in red, standing on the back of a large black whale, and holding in each hand a smaller whale of the same color. This central group was surrounded by drawings in black representing men in boats, birds, etc. Murdoch thought the red giant to be *Kikam-igo*, the divinity who controls the whales and other sea animals. The following is from Dr. Gordon's paper.

When I was in Alaska in 1905 I was able to obtain several examples of this object [whale's tail symbol] which are now in the Museum. I had no opportunity of seeing the ceremony, but from Mrs. Bernardi of Nome who had witnessed many Eskimo ceremonies I learned some of the facts about the ceremony connected with the whale hunt.

At that time and later I noticed that the whale's tail is a favorite device among the Alaskan Eskimo for carving on ivory or wooden implements and for tattooing on their persons and for charms. This use of the symbol which often at first sight appears to be for decoration has also a deeper religious significance. Many emblems are used in the whale ceremony; that which represents the animal's tail takes two forms.

Then follow drawings of the typical tail symbol and also of what he considered a conventionalized form of the same which resembles the New England ceremonials shown in figure 39. Those who have seen a school of sporting whales or a moving picture of one will doubtless recall the interesting sight presented as the tail and rear part of the body of the animal are thrown high in the air at intervals. This movement is often shown in the delineations of the Eskimo, and it could not fail to have strongly impressed itself upon the minds of our native people.

The occurrence of these symbols among the Eskimo of Alaska, together with the woman's semilunar knife, various forms of slate projectile points, and certain other artifacts, taken in connection with the occurrence of similar types in New England and other parts of the Northeast, is significant, especially as in the latter region they certainly belong to a pre-Algonquian occupation. I do not think, however, that the Eskimo ever inhabited any portion of New England.

In figure 37 are shown typical examples of the whale symbol, from New England. Occasionally unfinished specimens are found which show the process followed in their making. A piece of slate or other suitable stone is roughly chipped into the approximate form, the shaping is carried still further by pecking and grinding. When the form is about complete, drilling is begun at the upper or concave side, sometimes with a solid drill of flint or other material though usually with a hollow drill, probably of elder wood. A number of partially drilled specimens have been found showing the central core made by the hollow drill. To the layman it seems impossible to drill compact slate to the depth of three inches or more with a piece of hollow elder wood, cane, or the bone of a large wading bird, even with the help of sand and water. It required patience, but the process is perfectly practical, as the following experiment proved.

A section of elder wood about one half inch in diameter, with bark and pith removed, was cut square across. This formed a cylinder with walls less than one eighth of an inch thick. By placing a small amount of wet sand upon the slate and rotating the stick between the palms, a circular depression was started, which as it became deeper held the drill in place. The work was then carried forward more rapidly. The end of the drill being of wood catches and holds some of the sharp grains of sand till they crumble and others take their place, gradually cutting away the slate, and leaving a core in the center of the hole, which can easily be broken off and removed as the work progresses.

Probably the examples shown in figure 37 were mounted on the end of a staff as illustrated in the Beothuk drawing, o. Certain others from Maine and New Hampshire (figure 38), being smaller and lighter, were probably worn as personal ornaments. Several of these, c, e, f, i, j, were taken from graves of the pre-Algonquian cemeteries.

I have been unable to learn of the finding of one of these symbols in an Algonquian grave. They are undoubtedly pre-Algonquian. With the exception of the smaller examples (figure 38), they are usually surface finds that were doubtless plowed from shallow graves which passed unnoticed. In New England they are quite common. In time they will probably be discovered northward to at least the southern portion of Hudson Bay. I have recently examined a beautiful specimen of about the size and form of m, in figure 37. This was in the collection at Chateau de Ramezay, Montreal, and is recorded as having been found in 1854, in an Indian grave near the L'Assumption River, Parish of St. Paul de Lavaltrie, which is about twenty miles north of Montreal. As already noted several have been taken from a very ancient cemetery near Rancocas Creek, New Jersey.

Three unusually fine examples of this symbol are illustrated in g, h, i, of figure 37: g, is from North Preston, Connecticut, and is in the N. L. Bull collection at Hartford; b, was found by Dr. H. L. Watson near Amoskeag Falls and is in his collection at Manchester; i, is from Holderness, New Hampshire, and is in the cabinet of J. B. Sweet of Boston; l, forms a part of the Henry D. Thoreau collection now in the Peabody Museum at Cambridge. They are all of banded slate.

It may be well to mention here one of those coincidences of form which are sometimes brought to the attention of archæologists. Among the household utensils of the Lapps is a wooden implement of almost the exact shape and size of k, or l, in figure 37, having a stick about two feet long inserted in the perforation and projecting as a handle from the concave edge. This implement is used as a "whorl" in preparing milk foods, is rotated between the palms, and functions much after the manner of some forms of egg-beaters. There is of course no possible connection between this Lapp implement and the whale tail ceremonials, although the forms are nearly identical.

Another group of ceremonials which are somewhat less numerous than those described above and which have approximately the same distribution is illustrated in figure 39.

The drawings give a good idea of their relative sizes and shapes. They are usually without surface decoration, although sometimes one is found with crude cross-hatch lines which seem to have no special significance. The specimen shown in b, has an unusual design consisting of two curved patterns each made up of four parallel rows of dots. Near the base is also a row of notches. These notches and rows of dots are upon one side only. This specimen is of a reddish-yellow compact stone resembling slate, and was found on the Daniel Webster place in Franklin, New Hampshire.

One of the finest examples of this type of ceremonial that I have seen is represented in a. It is of greenish slate interspersed with black blotches. The wings are very thin, and the perforation is an excellent example of stone drilling. It was found in Danvers, Massachusetts, and is in the Peabody Museum at Salem.

Another interesting specimen from Massachusetts is shown in e. This is nearly seven inches in length and unfinished. It is finely pecked over the entire surface but no attempt has been made to grind or polish it. The drilling has been continued for about two thirds its length.

Mr. Norris L. Bull of Hartford has reported fragments of a small bannerstone much like figure 39, a, from the bottom of a shell-heap explored under his auspices at Niantic, another indication that the lower layers of some of our shellheaps were accumulated by pre-Algonquians.

It will be noticed that the ceremonials illustrated in c, d, are grooved upon either side and have no perforations. These grooves are obviously for the purpose of receiving the split end of the staff. This and the perforated form seem to occur in about equal numbers in New England.

Figure 40, g, is a copy of one of the drawings made by Shanaw-dithit, the Beothuk woman before referred to. The legend accompanying it is as follows: "Kuus (moon) handle painted red 6 feet long." Howley's text reads: "No. 3. This represents the half moon inverted, and is named 'Kuis.' There is no note of any kind to indicate what [other] significance was attached to it." [20] It seems evident that the other illustrations in figure 40 represent the same symbol and were intended also to be hafted in a like manner for ceremonial use. They are all carefully fashioned of slate. Specimen a, is from a pre-Algonquian grave on Lake Alamoosook, Orland, Maine; b, and c, are from graves of the same period at Oldtown, Maine; d, is from the vicinity of Norwich, Connecticut; e, is from Wakefield; and f, was found while digging the cellar for the Lyceum building at Salem in 1829.

In figure 41 are represented several ceremonials which evidently belong to the same general group as the ones above described. Those represented in f, g, and h, are probably variants of figure 37. Figure 41, h, is from a pre-Algonquian ("Red Paint") grave on the Hathaway farm, Passadumkeag River, Maine. It has several

[20] J. P. Howley, *The Beothucks or Red Indians*, p. 250.

notches along its lower edge; f, is also ornamented with small notches. The form g, while not common in New England, has a wider distribution to the westward. This remark also applies to the specimens in the upper row, and also to d. The remaining one, e, is uncommon. It bears a close resemblance to the objects placed upon the upper portion of the ceremonial staff, i, copied from Shanawdithit's drawing. The legend accompanying the drawing gives only the Beothuk name of the staff and its length: — "Ash-wa-meet. 6 feet long."

It may be well also to mention that Shanawdithit made a drawing of another staff of the same length as the above, the upper portion of which terminated in four, slightly truncated triangles placed one above the other. A staff, evidently of this form, was found in 1811 in a village on the Exploits River. It was shown to Lieut. Buchan by a Beothuk man who

pointed out a staff and showed that it belonged to the person that wore the high cap, the same that I had taken to be the chief; the length of this badge was nearly six feet, and two inches at the head, tapering to the end, terminating in not more than three quarters of an inch; it presented four plain equal sides, except at the upper end, where it resembled three rims one over the other, and the whole stained red.[21]

We now come to a final group of this general class of ceremonial objects, representations of which appear in figure 42. They are usually of slate, are carefully made, and the surfaces are polished to a greater or less degree. Occasionally one is found with a groove along its side as in d. This has led some to believe that it was used in finishing arrowshafts, which seems improbable, as the surface is usually polished and has no rasping qualities, like the well known forms illustrated in figure 99.

These more or less egg-shaped objects are fairly common in this region. They are undoubtedly pre-Algonquian. I know of but one that was found in a grave. This was taken by Dr. Moorehead from a grave on the land of M. Rollins, near Dover, New Hampshire. Two gouge shaped adze blades of typical form lay beside it.[22]

Pre-Algonquian Semilunar Knives. The cutting implements illustrated in figures 43 and 44 are fairly common in New England. They are usually of slate, the colors ranging through grays, greens, reds, and purple to nearly black. Occasionally one is made of fine-

[21] Howley, Ibid., p. 79.
[22] W. K. Moorehead, *A Report on the Archaeology of Maine*, p. 208, fig. 108.

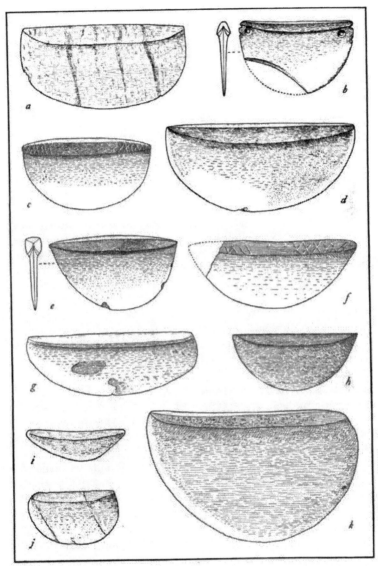

Figure 43. Semilunar Knives. Usually made of slate. a, b, c, d, h, i, Massachusetts; a, Wenham; c, Topsfield; d, Newton; h, Bradford. g, Maine; j, West Bath, Me.; f, East Jaffrey, N. H.; k, Manchester, N. H.; e, Hopkinton, R. I. a, b, e, f, h, i, k, Peabody Museum, Cambridge; c, Peabody Museum, Salem; g, i, Bowdoin College Coll. (about 1/4.)

grained sandstone. Many of the slates contain a good deal of silica which adds much to the efficiency of the cutting edge when properly ground. These knives are undoubtedly pre-Algonquian. In New England they may be grouped with the oldest artifacts of which we have knowledge. Disregarding for the moment the occurrence of certain forms among the Eskimo, their distribution is about as follows: New England, New Jersey, Pennsylvania, New York, and parts of Ontario northward to about the latitude of Ottawa. North of this point we have little archæological data upon which to base their distribution.

In the collections of McGill University at Montreal is a very fine example eight inches in length of the monolithic type, which came from the east coast of Hudson Bay. This is much like e, in figure 43. So far as I know these knives have not been reported from Quebec or the Maritime Provinces, but as these regions have not been very thoroughly explored archæologically they may yet be found. They seem to be most abundant in New England and New York. They bear a very close resemblance to the Ulu, or woman's knife of the Alaskan Eskimo, as will be seen by comparing the drawings with figure 145 of the Supplement. The hafted examples in the latter illustration show conclusively that the perforations in the New England specimens were for securing the handle with lashings of cord, sinew, or other substance.

Nearly all of the New England examples are either perforated to aid in the attachment of the haft, or the implements are monolithic; that is, the handle and the blade consist of a single piece. In some examples, as in figures 43, b, and 44, c, d, e, j, wooden handles were doubtless added to the monolithic form, but usually the perforated blades are without the thickened upper portion fashioned to serve as a grip.

Among the Eskimo, the handles, when present, are made of a separate piece, usually of wood or ivory. Among the Alaskan Eskimo and occasionally among the Northwest Coast tribes this primitive knife survives in its ancient form although its blade is often made of iron. The Eskimo to the east of Alaska doubtless used it in olden times but its form has become modified in later years.

That many of the knives found in New England were made in these states is conclusively shown from the fact that a considerable number of unfinished examples may be seen in our collections, some of them being roughly blocked out by chipping and others having partially ground surfaces. Both types of perforations, the drilled and the incised, when they occur on New England examples, are

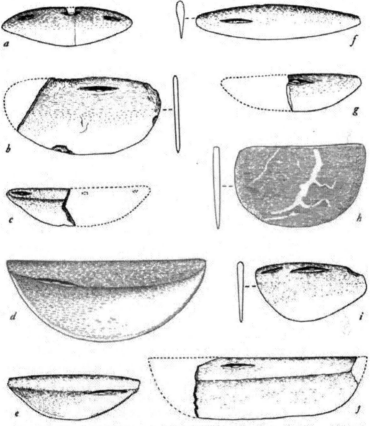

Figure 44. Semilunar Knives. a, c, d, f, h, i, j, Massachusetts: a, Danvers; c, Concord; d, Deerfield. e, Centerbrook, Conn.; g, Allingtown, Conn.; b, Tiverton, R. I. b, h, Peabody Museum, Cambridge; a, Peabody Museum, Salem; e, Peabody Museum, New Haven; f, i, d, Amherst College Museum; c, g, Andover Museum; j, National Museum. (about 1/4.)

identical with those from Alaska. The incised perforation is made by scraping two depressions opposite each other, one upon either side, until the incisions meet. In figure 44, f, is an unfinished perforation. Both grooves are cut, but they do not join.

The New England knives vary greatly in size. The smallest

that I have seen measures two and one half inches in length. It was found on an old site in Wayland, Massachusetts, by Mr. C. C. Ferguson and is now in his collection. The largest is in the Museum at Amherst College. It is twelve and three quarters inches in length, and five and three quarters inches in width. It is made of gray-green slate and was found in Belchertown, not far from Amherst. The great majority of these tools are four to six inches in length.

So far as I know none of these implements has been found in a grave, or at least in what was recognized to be a grave. They have, however, been obtained from sites from which other well-known types of pre-Algonquian implements have been taken.

Tools of this general type in recent use among the Eskimo and tribes of the Northwest Coast are usually called fish knives for they were generally employed by women in splitting salmon and other fish for drying. This, however, is but one of the many uses for which the tool is fitted. Our New England examples may be considered general utility tools used by the women for many purposes, such as slitting fish, skinning and cutting up animals, cutting dressed skins for clothing, belts, bags, etc., and for various other domestic purposes. It should be remembered that they are of the same form as the old fashioned saddler's knife. Perhaps the most perfect specimen so far recovered is illustrated in figure 43, h, one fourth natural size. It is made from a piece of dark purple slate, and it looks as fresh as though just from the hands of its maker.

It was plowed up in a swamp at Bradford, Massachusetts, on the Merrimack, and given to the Peabody Museum of Cambridge some fifty years ago. Its perfect preservation is due to its having lain in still water or soft mud where it was free from erosion. Its cutting edge is perfect, and with it I have cut Indian dressed buckskin, birch bark and other material as neatly as with a steel knife of average sharpness.

As a rule these semilunar knives are without ornamentation. The upper portion or handle of the monolithic form, however, is sometimes decorated with incised lines or cross-hatch markings much like those in figure 43, c, f. I have seen several with similar ornamentations. Perhaps these lines serve also to make the grip more secure.

These cutting implements attained a high development in New England. Nowhere else do they have so great a range in size.

They are essentially a woman's tool, and their apparent absence from graves of the inhumation type is not easily explained. It should be borne in mind, however, that the Beothuk, probably an offshoot of the ancient people who formerly occupied most of northeastern America had three principal methods of disposal of the dead: burials upon the surface; scaffold burials, usually in well made box-like structures of poles or logs; and inhumation. The latter method seems to have been most common in New England, but to what extent the two former methods were followed can only be surmised. It is very probable that many of our surface implements came from scaffold burials or from burials on the surface, while the majority were doubtless plowed or washed from shallow graves beneath the surface.

Pre-Algonquian Miscellaneous Objects. In figure 45 are several tools of unknown use, all of slate with the exception of b, which came from the shore of Chesuncook Lake in Maine. From graves at Veazie dam, near Oldtown on the Penobscot River, c, d, and f, were taken; a, is also from the Penobscot Valley but the exact locality is unrecorded. The lower portions of a, and c, are curved, the latter being ground to an edge. The end of e, is also ground to an edge. The less symmetrical example, d, perforated at its upper extremity, may be a sharpening stone somewhat analogous to those in figure 46. What seems to be a handle of some sort appears in f. The lower part (at the left) is less carefully finished than the rest of the surface.

Often accompanying adze blades in the old cemeteries are slate pendants, showing unmistakable use as sharpening stones. These were doubtless used for keeping the cutting edges of adzes and other tools in good condition. They are usually, though not always, perforated at one end for the purpose of suspension. Three of them are illustrated in figure 46. The two upper ones are from the old cemetery on the west side of the Kennebec River at Waterville, and c, is from a grave at Mt. Desert Ferry. Similar though somewhat narrower tools are often found in other portions of New England.

In figure 47 are illustrated two bow-drill rests from southern New England. They are both surface finds. The one at the left, a, is from near Taunton, Massachusetts. It is of a type in common use among the Alaskan Eskimo, where they are generally set into a socket in an oblong wooden holder made to be held firmly between the teeth or in the hand. One end of this wooden holder is often perforated for the attachment of a thong which is used for binding together the parts of the drill when not in use.

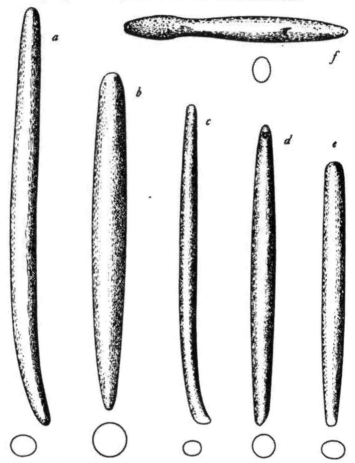

Figure 46. Implements of Unknown Use. All of slate with the exception of b. a, b, c, d. f, Maine: a, Penobscot valley; b, south end of Lake Chesuncook, A. E. Marks Coll.; c, d, f, from pre-Algonquian graves near Veasie Dam, Oldtown, H. A. Harnden Coll.; e, Manchester, N. H., G. B. Sanford Coll. (about 1/2.)

A second drill-rest, from Slate Hill, Middleton, Rhode Island, is figured in b. This is complete in itself and was doubtless intended to be held in the hand only. The hole for the reception of the upper end of the drill shaft is on the concave side, and there is a groove around one end also for the thong used for wrapping the parts of the drill together when laid aside.

In figure 48, one third natural size, is illustrated an object wrought from greenish slate taken from a pre-Algonquian grave in an old cemetery on the Holway farm near the head-of-tide, Narramissic River, Orland, Maine., by E. O. Sugden about 1900. It still shows signs of the red paint in which it lay. It is

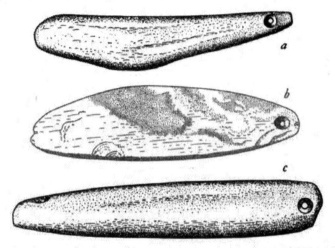

Figure 46. Sharpening Stones. From pre-Algonquian graves in Maine. a, b, Waterville; c, Mt. Desert Ferry. Peabody Museum, Cambridge. (1/3.)

now in the Museum of the American Indian, New York. This object is about five sixteenths of an inch in thickness, and is perforated by a rectangular opening, and two small holes near the bottom apparently for the passage of binding cords. The two opposite sides are each furnished with a groove somewhat less than one eighth of an inch deep. The object has the appearance of having been fitted into a socket furnished with tongues which projected into these grooves to assist in holding it firmly in place. The specimen reminds us quite forcibly of the ivory or bone rest for the Eskimo whale harpoon which is lashed between the forward ends of the gunwales of the umiak used in hunting this animal, and serves to support the forward part of the harpoon, also as a guide for the line after the whale is struck.

Fire-making Sets. One of the most characteristic groups of implements from the pre-Algonquian graves consists of fire-making sets, each set originally composed of two lumps of iron pyrites, or one lump of this mineral and one of flint. By striking the two together after the manner of a flint and steel, sparks were produced which, when caught upon properly prepared tinder, and gently blown, produced fire.

A large proportion of the graves contained one of these fire-making outfits. I have recovered many of them and in every instance the pyrites had become wholly disintegrated owing to the long period which had elapsed since they were buried. If the pyrites were fairly pure, only a yellow powder remained, which has sometimes been mistaken for paint.

Figure 47. Rests for top of Bow-drill. a, From vicinity of Taunton, Mass.; b, Slate Hill, Middletown, R. I. Peabody Museum, Cambridge. (1/3.)

If the pyrites originally consisted of disseminated crystals in a matrix of quartz or other stone, the cavities contained a small quantity of yellow powder only. The purity of the pyrites varied considerably in different graves, and sometimes the impurities were so abundant that the lump retained its original form and appeared as a cinder-like crust permeated with minute sponge-like cavities. Two of these sets are illustrated in figure 7, each pair originally consisting of a lump of impure pyrites and a smaller hammerstone of flint.

This type of fire-making set, or strike-a-light, as it is often called, was known throughout the Eskimo area and also to the people who came in contact with the Eskimo, including the Beothuk of Newfoundland. The Algonquian Indians of southern New England also used fire-making sets of flint and pyrites, having probably adopted them from their more northern neighbors.

Gosnold, Brereton, Morton, and Williams all mention the use of firestones, Brereton's account is the best. Writing of the Indians near Buzzard's Bay he says:

They strike fire in this manner; every one carrieth about him in a purse of tewed leather, a mineral stone . . . and with a flat emery stone . . . tied fast to the end of a little stick, gently he striketh on the mineral stone, and within a stroke or two, a spark falleth upon a piece of touchwood (much like our sponge in England,) and with the least spark he maketh a fire presently.[22]

Josselyn calls this touchwood, spunk, and says it is an excrescence which grows out of the black birch.[24] Both Josselyn and Gyles saw the firedrill also in use in New England. It was probably likewise to be found over the entire area of the distribution of the strike-a-light. The latter method seems to have been the favorite, however, for Jenness, writing of the Copper Eskimo tells us that

the thong drill used by all other Eskimos is known to them, but they never employ it except in an emergency, because of the labor involved and the difficulty of obtaining suitable wood.[25]

There are several Eskimo fire-making sets of pyrites in the Peabody Museum at Cambridge from Greenland, Labrador, and the Coronation Gulf region. In the set from the last locality, each lump of pyrites is enclosed, with the exception of one side, in a tight fitting jacket of skin with the hair outermost. The tinder, which consists of seeds of the cotton-grass (*Eriophorum*) is kept in a small receptacle of skin. There is also a skin disc upon which are grouped a few heads of cotton-grass ready to receive the sparks. This outfit is all enclosed in a skin bag as a protection from dampness. Dried moss is also used for tinder. In the set brought from Greenland by Peary the moss was enclosed in a greasy bird skin, which together with the rest of the outfit was kept in a skin bag.

Red Paint. The almost universal use of red ocher by the pre-Algonquian people of New England, as shown by its presence in practically all of the graves thus far opened, is another indication of their probable relationship to the Beothuk of Newfoundland to whom the term Red Indian was given by the early navigators who visited that island. They were so named, not because their skins were naturally of a reddish hue, but because their persons, and nearly everything belonging to them, were painted with this pigment. A similar custom, though less marked, was followed in more recent times by certain of the Tinne, notably the Kutchin of northern Alaska.

[22] Brereton, *Account of Gosnold's Voyage*, Mass. Hist. Coll. 3rd series, Vol. VIII, p. 91.

[24] John Josselyn, *New England's Rarities*, Veazie reprint, p. 100.

[25] D. Jenness, *The Life of the Copper Eskimos*, p. 108.

The Beothuk had abundant outcrops of this red sesqueoxid of iron in Newfoundland and several places around the coast are still pointed out where the Indians procured this red ocher. One of these, in Conception Bay, is known as Ocher Pit Cove. Another is Ocher Island, in Bay of Exploits.

Our New England tribes, and especially those of Maine, doubtless obtained their red paint largely from the extensive outcrops near the Katahdin Iron Works in the central part of the state. Dr. Moorehead, who visited the locality in 1915, found an outcrop of this pigment at the foot of a high elevation or long ridge about half a mile from the small settlement at the Works. He also found numerous depressions at Olamon, on the Penobscot, where the older residents claim that in earlier days red ocher was dug up and taken away.[26]

Figure 45. Object of slate somewhat resembling the ivory harpoon rest and guide for line fastened between the forward ends of Eskimo umiak gunwales. From pre-Algonquian grave on the Holway farm, Orland, Me. (1/2.)

A considerable portion of the paint in the graves was doubtless deposited in bags or other receptacles, but it also seems to have been occasionally strewn in the bottom of the excavation, perhaps as a part of the burial ceremony. Occasionally the thin layer continues for some distance, as in figure 12, Sections 9 and 10, where it extended for at least fifteen feet.

The use of red paint by the New England Indians was not confined to the pre-Algonquian group. It also occurs in many of the graves of the Algonquians who prized it highly for personal adornment. Its use, however, was less prevalent among the later tribes.

[26] W. K. Moorehead, *A Report on the Archaeology of Maine,* pp. 221, 222.

THE OLD ALGONQUIAN GROUP

W E have called this group of artifacts old Algonquian. That the Great Earthwork Builders centering in Ohio were members of this great stock is more than probable. Types of artifacts characteristic of this mound culture are distributed throughout most of the Algonquian area south of the Great Lakes and the St. Lawrence from Wisconsin eastward to Maine, and various phases of Algonquian mythology are well represented in certain ceremonial objects from the great mound groups. They are the earliest people that may be assigned with confidence to this stock.

The expansion of the people of this group is probably responsible for pushing the pre-Algonquian inhabitants eastward and finally driving them from New England.

The approximate extent of this culture is shown in figure 2. It attained its height at a period antedating by many years the arrival of the Whites in the Ohio Valley.

During the period between the abandonment of the principal mound groups and the arrival of the French, southern Ohio seems to have been occupied principally by the Mosopelea, eight villages of which are located on Franquelin's map of 1684. La Salle tells us that these towns were destroyed by the Iroquois.[27] One of these villages was probably at Madisonville on the extensive village and cemetery site, which, as shown by a few artifacts of European origin from the graves, was occupied down to the beginning of the historic period.

The material culture of the Madisonville people was like that shown by numerous other sites in southern Ohio and was very different from the culture of the builders of the great earthworks. There are certain features which seem to connect it with the Muskhogean group to the south, among whom the surviving Mosopelea found refuge, after the destruction of their villages by the Iroquois. As shown on the map, the old Mound-builder culture extended on the north to the Great Lakes and also included southern Ontario. On the west it embraced the greater portion of Wisconsin and Illinois; on the south Virginia and a part of Tennessee; while to the east it extended over the Middle States and nearly all of New England.

[27] C. A. Hanna, *The Wilderness Trail*, vol. II, p. 97.

The most extensive and the greatest number of mounds and earthworks were in the central portion of the area; they became more scattered and less prominent toward its outer limits. East of central New York few if any mounds or stone-lined graves were built, but typical Mound-builder artifacts occur in eastern New York and in certain graves, cemeteries, and other sites throughout most of New England. Outside the area shown in figure 2, an occasional artifact belonging to this culture occurs, but they are rare.

By turning to figure 3 which shows the distribution of our northern Indian groups at the time of the arrival of Europeans, it will be seen that the war-like Iroquois had displaced these older inhabitants in the region of Lakes Erie and Ontario and the valley of the St. Lawrence River. The period of occupation by the Iroquois seems to have been sufficient for their characteristic material culture to have developed, for these artifacts are not found outside this area in sufficient numbers to indicate more than an occasional visit or brief occupation.

The great mound settlements of Ohio formed, so to speak, the Metropolitan District of this northern Mound-builder group. It was in this section, under favorable conditions, that the people were able to develop their native arts and industries to a high degree of excellence. It is in the Metropolitan District of any province that we look for the most advanced attainment of any people.

Many of the artifacts from the Ohio mounds are identical with certain New England types, and others are but an elaboration of simpler forms from these and other states which make up the outer border of this culture area.

The more important of these types are as follows: platform tobacco pipes; tubular pipes and shaman's tubes; hollow amulets; bird amulets; bar amulets; tablets or toggles with two perforations; and native copper implements and beads. An interesting method of pottery decoration common in both sections is the zigzag design shown in figure 112, a, b.

In New England, the artifacts belonging to this culture are more abundant in the western and southern portions than in Maine. Numerous burial places have been destroyed in building dams, making roads, grading, etc. The more important cemeteries seem to have been near the natural falls of the larger rivers, at sites later chosen by the Whites for building dams and establishing great manufacturing enterprises. I know of but one instance in New England, where a cemetery of this culture has been explored by a person competent to record in a proper manner the facts revealed.

Many of the artifacts from these burial places, however, have finally found resting places in the cabinets of local historical societies, in private collections, and in the museums of our colleges and universities.

Burial Places at Holyoke and Vicinity. The following account of a burial place situated on the west bank of the Connecticut River at Holyoke, which belonged to this culture, is from the Historical Magazine of January, 1869. It was originally published, I believe, in the Springfield Republican.

In grading the ridge just east of Holyoke depot for building lots the workmen of Bowers and Washer opened an Indian burial ground, on Friday, and since that time skeletons and relics have been found more or less every day, and the mine shows as yet no signs of exhaustion. In all about twenty skeletons have been unearthed, but none of them are entirely complete, and many crumbled to pieces upon exposure to the air. Some of the bones are those of infants, and some are large and full grown men. The bodies had been buried in a sitting posture, with the knees drawn up against the breast and encased in a paste of peculiar red clay or ocher so that frequently the place where the body had been deposited was clearly defined, although it had entirely disappeared, bones and all. One skeleton, however, was stretched at full length; and from the great size of the frame and the unusual position, it evidently had belonged to some chief, famous warrior, or medicine man. The soil in which these remains are found is composed entirely of fine sand, deposited there at some remote age, by the Connecticut which flows close by. As it is free from alkali, the corpses buried in it would remain without decomposition for a long time, and the bones be preserved intact during a very extended period. This, and the fact that it is known that no Indian settlement has existed in Holyoke for some 200 years, gives the bones and relics a very respectable antiquity.

Buried with these skeletons were found a great many Indian utensils, ornaments, and weapons. The most noticeable of these were flint arrowheads, copper spearpoints, copper beads made in the form of triangular prisms, a large dish hollowed out of soapstone, with handles at the sides and much black on the bottom by use in the fire, pipes of the same stone, skilfully and cunningly wrought, tomahawks of flint, vermillion war paint, and generous strings of wampum.

In the above account it seems clear that the words *twenty graves* should be substituted for "twenty skeletons" for it goes on to say that "frequently the place where the body had been deposited was clearly defined although it had entirely disappeared bones and all." This is a characteristic feature of numerous graves of this period.

A number of the implements and ornaments found in this cemetery were brought together by Professor Hitchcock of Amherst College and placed in the museum of that institution. A few of the more important of these are shown in the following illustrations: two shaman's tubes, figure 50, g, h; copper implement or nose pin, figure 59, s; copper and shell beads, figure 60, c, d, e, f, and figure 61, c; and a so-called bar amulet, figure 56, b. There were numerous other implements including two soapstone cooking pots, chipped flint knives, etc. The shell beads from this cemetery in the Amherst collection number more than thirty. They are badly disintegrated, only a few retaining their original size and form. The most perfect one is shown in the illustration.

It is probably made from a large *Fulgur carica* which occurs as far north as the New England coast. The beads of native copper were mostly of small size, figure 60, d, being about the average. There were seventy-two of these and three of a larger size.

It will be noted in the above description of the cemetery that in some of the graves the bones had entirely disintegrated and that where the body had laid was clearly marked by the presence of discolored earth and a "paste of peculiar red clay or ocher." This paste-like appearance is not an uncommon feature in old graves, and the pinkish color does not seem to be wholly the result of the presence of red paint which may have been deposited with the body.

One mile to the northwest of this cemetery on the bank of the Connecticut, a workman of the Holyoke Water Power Company unearthed a grave of approximately the same period as those above described. The skeleton had disintegrated, the only parts found being a portion of a jaw and a small piece of a bone which could not be identified. In this grave were also found copper and shell beads, figure 60, a, b, which originally formed a necklace about a foot long, every fifth bead being of shell followed by four of copper. There were also a few small "conch shells" (Marginella) like figure 61, d, and two shaman's tubes of purplish-red sandstone, figure 50, d, e. The objects from this grave are now in the Museum of the Holyoke Library Association.

In 1901 a grave was opened at South Hadley Falls by Mr. W. J. Howes, which contained two tubes and many beads of shell and native copper. The tubes were similar in shape, and proportionate one to another in size as the above. The only bones found were fragments of the skull and three pieces of arm bones. There were also three chipped arrowpoints and a knife, all of black flint.

Burial Place at Swanton, Vermont. Another old cemetery of this culture was located upon a sandy ridge about two miles north of Swanton, northwestern Vermont. This is described by George H. Perkins in the Proceedings of the American Association for the Advancement of Science for 1873. It was discovered about the year 1861, and was subject to the usual despoilations by relic hunters over a period of several years. Numerous graves were opened at various times and a considerable number of artifacts carried away. A few of them are in the Museum of the University of Vermont at Burlington, and others in the state collection at Montpelier. Some are in private collections. Many of course are scattered.

From the account by Perkins, partly obtained by him from people who had dug for implements at various times, we learn that at least twenty-five graves were opened. The skeletons were much decomposed. Only two bones, a femur and a radius, were entire, though several others were nearly whole, among them about half a skull. The sand beneath where the bodies rested, was, with two exceptions, a dark red or reddish brown, and in the exceptional cases, black. This red discoloration was thought to have been caused by the presence of red ocher, which in prehistoric times was highly valued by all Indians who were able to obtain it.

Some of the more important artifacts recovered are as follows: Ten or twelve Shaman's tubes, three of which are shown in figure 50, a, b, c, also two plugs, m, n, which belong with the first two tubes; about thirty shell beads, the largest and best preserved being illustrated in figure 61, b; Marginella shells like d, in this illustration; copper beads, and two copper pins, which are shown in figure 59, q, r; two bird amulets, figure 55, k, l; and the discoidal gaming stone, figure 57, b.

In addition to the above there were one or two grooveless axes, some bar amulets and "boat-stones," arrowmaker's stones, tablets with double perforation, and chipped knives. The drawings of such of the above artifacts from these graves as are given in our figures, are with one or two exceptions from the illustrations of Professor Perkins.

Burial Place near Orwell, Vermont. During the summers of 1933–34 nineteen graves of this old culture were opened under the auspices of the Museum of the American Indian, Heye Foundation, New York. The work was conducted by Mr. Godfrey J. Olsen, who very kindly prepared the notes from which the following brief account is taken. The burial place was situated on the low terrace of the eastern shore of Lake Champlain nearly opposite Fort Ticonderoga. The graves were at a depth of four to seven feet, and under a stratum of undisturbed sand some thirty inches in thickness which had probably been deposited by floods since the graves were made. As is usual in the old graves of this culture the bones had largely disappeared through disintegration, fragments only being found in four of them, and these showed evidences of cremation. Most of the graves contained a considerable amount of pigment, either red ocher or graphite. There were also nodules of hematite and pieces of iron pyrites, the latter being probably the remains of fire-making sets.

The artifacts consisted of chipped arrowpoints, several adze blades and grooveless axes, a bird amulet, three bar amulets, two "boat-stones" or hollow amulets, native copper beads, a nose pin or awl and a "celt" both of native copper. There were also thirteen shaman's tubes, three of stone and the others of clay. Some graves contained but one, one grave contained two, the longest measuring seventeen inches, a third burial contained three. In several of the tubes was a small plug either of stone or terra cotta, at the small end of the perforation. Some of the tubes were encrusted on the inner side with a layer of carbonized material, probably caused by the burning of tobacco or other "medicine," the smoke of which was blown upon the patient.

Other graves of this period. About 1840 students of the Theological Institute, then located at East Windsor Hill, Connecticut, discovered at the west end of the Institute grounds on the bank of the Connecticut, what seemed to have been a burial place although no bones are mentioned. A soapstone dish of about a pint capacity, a fine bird amulet, and several other articles were found. The hill has since been cut into by the river beyond the place where they were unearthed.

Perhaps the finest lot of artifacts reported to have been taken from a single New England grave belonging to this old culture is now in the Norris Bull collection at Hartford.

The grave was found in a sand knoll at East Windsor, not far from the Scantic River. It contained a bird amulet, figure 55, j, eight slate tablets or gorgets, two of which appear in figure 52, g, h, a dozen or more chipped knives and projectile points, and a small chipping hammer. Mr. Bull informs me these were arranged around what was originally the body, no bones remained, although some of the white powder left by their decomposition was in evidence.

Mr. Bull also tells me that in the general locality of Windsor and East Windsor several pendants and gorgets of green, black-banded Huronian slate have been found where sandy banks have been washed away, or turned up by the plow in places where the original soil level has been lowered by working or erosion. These he is inclined to regard as grave inclusions. This theory is confirmed by my own observations in various sections of New England. It is probably a fact that most of the better class of artifacts of types customarily placed in graves and which are often found on the surface of sand fields and other places subject to erosion, originally were placed in graves.

In the Connecticut Historical Society's collections at Hartford are several objects from a burial place on the west bank of the Connecticut at Windsor Locks. Here again we have a shaman's tube, figure 50, f, several large shell beads, one is shown in figure 61, a, a few beads of native copper, and some Marginella shells, a combination occurring in several widely separated localities.

In 1871 three graves were found in Beverly while digging away a large gravel hill and several implements were secured including three platform pipes, the most perfect of which is shown in figure 49, g. Two of these came from one grave. The other objects from the three graves were a large and a small leaf-shaped flint knife, two adze blades of the usual Algonquian form, three arrow maker's stones, one of which appears in figure 58, b, another similar stone but without the perforation, three worn and grooved pieces of sandstone, and a piece of sandstone upon which is incised a crude design, such as a child might draw to represent a ladder and a tent. In addition there were several quite large pieces of mica. Traces of red ocher were noticeable on some of the implements and in the earth of the graves. The only bones found in the three graves were a small portion of a skull, and the enamel of one molar tooth.[28]

It is an interesting and suggestive fact that numerous artifacts belonging to this group are recorded as having been found at con-

[28] Bulletin of the Essex Institute, vol. III, pp. 123–125; also vol. XXVII, p. 89.

siderable depths while excavating, no bones or other indications of a grave being noticed. The bones had doubtless disappeared through disintegration.

Good illustrations of these finds are the platform pipe, figure 49, a, found four feet below surface while digging for the foundation of the Miles Standish monument at Duxbury, and the native copper knife, figure 59, f, from four and one half feet beneath the surface in a sand bank at East Pepperell, Massachusetts.

If these had been found by trained observers, discolored earth and perhaps other indications of graves would probably have been noticed. Artifacts belonging to this culture are found in nearly every local collection. They cover most of New England but occur less frequently in Maine.

In addition to the artifacts above noted which were placed in graves with their owners, many ordinary every day tools were undoubtedly in common use, such as grooved and grooveless axes, adze blades, net sinkers, chipped implements, pestles, and other common forms. Pottery vessels, doubtless placed in some of these graves seem to have been generally overlooked, but soapstone pots were occasionally found.

The occupation of New England seems to have been continuous from the time of the arrival of the outposts of this central culture which we have called old Algonquian, down to historic times at which period the Algonquians occupied a greater area in North America than any other linguistic group. This culture became somewhat modified in New England during this long occupation, but some of its features persisted into historic times.

Agriculture was introduced by this group and the tradition given by Roger Williams[29] that the crow brought our Indians a grain of corn in one ear and a bean in the other from the field of the great god Kautántouwit in the Southwest, whence came all of their corn and beans is both interesting and significant.

Before giving a general account of the material culture of the New England Algonquians as a whole, some of the more characteristic artifacts of this old group will be described.

Platform Tobacco Pipes, Old Algonquian. The platform pipe, examples of which are illustrated in figure 49, is perhaps the most ancient New England form. Like many other types of arti-

[29] Roger Williams, *Key into the Language of America.* Coll. Rhode Island Hist. Soc., vol. I, p. 86.

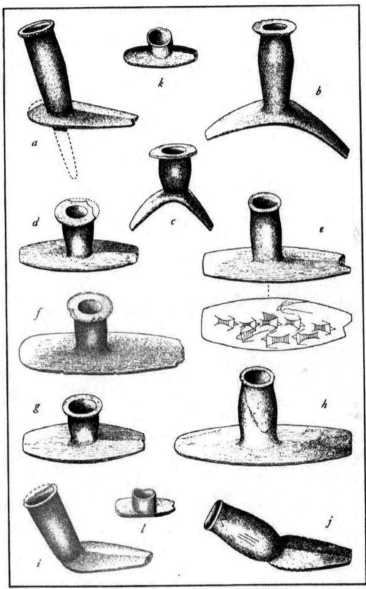

Figure 49. Platform Tobacco Pipes. a, b, d, e, g, h, i, k, l, Massachusetts: a. Duxbury; b, Billerica; d, Plymouth; e, Revere; g, Beverly; h, Newton; k, Martha's Vineyard; l, Treadwells Island, Ipswich. c, Westerly, R. I.; f. North Chatham, N. H.; j. Popham Beach, mouth of the Kennebec. a, Pilgrim Hall, Plymouth; b, Tolman Coll.; c, Rhode Island Hist. Soc.; i, Peabody Museum, New Haven; d, e, f, g, h, k, l, Peabody Museum, Cambridge; j. Maine Hist. Soc. a, c, d, e, g, Are from old Algonquian graves. (1/3.)

facts common to the old Algonquian area they attained their highest excellence among the Great Earthwork Builders. The well known effigy pipes of these mounds, ornamented with well executed sculptures of birds, animals, and reptiles, are the highest development of this type.

Most of the New England platform pipes are made of some variety of steatite, chlorite, or serpentine, much of it probably of local origin, and they range in color from gray through various shades of yellow and green, to nearly black. Several have been taken from graves uncovered while excavating, but most of them are without special data except as to the general locality where found.

They are frequently quite fragile and many fragments may be seen in our collections. Sometimes specimens are found with two or three holes drilled along the broken edge of the platform, showing that the piece which had been broken off had once been joined to the pipe by lashing with cord or sinew.

A pipe of unusual interest is illustrated in a. It is nearly black and was found four feet beneath the surface while excavating for the foundation of the monument erected to the memory of Miles Standish, at Duxbury, near Plymouth. It is now in Pilgrim Hall, Plymouth.

This is the only example that I have seen from New England which had a handle projecting from its base. This handle has been broken off near the base. The dotted line, however, shows the probable extent of this feature, which is present in only a few pipes of the platform type. Parker figures one with a shorter and more bulging bowl from a "Mound-builder's" site in central New York, and McGuire illustrates another much like the latter from a mound in London County, Tennessee. Variations from this are reported from Wisconsin, New York, and other sections. In most pipes of this form the handle is longer than the bowl.

Platform pipes having a curved base are rare in New England. The example illustrated in b, is in the Concord River Valley collection of the late Adams Tolman, now in the public library at Concord, Mass. This was found in what was locally known as the "Sand Plain" near the Shawsheen River in Billerica. The material is the same as that of most of the platform pipes of this region, a very dark steatite, and the bowl has the broad thin rim which occurs so frequently. Another, now in the Peabody Museum at

Cambridge, was for many years in the collection of the Massachusetts Historical Society.

An especially fine pipe of this class from a grave in Westerly is shown in c. The base has the most pronounced curve of any that I have seen, and it is very obvious that it could not be smoked with any degree of comfort except by a person in a reclining position. We may assume, therefore, that pipes of this form were not used when the smoker was standing or sitting upright.

Platform pipes with curved bases are found as far west as Wisconsin and they occur in many of the mound groups especially in Ohio. Mills obtained several of this general form made of red pipestone with long slender bowls and curved platforms, from the Tremper Mound near Portsmouth, Ohio, of which he gives excellent illustrations.[30]

Typical New England platform pipes are usually from graves but unfortunately the importance of carefully noting the conditions under which they were recovered rarely entered the mind of the discoverer, and as the majority were found many years ago while road building, grading, or excavating for buildings, our knowledge regarding the graves or the types of implements found in them is naturally meager.

The pipe shown in d, was found in a grave at Plymouth; e, from a grave at Revere Beach, has several figures, probably flying birds, incised upon the bottom of the platform. These are doubtless totemic; f, was plowed up in North Chatham, New Hampshire. In 1871 three graves were found in Beverly while digging gravel. Several artifacts were discovered, including three platform pipes, the most perfect of which is illustrated in g. Two of these were from one grave. The reddish yellow mottled steatite pipe, h, came from the old Boston Museum and has upon the under side the name *Nonantum*, in much faded ink. Nonantum was one of the seventeenth century villages of the Praying Indians situated in Newton. It was here that John Eliot established his church in 1646. The pipe is doubtless much older than this historic village.

A few unfinished platform pipes in process of making have been found in New England which indicates that many of those recovered were doubtless made within the borders of our territory.

The form of the pipes represented in i, and j, is less common in

[30] W. C. Mills, *Explorations of the Tremper Mound.* Certain Mounds and Village Sites in Ohio, vol. II, part 3.

New England than the typical platform variety, but probably belongs to the same period. Indeed, an examination of the platform pipes in our collections including many fragments, shows that the projection beyond the bowl, opposite the stem, varies from one fourth inch to two inches or more. A comparison of the platform of i, with that of a, illustrates the slight difference in certain examples of the two types. Both varieties are usually made of steatite or serpentine. The form without the platform extension is occasionally found throughout the eastern half of the old Algonquian culture area and as far south as Tennessee. The example shown in i, is in the Peabody Museum at New Haven and is from Massachusetts. The one figured in j, was found on Popham Beach at the mouth of the Kennebec River and is in the Maine Historical Society's collection at Portland. Platform pipes are rarely found east of New England. One has been reported from Musquodopoit Harbor, Nova Scotia, and another from Albert County, New Brunswick.

While the platform pipe was the prevailing form among the old Algonquians, there is little evidence of its continued use by the later people of this stock. I know of no example from an historic grave. Dr. E. E. Tyzzer obtained the one illustrated in figure 107, e, from about eight inches beneath the surface of a shellheap on Harbor Island, Brooklin, Maine. It is apparently of steatite and has been artificially colored a deep glossy black, the effect being the same as the finish produced by the use of a paint made from the juice of the Rocky Mountain Bee Plant, or Guaco, on the black ware of the Rio Grande pueblos where the color is fixed by firing.

We are told by Zeisberger, when among the Delaware, about 1780, that visiting Cherokee brought with them many tobacco pipes for trade. When completed they were blackened in such a way that they retained their color. That this pipe did not originate in New England seems probable. There are two oval depressions near the end opposite the stem similar to those on the bowls of c, and d, of the same figure, which were probably prepared for shell inlay.

Shamans' Medicine Tubes and Pipes, Old Algonquian. A group of objects of unusual interest is represented, one third their natural size, in figure 50. They are usually made of various kinds of stone fairly easy to work, including slate, argillacious shale, sand-

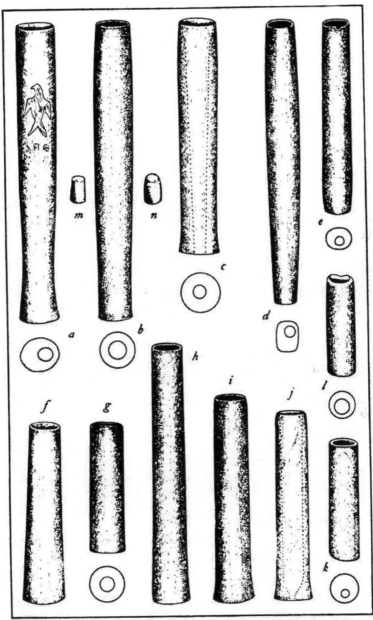

Figure 50. Shaman's Tubes. a, b, c, Swanton, Vt.; d, e, g, h, Holyoke, Mass.; i, Turners Falls, Mass.; f Windsor Locks, Conn.; j, Manchester, N. H.; k, l, Orland, Me.; m, n, stone plugs for tubes a, b. a–h, From old Algonquian graves. a, m, after G. H. Perkins; b, n, k, l, Andover Museum; c, American Museum, New York; d, e, Holyoke Public Library; g, h, i, Amherst College Museum; f, Connecticut Hist. Soc. (1/3.)

stone, clay-iron-stone, soapstone, and sometimes of clay. In their production they appear to have been worked from pieces of selected material into cylinders of nearly the form desired by pecking and grinding. They were then perforated by drilling, probably with a wooden drill, used with sand and water. In most of the specimens examined the perforation gradually diminishes in diameter toward its smaller end as indicated by broken lines in c. The sides of the perforations are often irregular, the striae produced by the drill being very pronounced. In other examples the walls are of nearly uniform thickness throughout the greater part of their length as in j, the narrow hole at the lower extremity being made with a smaller drill. In most of the specimens the marginal end of the wider opening is slightly enlarged by reaming or scraping, this portion being usually very neatly finished.

Tubes of this general type are distributed over a considerable portion of the Algonquian area south of the Great Lakes and the St. Lawrence River, and are also not uncommon in Ontario. In New England they occur as far east as the Penobscot Valley but are more common in the western half of these states.

In Ohio and eastward to central New York they are found in burial mounds and isolated graves and on old sites of this culture, associated with bird and bar amulets, perforated slate tablets, platform and elbow pipes, and implements and ornaments of copper. East of central New York, burial mounds were rarely, if ever built, but the artifacts belonging to this culture are found eastward from this point to central New England and occasionally, though rarely, in Maine.

All of the tubes in this illustration except i, and j, were taken from graves, and with the exception of k, and l, by untrained collectors who naturally failed to obtain data necessary for a clear knowledge of the contents of the individual graves or of the relation of one grave to another. Fortunately, enough has been recorded in local newspapers and elsewhere to give us a fair idea of the burial places from which the tubes and the principal types of artifacts associated with them were found.

The specimens a, b, and c, were obtained with several others from the cemetery near Swanton, Vermont, a brief account of which we have already given. The first of these is of special interest as it has a picture, probably of the thunderbird, incised upon it, below which appear marks bearing a general resemblance to some of the later characters in use among the Cree and Micmac. This is the only one of the tubes illustrated that has not been personally examined by the writer, the drawing being a copy of an illustration accompanying Professor Perkins's account of the Swanton cemetery.[31]

The symmetrical tube, b, is of reddish sandstone, and is now in the archæological museum at Andover, Massachusetts. An interesting feature is the well wrought plug of the same material as the tube which was found in the small end of the perforation. This does not fit snugly, but is small enough to pass easily through. Perkins figures a similar plug which is copied in m, but he does not make it clear whether or not it belonged to tube a.

He writes:

Into this small end of the bore was inserted a stone plug, like figure 12; these plugs were not all carefully made and did not often entirely fill the aperture; in one or two cases a small quartz pebble with little or no working was used, though most are of sandstone. They are from .75 inch long and .5 inch in diameter to not more than .5 inch long and .4 inch in diameter at the larger end.

Several of the tubes from the graves at Orwell, Vermont, also had a stone plug, some of which according to Mr. W. C. Orchard, Museum of the American Indian, New York, are too large to pass through the perforation at the small end of the tubes.

A third tube from the Swanton burial place is illustrated in c. This is in the collections of the American Museum, New York.

We have no knowledge of the number of tubes found in any single grave; the number of graves containing one or more tubes; or the types of articles associated with them in the different burials of the Swanton cemetery. We do know, however, that large shell beads, apparently made from the columella of *Fulgur carica*, figure 61, b, shells of the *Marginella*, d, and implements of native copper, were taken from some of the graves and that like objects have been found associated with similar tubes in other old New England burial places.

The two sandstone tubes illustrated in d, and e, were taken from the grave unearthed by workmen of the Holyoke Water Power Company, previously described.

The two tubes illustrated in g, h, are from the old burial place east of the railroad station at Holyoke, also described above. The

[31] G. H. Perkins, Proc. of the Am. Assoc. for the Advancement of Science. vol. XXII, pp. 76-100.

more important artifacts from this site are in the Museum of Amherst College, including the two tubes, a necklace of thirty large shell beads, the best preserved of which is shown in figure 61, c; seventy-two small beads, two large ones and one with triangular cross-section, figure 60, c, d, e, f, all of native copper; and a pin or nose ornament of the same metal.

The tube illustrated in f, is from a grave at Windsor Locks, Connecticut, and is in the cabinet of the Historical Society of that state at Hartford. Exhibited with it are several large shell beads, a few small beads of native copper, also a few Marginella shells, like those found in the Swanton and Holyoke graves. This grave was discovered in 1871.

Most of the tubes in private collections are without data save as to general locality. Specimen i, is from Turner's Falls, on the Connecticut River, and j, of banded slate, is from Amoskeag Falls, Manchester, New Hampshire, and one has recently been acquired by the Peabody Museum at Salem from Lake Winnepesaukee, made of clay-iron-stone. This probably originated in Ohio. The two small examples, k and l, were obtained from two graves on the south shore of Lake Alamoosook, in Orland, Maine, during the exploration of the "Red Paint" cemetery by the Andover Museum. These graves were thought by Dr. Moorehead to be intrusive and it is interesting to observe that beads of native copper were found in both.[32]

While there is, perhaps, no conclusive evidence that the above described tubes were parts of shamans' outfits, there are indications which point strongly to such use. The shamans were men of influence and wealth. In several of the graves containing these tubes, beads of massive shell, and of native copper, were found, also Marginella shells which were probably a recognized part of a shaman's outfit. Massive shell beads are rare in New England.

An interesting point to consider is the stone plugs and pebbles found in the perforation at the small end of some of the tubes at Swanton and Orwell. Similar objects may well have been present in the tubes from other cemeteries but were overlooked.

Now what could have been the function of these stone plugs? Some of them were small enough to pass easily through the smaller end of the tube in which they were found. Others were too large to do so. They doubtless were used with the tube in some

[32] W. K. Moorehead, *A Report on the Archaeology of Maine*, pp. 46–49.

manner during the healing ceremony. The sick were given to understand that the cause of their illness was the sticks, thorns, pebbles, or other objects in their bodies which the shamans extracted through the skin by sucking, usually with the aid of tubes of some kind. Henry saw the quill of a feather apparently sucked from the body of a child, and which was taken from the bone tube used by the doctor. Sometimes the surface of the skin over the afflicted part was scarified by scratching or scraping with a sharp flint preliminary to applying the tube. This would enable more or less blood to be drawn to the surface of the skin, which would render the delusion more perfect.

The eastern Algonquian shamans were notorious jugglers. Sometimes the offices of shaman and chief were combined in a single individual, as in the case of Passaconaway of the Pennacook, who was a most noted powwow of this section. Their exhibitions made a great impression upon the early colonists, and Roger Williams says that after once being present at the incantations of a priest, he durst never be an eye-witness, spectator, or looker on, lest he become a partaker of Satan's invocations.

The treatment of a patient was usually carried out with incantations and the accompaniment of a drum or rattle. The Indians paid the doctor in presents of robes, furs, or other valuable objects for his services.

Alexander Henry,[33] fur trader among the Indians, 1760–1776, gives the following interesting account of the treatment of a sick child by an Ojibwa medicine man: —

I was once present at a performance of this kind, in which the patient was a female child of about twelve years of age. Several of the elder chiefs were invited to the scene; and the same compliment was paid to myself, on account of the medical skill for which it was pleased to give me credit.

The physician (so to call him) seated himself on the ground; and before him, on a new stroud blanket, was placed a basin of water, in which were three bones, the larger ones, as it appeared to me, of a swan's wing. In his hand, he had his *shishiquoi*, or rattle, with which he beat time to his *medicine-song*. The sick child lay on a blanket near the physician. She appeared to have much fever and a severe oppression of the lungs, breathing with difficulty, and betraying symptoms of the last stage of consumption.

After singing for some time, the physician took one of the bones out of the basin: the bone was hollow; and one end being applied to the breast of the patient, he put the other into his mouth, in order to remove the disorder

³³ Alexander Henry, *Travels and Adventures in Canada and the Indian Territories*, Bain edition, pp. 115–117.

by suction. Having persevered in this as long as he thought proper, he suddenly seemed to force the bone into his mouth, and swallow it. He now acted the part of one suffering severe pain; but, presently finding relief, he made a long speech, and after this, returned to singing, and to the accompaniment of his rattle. With the latter, during his song, he struck his head, breast, sides and back; at the same time straining as if to vomit forth the bone.

Relinquishing this attempt, he applied himself to suction a second time, and with the second of the three bones; and this also he soon seemed to swallow.

Upon its disappearance, he began to distort himself in the most frightful manner, using every gesture which could convey the idea of pain: at length, he succeeded, or pretended to succeed, in throwing up one of the bones. This was handed about to the spectators, and strictly examined; but nothing remarkable could be discovered. Upon this, he went back to his song and rattle; and after some time threw up the second of the two bones. In the groove of this, the physician, upon examination, found, and displayed to all present, a small white substance, resembling a piece of the quill of a feather. It was passed round the company, from one to the other; and declared, by the physician, to be the thing causing the disorder of his patient.

In the above instance three bone tubes were employed. It should be noted that two tubes were recovered from a grave at Holyoke, figure 50, d, e, also from a burial at South Hadley and at Orwell, each pair being made up of one long tube and a shorter one. At Orwell three tubes were taken from one grave.

In more recent times the Ojibwa and Potawatomi used a small horn of a steer or heifer for this purpose.

Medicine tubes of stone of the type found in New England had apparently gone out of use in this section before the colonial period. C. C. Jones[34] has brought together a number of references to the similar use of tubes by the southern and western medicine men, and quotes Ribas as saying "they give the sick to understand that the causes of their illness are the sticks, thorns, and pebbles in their bodies which they take out. This is false. They have the things in the mouth, or held craftily in the hand, and afterwards exhibit them."

The material of which tubes were made is mentioned in these quotations in one instance only as follows:

Venegas confirms the observation of Baegert with regard to the use of stone tubes by the medicine-men of the California Indians:

"One mode was very remarkable, and the good effect it sometimes produced heightened the reputation of the physician. They applied to the suffering part of the patient's body the *chacuaco*, or a tube formed out of a very hard black stone; and through this they sometimes sucked, and other times blew,

[34] C. C. Jones, *Antiquities of the Southern Indians*, pp. 362-364.

but both as hard as they were able, supposing that thus the disease was either exhaled or dispersed. Sometimes the tube was filled with *cimarron*, or wild tobacco lighted, and here they either sucked in or blew down the smoke, according to the physician's direction."

It is not improbable that tobacco may have been used ceremonially as above described with some of our longer New England tubes, for a carbonized substance was found adhering to the inner side of one of the two tubes (figure 50, d, e) from the grave unearthed by the workmen of the Holyoke Water Power Company, and some of the clay tubes from the graves at Orwell, Vermont, also contained a crust of carbonized material.

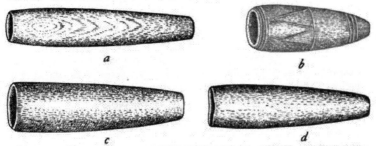

Figure 51. Tubular Pipes. a. From Lawrence, Mass.; b, from shellheap, Frenchmans Bay, Me.; c, from near Concord, Mass.; d, Rhode Island. a, Banded slate; b, terra-cotta; c, d, clay-iron-stone. a, b, d, Peabody Museum, Cambridge; c, Amherst College Museum. (1/3.)

Another group of tubes bearing a general resemblance to those above described, but being shorter in proportion to their diameter, is illustrated in figure 51. Perhaps no clear distinction should be drawn between the two groups. The shorter examples, however, especially the one illustrated in b, closely approach in outline the more or less conical tobacco pipes which occur in various sections westward to the Pacific coast, and which were used until recent times by the Mohave, Pueblo, and certain other tribes of the West, for tobacco smoking, and also by the priests and shamans for blowing the smoke of tobacco and other herbs during incantations and ceremonies. In the Peabody Museum at Cambridge are twenty or more of these conical stone pipes from graves of the Santa Barbara region of California, several of which have a short stem made by inserting a small hollow bone an inch or two in length into the opening of the smaller end, where it is fastened with asphaltum. Among the most interesting artifacts of northern California are the stone shaman tubes or pipes of the Karok,

Yurok, and Hupa Indians. Some of them are nearly a foot in length and one inch or less in diameter at the larger end. Wooden pipes of the same form and of equal symmetry are still in use; in these the bowl proper is usually of steatite or serpentine and of the same diameter as the stem where it joins the bowl, being in reality a continuation of the stem. The smaller tubular tobacco pipes in general use among the laity are about one half the length of the pipes of the shamans, but are equally well made.

The tube of banded slate, a, figure 51, is from Massachusetts; b, is of terra-cotta and was found by Professor Bates in a shell-heap in Frenchman's Bay; c and d are of clay-iron-stone, the former from near Concord, Massachusetts, and the latter from Rhode Island. We are indebted to Gerard Fowke for the following account of this or a similar material:[35]

It occurs in Ohio in bowlder-like masses scattered through beds of dark brown clay. The color is light gray sometimes tinged with yellow. When first quarried at a depth of three or four feet it resembles steatite in appearance. It is then not harder than chalk or gypsum, but on exposure to the air it solidifies as the water evaporates, and in a short time becomes as hard as slate. When first taken from the ground the material is easily worked. Different varieties of this clay-iron-stone, some of which quite closely resemble red pipe-stone from the famous quarry in Minnesota, were used in making medicine tubes and some of the finer tobacco pipes from the Ohio mounds.

The specimens here recorded of this substance were probably made by the Ohio Indians and found their way to New England in ancient times. While the tubes shown in figure 51 may have been used with tobacco ceremonially, and perhaps by individuals for smoking, it seems well to group them with the ceremonial tubes of the shamans instead of with tobacco pipes.

Tablets with Double Perforations, Old Algonquian. Figure 52 shows a series of tablets with double perforations which may be considered typical not only of New England but of the entire old Algonquian area. In the East they are usually made of slate though other varieties of stone are sometimes substituted. Like most objects belonging to this period they seem to have generally passed out of use before the beginning of the sixteenth century. One or two fragments have been found in the shellheaps, and a

[35] Gerard Fowke, *Archaeological History of Ohio*, pp. 577–578.

part of one, figure 131, c, used in making a mould for lead buttons, is from a post-colonial grave at Kingston, Massachusetts. It is very probable, however, that the fragment was found on the surface and appropriated by the finder for this purpose. These tablets are

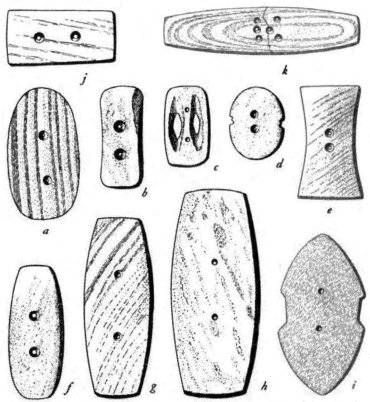

Figure 52. Perforated Tablets. a, g, h, k. From old Algonquian graves. a, b, c, f, k, Massachusetts: a, Salem Neck; b, c, Springfield; f, Hadley; k, Cape Cod. d, g, h, i, Connecticut: d, Windsor; g, h, East Windsor Hill; i, East Hartford. e, j, Vermont. a, Peabody Museum, Salem; b, k, Peabody Museum, Cambridge; c, d, f, i, Amherst College Museum; g, h, Norris L. Bull Coll. (About 1/3.)

quite common throughout the area specified, especially south of the Great Lakes, where they are frequently found with skeletons in the mounds. In Ohio they are sometimes made of native copper and similar though larger tablets, also of native copper, are often associated with burials in the larger mound groups.

The smaller slate tablets also occur with mound burials. Dr. Moorehead found one similar to f, lying between the femora of a skeleton which may have fallen from the wrist. In another instance he obtained one much like e, which was lying on a skull. Dr. Mills obtained a similar one from the right wrist of a burial in the Adena Mound[36] near Chillicothe, Ohio, and on the wrist of another skeleton in this mound was a tablet or bar like d, in figure 53, excepting that it had the usual double perforation. This bar was held in place by two native copper bracelets, each end of the bar being pushed between a bracelet and the wrist, where it seems to have been secured with cord passing through the holes in the bar. Portions of this binding cord were preserved by contact with the copper.

In New England, like many other artifacts of the same period, they are rarely found with skeletons, because the latter have usually disappeared through disintegration. The beautiful specimen of banded slate, k, was taken from an ancient grave at Cape Cod by Mr. F. P. Orchard of the Peabody Museum at Cambridge. It was found but a few inches from the surface in sand somewhat discolored, and near it were what seem to be fragments of disintegrated firestones of pyrites. Only one piece of bone was noticed. This was too small for identification. The tablet originally had the usual two central perforations. It became broken through one of these holes. To repair it the Indian had drilled four additional holes for the lashings which had bound the two parts together.

These carefully made objects were doubtless worn either attached to some part of the person, or to the clothing. They are commonly called gorgets but it is doubtful if they were so worn.

In d, and i, of figure 52, there are side notches, an unusual feature, and in c, two additional perforations were made subsequent to the original completion of the tablet. These two larger perforations probably had a function similar to the side notches in d and i, which seem to have been for the purpose of binding some object to the tablet.

In the American Museum, in New York, there are two specimens similar to g, the larger of which is about four and one half inches long. These were obtained from the Munsee Reservation in Canada and are said to have been used by the Munsee women to

---

[36] W. C. Mills, *Excavations of the Adena Mound. Certain Mounds and Village Sites in Ohio*, vol. I, part I, pp. 14, 18.

fasten their hair braids at the back of the head. The Munsee are a branch of the Delaware, and are, of course, Algonquian.

Lucien Turner [37] describes and figures two wooden forms for women's hair, about the size and shape of e, but without the two central holes, that he found in use among the Nascapee, another Algonquian group living in Labrador. The ends were slightly more concave than in e, however.

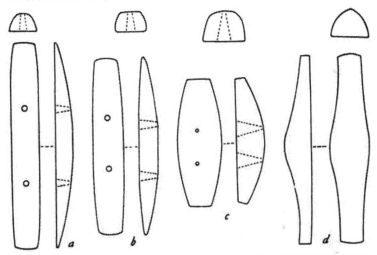

Figure 53. Slate Bars, usually having two perforations. a, Connecticut Valley; d, Montague, Mass.; b, East Windsor, Conn.; c, Dover, N. H. a, d, Amherst College Museum; b, Mattatuck Hist. Soc., Waterbury. (About 1/3.)

Whatever may have been the use of these well finished stone objects they were certainly highly valued for they seem to have been universally distributed throughout the area.

Another group of objects of the same general class, although relatively narrower and thicker, is illustrated in figure 53. They usually have two perforations, the openings of which are very small on the convex side and much larger on the opposite or flatter side.

We have already referred to the finding of one like d, of this figure, on the wrist of a skeleton in the Adena Mound in Ohio, by Dr. Mills, where it was held in place by two copper bracelets. The Adena specimen, however, was supplied with the usual two perforations.

[37] L. M. Turner, Eleventh Rpt., Bureau of Am. Eth., p. 320.

In a third group are the hollow amulets, commonly called "boatstones," a misnomer which should be discarded. Examples are shown in outline in figure 54. In New England they are generally made of slate, but other varieties of stone are sometimes chosen. They are usually very carefully made, and nearly always have two

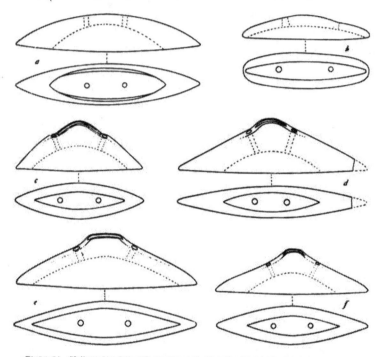

Figure 54. Hollow Amulets, "Boat Stones." Usually furnished with two perforations. a, Banded slate, vicinity of Framingham, Mass., Framingham Hist. Soc.; b, greenish slate, Massachusetts; c, chlorite, Connecticut Valley, Amherst College Museum; d, red slate, West Springfield, Mass., Andover Archaeological Museum; e, banded slate, Silver Lake, Conn., Peabody Museum, New Haven; f, Unionville, Conn., N. L. Bull Coll. (About 1/3.)

perforations through which a cord was passed apparently to secure the amulet to some object or to a base of some kind. The more perfect ones have a groove at the top through which the cord ran. Sometimes the groove is lacking as in a, and b. Like the two previous groups these objects are distributed throughout the old Algonquian area. In Ohio they attained their highest development, culminating in the beautiful hollow effigies of birds and animals from the great mound groups.[38]

In the remarkable deposits of sacrificial objects discovered by Dr. Mills in the Tremper Mound of Scioto County, Ohio, there were many platform pipes having bowls in form of birds and animals, also several of the New England type including some with curved bases. There were also several of these hollow amulets or "boat-stones," some of native copper, others of stone.

One of the latter was much like b, of figure 54, but broader in proportion to its length, with the opening more oval in outline. There was a broad but shallow dorsal groove running the length of the upper side, the remaining portion of the back being ornamented with crosshatching. There was another example with the two perforations somewhat farther apart but with a hollow of the same size and shape. This represented a beaver. The copper examples were especially interesting. The following is from the report of Dr. Mills.[39]

The boat-stone shown in figure 90 is an effigy of the beaver in the act of swimming, showing only that portion of the animal which would appear above the surface of the water. The head, with its small ears, the round stout body and flat well marked tail, are characteristic of the beaver. Figure 91 shows the underside of the specimen, somewhat resembling a canoe or boat, whence the name of the type. . . Boat-shaped objects of copper are shown in figures 94 to 97. Figure 94 shows a very finely wrought specimen, pierced with a hole at each end. The edge at each side is turned under, forming a curved ridge. Figure 95 shows the opposite side of the above specimen, which contains a quantity of broken quartzite pebbles attached to it by corrosion of the copper. Figure 96 shows another copper boat-shaped specimen, filled with round quartzite pebbles, white and pink in color.

It will be noted that in the specimen just described the pebbles were broken, while in this one they are perfect, all uniformly rounded and about the size of small peas. The specimen is pierced with two holes near the center, similar to the boat-shaped objects of stone. Figure 97 shows another boat-shaped specimen, pierced with two holes near the center. No pebbles were found in this specimen, as it was placed in the cache upside down. No doubt originally its contents were similar to those of the two others, as the pebbles were found in abundance in the cache but no significance attached to them at the time.

It seems reasonable to assume that these hollow objects, whether found in New England or in other portions of the old Algonquian

[38] C. C. Willoughby, *Art of the Great Earthwork Builders of Ohio*, plate XI. Holmes Anniversary Volume.

[39] W. C. Mills, *Explorations of the Tremper Mound*. Certain Mounds and Village Sites in Ohio, vol. II, part 3, pp. 206-210.

area, including the great mound groups of the Ohio region, were amulets of some sort, and that the hollow portion was for the purpose of holding "medicine." They may have been fastened to the clothing or to some object of personal adornment, or perhaps used by the shamans. As indicated by those in form of birds and animals, their normal position must have been with the hollow side downward, so they were doubtless fastened in that position to a base or object of some kind which would serve to hold in place the pebbles or other magic material with which they were doubtless filled.

They are rarely found with skeletons. In Ohio the finer effigy forms have usually been taken from altars or sacrificial deposits where the property of notables was placed at the time of the cremation of the owners' bodies.

Bird Amulets, Old Algonquian. The highly conventionalized effigies illustrated in figure 55, undoubtedly represent birds. They are comparatively rare in New England, being confined principally to the southern and western portions of these states. They are usually made of slate, the banded variety being preferred when obtainable. The eyes, when present, are represented by knob-like projections which are quite prominent. The base is flat or nearly so, and near either end is a perforation made by drilling two holes from opposite sides of the angle at this point until they intersect.

These perforations are doubtless for the passage of cords used for securing the effigy to the person or to a portion of the clothing. In k, and l, a single drill hole near either end forms the perforation.

These effigies undoubtedly belong to the old Algonquian culture represented by the burials at Swanton, Orwell, Holyoke, East Windsor, Manchester, and many other localities. The two shown in k, and l, are from the cemetery at Swanton, Vermont, and j, made of banded slate, is from the one at East Windsor, Connecticut; f, and the two fragments, figured in e, were found near the base of a large boulder mortar at Woodbury, Connecticut. The other specimens illustrated are mostly surface finds, some of them having undoubtedly been plowed out of shallow graves from which the bones had disappeared.

The area of distribution of these interesting artifacts extends from central New England westward to Illinois and central Wisconsin, and from central Ontario southward to the Ohio River and southern Pennsylvania. A few have been found outside the area,

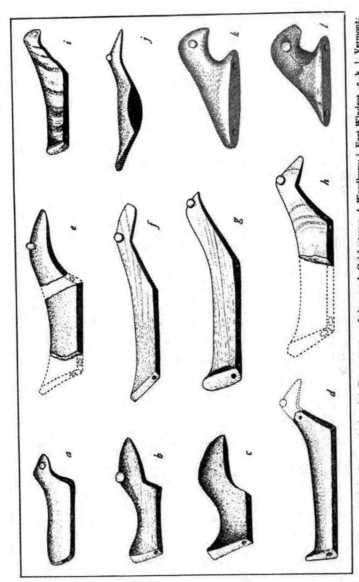

Figure 55. Bird Amulets. a, b, d, e, f, j, Connecticut: a, Lebanon; d, Colchester; e, f, Woodbury; j, East Windsor. c, k, l, Vermont: k, l, graves at Swanton. i, Westerly, R. I.; g, New Hampshire, figured by Schoolcraft; h, Newburyport, Mass. a, d, Slater Museum, Norwich: b, f, k, American Museum, New York; e, i, University of Vermont. e, j, N. L. Bull Coll.; h, i, Peabody Museum, Cambridge. (1/3.)

notably in Kentucky and Tennessee. The public and private collections within this area show many examples. Probably four or five hundred would be a conservative estimate, as some two hundred are recorded from southern Ontario alone.

The material is chiefly slate. The banded variety was extensively used. Another favorite stone was porphyritic syenite, the scattered crystals of this mineral contrasting pleasantly with the darker, variously colored matrix. The New England examples are chiefly slate, though some are of limestone or steatite.

The three principal types of these effigies occurring throughout the area as above given are also found in New England and are represented in the illustrations. Of the first group, without the eye-like projections, c, and i, are examples; those of the second group are provided with these projecting eyes, some of which are large and prominent; in the third group are included those shown in k, and l, which represent the head and neck only. This form is rare but is found sporadically throughout the area mentioned. An excellent example made of porphyritic syenite was taken from one of the altars of the great mound of the Hopewell group near Anderson, Ohio, and is now in the Field Museum.

Very few bird amulets have been found in mounds or recognizable graves. When occurring in graves they seem to have been often accompanied by implements or ornaments of native copper, or at least such objects were found in some of the neighboring graves of the same period.

Various theories have been advanced as to the probable use of these curious effigies, most of which may be dismissed as not worthy of serious consideration. The example illustrated in g, from New Hampshire, is copied from one of Schoolcraft's plates in part 4 of his great work. On page 176 he refers to it in the following words. "In figure 2 is delineated a curiously shaped stone knife handle designed to confine the cutting edges of flint or obsidian blades." This writer, who, it will be remembered, married a half-blood Ojibwa woman, was of course familiar with the curved steel knife in almost universal use among our northern tribes during the past century.

The wooden handle of this knife bears a certain resemblance to the body and tail of this bird effigy of stone. In using this steel knife the Indian always draws it towards his body. The handle is grasped in the hand with the blade projecting from the side opposite the thumb. The top of the handle projects to one side and is formed especially for the thumb to rest against. This projection resembles the tail end of the effigy but is usually longer.

Mr. W. C. Orchard of the Museum of the American Indian tells me he saw a portion of one of these bird amulets hanging in an Ojibwa cabin, and was told by the owner that it was a part of an ancient knife handle. The assumption was undoubtedly due to the resemblance of the fragment to the wooden handle of the modern curved steel-bladed knife of Indian make. An examination, however, of any large group of these effigies shows conclusively that they could not have been used for this purpose. A large proportion of them are far too short. All of them are unsuited for the attachment of a flint blade. This, taken in addition to the fact that no example has been reported as having been found in conjunction with a blade, seems to preclude the possibility of such use.

In the Smithsonian Report for 1873, p. 371, Mr. Henry Gillman figures and describes one of these amulets from Grossepoint, Lake St. Clair, Michigan. Mr. Gillman was an archaeologist of Detroit and did considerable field work in Michigan and other sections. He brought together the Ojibwa ethnological collection now in the Peabody Museum at Harvard.

Mr. Gilman says

I have learned, through an aged Indian, that in olden times these ornaments were worn on the heads of Indian women, but only after marriage. I have thought that these peculiar objects, which are always made of some choice material, resemble the figure of a brooding bird; a familiar sight to the "children of the forest;" that thus they are emblematic of maternity, and as such were designed and worn.

When writing his *Primitive Industry*, Dr. C. C. Abbott asked for information with reference to these bird-shaped stones through a local publication. Soon after, he received from Colonel Charles Whittlesey of Cleveland, the well known pioneer archæologist, the following:

Dr. E. Stirling, of this city, says, such bird effigies, made of wood, have been noticed among the Ottawas of Grand Traverse Bay, Michigan, fastened on the top of the heads of women, as an indication that they are pregnant.[40]

In my search for evidence bearing upon the use of these objects I have found the following which seems worth recording. It is well known among students that the native Indian flageolet is

[40] C. C. Abbott, *Primitive Industry*, pp. 370, 371.

primarily a lover's instrument which is used by the young swain for calling his sweetheart to their secret trysting place. Special love calls are composed for the purpose and when the girl hears her lover's call she knows that he awaits her coming. The use of this flageolet was widespread, not only among the Algonquians but also various neighboring tribes.

The tone of this instrument is regulated by the adjustment of a small block over the sound hole, which is usually held in place by several windings of string or thong, so that it may be adjusted by the player. While the general shape of most of these block slides is plain and may have no special significance, others are in the form of birds which resemble the bird amulets of stone. (See Supplement, figure 146.)

There may, of course, be no connection between the two groups of effigies. On the other hand, the occurrence of these bird forms upon instruments of courtship, and their recorded use by women as symbols of pregnancy certainly seem to indicate a relationship.

While only a co-incidence, and having no bearing whatever on the use of our bird amulets, it may be of interest to mention that an almost identical bird effigy made of wood was in ancient times worn attached as a bracelet by the anaana, or praying-to-death sorcerers of the Hawaiian Islands.

Miscellaneous Stone Objects, Old Algonquian. *Bar Amulets.* Examples of a group of objects which are generally considered as being more or less closely related to bird amulets are represented in figure 56. They have the same general distribution as bird amulets but are far less common. In New England they are rare. They are usually made of slate and are perforated in the same manner as the bird stones. Abbott and some other writers regard them as highly conventionalized bird forms. They undoubtedly belong to the same period and people as the bird amulets. The specimen shown in b, is of banded slate and is from the old cemetery at Holyoke described on page 83. The one illustrated in a, is from Bristol, Connecticut.

Chunkey Stones. Finely wrought gaming stones of the type illustrated in figure 57 occur occasionally in New England but they are rare. They are abundant, however, in the more southern sections east of the Mississippi River and were doubtless introduced into New England by the old Algonquian people as is evident from the fact that b, of this figure is from a grave in the cemetery at Swanton, Vermont. It is made of white quartz and is a most admirable example of stoneworking.

The game was called chunkey by the Cherokee and was played as follows: Each party had a pole about eight feet long which

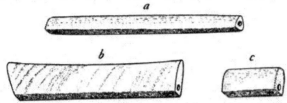

Figure 56. Bar Amulets. a, Bristol, Conn., N. L. Bull Coll.; b, Grave at Holyoke, Mass., Amherst College Museum; c, Attleboro, Mass., J. A. Richardson Collection. (1/3.)

tapered at either end to a flat point. The players set off abreast of each other. One of them hurled the stone disc on its edge in as direct a line as he could, and each contestant then darted his

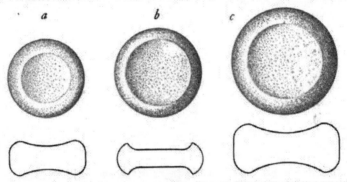

Figure 57. Gaming Stones. a, Danbury, Conn., N. L. Bull Collection; b, from grave at Swanton, Vt., after G. H. Perkins; c, Waterbury, Conn., Mattatuck Hist. Soc. (1/3.)

pole with proper force, as near as he could guess, so that its end might lie close to the stone when it stopped rolling. The player whose pole lay nearest the stone scored. In this manner the players might keep running at half speed most of the day, staking their various possessions on the result of the game.

The specimen shown in a, is from Danbury, Connecticut, and the one figured in c, is from near Waterbury in the same state.

Arrowmakers' Stones. There is a group of tablet-like objects, usually perforated near one end, apparently for suspension and showing unmistakable use as implements, which are occasionally found in old Algonquian graves. They are usually of slate, are occasionally without the perforation, and sometimes though rarely show no signs of use. Several of these implements are illustrated in figure 58. They all have more or less distinct marks on some portion of the surface, apparently the result of lightly striking some hard substance. These marks may appear on one or both edges, on the lower end, or upon the side, as shown in f.

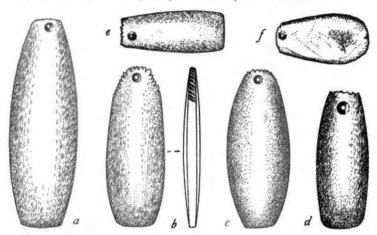

Figure 58. Arrowmaker's stones. All from Massachusetts: a, Newburyport; b, Grave at Beverly; c, Plymouth cemetery; d, Nonantum (Newton); e, Connecticut Valley; f, East Boston, Wood End Park. a, d, f, Peabody Museum, Cambridge; b, Peabody Museum, Salem; c, Pilgrim Hall, Plymouth; e, Amherst College Museum. (1/3.)

On the upper end of many are abrading grooves often quite distinct, sometimes hardly distinguishable, which may have been used in stripping sinew or preparing it for use in binding the ends of arrow shafts or in feathering arrows, or for some similar purpose.

Thomas Wilson[41] figures one of these from Norwich, Connecticut, which is very neatly ornamented with straight and zig-zag lines made by a series of small dots drilled into its surface.

In studying the implements shown in this illustration, comparison should be made with the much coarser tools illustrated in figure 98, which seem to have had a somewhat similar function.

Native Copper Implements and Beads, Old Algonquian. Artifacts of this group seem to have been nearly all imported into New

[41] T. Wilson, *Prehistoric Art*, Rpt. of the U. S. National Museum for 1896, p. 453.

England from Wisconsin and Michigan by the old Algonquian people. They are frequently found in graves of this period, and it may be assumed that most of them which have been recovered were originally placed in such graves.

The tools illustrated in figure 59, with the possible exception of g, are of types found throughout most of the old Algonquian area. They are rare in Maine and New Hampshire. Perkins reports that in the two major archaeological collections of Vermont there are not more than twenty-five. In Massachusetts and other sections of southern New England they are by no means common.

Parker states that in New York probably not more than two hundred and fifty implements of this class have been recovered.[42] He says they have not been found on Iroquoian sites. Wintemberg reports many from Ontario and a few from Quebec.[43]

As one goes westward from New England they increase in number, and in Wisconsin and upper Michigan, their center of distribution, they are very common. Mr. Charles E. Brown, Dean of the Museum of the Wisconsin Historical Society states that the number of these artifacts already recovered from the fields, village sites, graves, and mounds of that state is very large, probably exceeding in number those obtained from the balance of the United States. He estimates the number collected in the state up to about 1910 at not less than twenty thousand.

These artifacts were made from the copper obtained from ancient Indian mines in the Great Lakes region, or from nuggets brought from outcrops by glacial action, which are distributed over a considerable area south of the lakes. Workshops where these articles were made have been located in many parts of Wisconsin.[44]

The specimens illustrated are all undoubtedly from the Great Lakes region and were either obtained by trade or were brought to New England by immigrants from the West.

These were all made by the simple processes of hammering, cutting, annealing, and grinding. One can shape native copper up to a certain point by hammering, but beyond that point it

[42] A. C. Parker. *The Archaeological History of New York*, State Museum Bulletins, nos. 235–238, p. 238.

[43] W. J. Wintemberg, Bulletin 67, Department of Mines, Canada, pp. 79–81.

[44] For an exhaustive study of this subject see *Copper: Its Mining and use by the Aborigines of the Lake Superior Region*, by G. A. West, Bulletin, Public Museum of Milwaukee, vol. 10, no. 1.

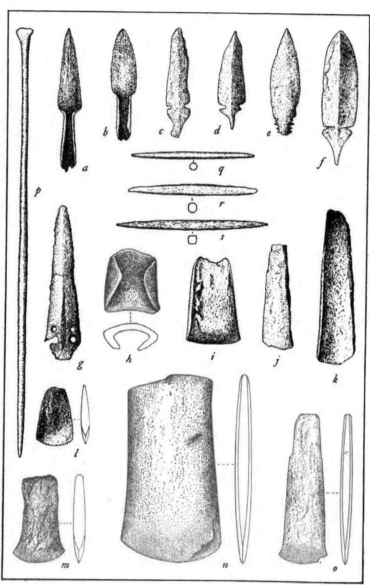

Figure 59. Implements of Native Copper. a–g, Knives and projectile points; h, "spud," probably used as an adze blade; i, j, k, adze blades; l–o, axe blades; p, pin; q–s, probably nose pins. a, d, e, j, k, q, r, Vermont: a, Williston; d, q, r, burial place at Swanton; j, k, Milton. i, Lewiston, Me. c, f, g, l, o, s, Massachusetts: c, West Millbury; f, East Pepperell; g, Merrimacport; l, Wakefield; o, Gill; s, grave at Holyoke. b, h, m, n, p, Connecticut: b, Lisbon; h, Southbury; m, East Windsor; n, Essex; p, Plantsville. a, d, e, j, k, q, r. After G. H. Perkins. (About (1/3.)

becomes brittle and will crack. This tendency can be overcome by annealing. By alternate hammering and annealing, and by cutting and scraping with sharp flints, and grinding with gritty stones and sand the metal can be wrought into almost any form. During Hearne's journey to the Coppermine River in northern Canada in 1771 he found the Indians of that region using native copper. He says, "By the help of fire and two stones, they can beat it out to any shape they wish."[45]

Copper, of course, cannot be tempered, but it can be hardened and brought to a good cutting edge by hammering and grinding. The hammering, however, must not be excessive.

Figure 59, a, b, are typical spear points, each having a socket for the reception of the end of the shaft. In a few examples there is a perforation near the bottom of the socket for a pin, to hold the point more securely to its shaft; a, is from Williston, Vermont, and b, from Lisbon, near Norwich, Connecticut. The spearpoints or knives, c, d, e, f, were intended to be set into a socket in the end of the haft where they were secured by wrappings of cord or thong; d, is from the burial place at Swanton, Vermont; f, was found in a sand knoll four and one half feet from the surface in East Pepperell, Massachusetts, and is probably from an old Algonquian grave.

The unique specimen figured in g, is from an old site on the bank of the Merrimack, at Merrimackport, Massachusetts. It is probably a knife, and was lashed to its handle through two perforations near its base, one of which has been torn out. In repairing this damage two more perforations were made just above the others. This is now in the Andover Museum. In all of the above specimens one side is flat. On the opposite side the blade is bevelled from a central strengthening ridge to either edge.

The specimen shown in h, is the only example of the "spud" which I have seen from New England. Beauchamp figures a similar one from Seneca River near Port Byron and says it is thus far unique in New York. The socket formed by the turned over sides is, of course, for the end of the haft. This was found at Southbury, Connecticut, and is in the American Museum, New York. The copper adze blade illustrated in i, is the only example from Maine that has come to my knowledge. It was found in Lewiston. This and the point f, are in the Peabody Museum at Cambridge. The

<hr>

[45] Samuel Hearne, *A Journey to the Northern Ocean*, p. 175.

two crude blades j, k, are from Milton, Lamoille Valley, Vermont, and are in the Museum of the University of Vermont.

The copper axes l, m, n, o, are good examples of this useful implement; l, found in Wakefield, Massachusetts, is now in the Peabody Museum at Salem. It is perforated near its upper end, and owing to its rarity and small size may well have been worn by its last native owner as an ornamental pendant.

The blade illustrated in m, is from the old Algonquian burial place at East Windsor, Connecticut. Perhaps the finest axe blade thus far reported from New England is shown in n. It is from Essex, Connecticut, and is in the Norris L. Bull collection, Hartford. Another finely proportioned blade, o, from Gill, Massachusetts, is in the Peabody Museum at New Haven.

Figure 60. Native Copper Beads. a, b, From grave, Water Power excavation, Holyoke, Mass., Holyoke Library Association Coll.; c–f, from grave east of Holyoke R.R. Station, Amherst College Museum. (1/1.)

The copper pin, p, is from Nonx Springs, Plantsville, Connecticut, and is also in the Bull collection. It is sixteen inches long, and has a flattened head, an unusual feature in this class of objects which are quite common south of the Great Lakes.

Three short pins are figured in q, r, s. The first two are from the burial place at Swanton, Vermont, and the last, s, is from the one at Holyoke, Massachusetts. Perkins reports that the pin shown in r, was found between the teeth of a skeleton, which seems to point to its use as an ornament worn through the septum of the nose, after the manner of the ivory pins of the same form worn by the Tinne Indians of Alaska.

From the old burial places also came many beads wrought from native copper. These, like the copper implements, were doubtless also brought from the Great Lakes region. Examples are shown in figure 60. Those at the left, a, b, are part of a necklace of copper and shell beads from a grave unearthed by workmen of the Holyoke Water Power Company and described on page 84. The copper and shell beads alternated, every fifth bead being of shell followed

by four of copper. The other beads in the illustration, c-f, are
from a grave in the burial place east of the railroad station at
Holyoke. This necklace is in the museum at Amherst College.
It was apparently made up of two large native copper beads, e, f,
one in the form of c, and seventy-two smaller ones similar to d.
There are also more than thirty shell beads, most of which are
quite badly disintegrated; one of the best preserved of these is
shown in figure 61, c. Parts of another necklace of copper and shell
beads came from a grave at Windsor Locks, Connecticut. In the

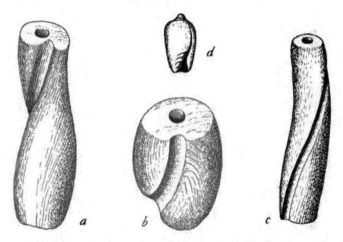

Figure 61. a–c, Massive Shell Beads; d, Marginella shell. a, d, grave at Windsor Locks,
Conn.; b, grave at Swanton, Vt.; c, grave at Holyoke, Mass. The beads are probably from
the columella of *Fulgur carica.* (1/1.)

Bull collection are approximately seventy-five to one hundred
native copper beads of the above types. They are a part of a
quart or more found in Essex, Connecticut.

A few copper nuggets from glacial drift have been reported
from New England, but I know of no evidence that such nuggets
were known to or used by our tribes for the production of ornaments or implements. Small nuggets have also been found in the
Maritime Provinces but they are not common. Dr. Fewkes found
a copper bead in a shellheap on Prince Edward Island and he
mentions eighteen copper specimens in the Provincial Museum at
Halifax from the vicinity of Lunenburg, Nova Scotia. "They

consist of nuggets of copper, some of which are somewhat hammered, well made knife blades, and pointed implements." [46]

From the above we may assume that some of the tribes of the Maritime Provinces practiced to a limited extent the art of working copper, and that the material used was native to their region.

During the interval between the years 1500 and 1600, our New England tribes obtained much European sheet copper and brass from fishermen and traders. Many personal ornaments and a few utensils were wrought from this material. A description of some of these will appear under another heading.

[46] J. W. Fewkes, *A Prehistoric Shellheap on Prince Edward Island*, Am. Antiquarian, January 1896.

THE ALGONQUIAN GROUP
IN GENERAL

WHILE it is possible to draw a fairly distinct line between most of the groups of artifacts of the pre-Algonquians and their successors, one would expect to find less distinction between the material culture of the old Algonquian group and that of the tribes encountered by the voyagers of the early days of the sixteenth century.

The artifacts which we have designated old Algonquian formed, of course, but a small part of the imperishable objects used by them in their daily activities; they were the highly prized personal belongings which were buried with them. It seems doubtful if all the types we have described continued in use in New England for a very long period after the northern invasion of the Iroquois.

We will now give an account of the more important groups of objects pertaining in general to the Algonquians who occupied New England down to proto-historic times, including many articles not previously described undoubtedly belonging also to the older tribes of this stock as well as to their successors.

Chipped Implements. Up to the present time we find no evidence that a paleolithic people have inhabited New England, although many so-called implements have been found which bear a certain resemblance to the ancient paleoliths of Europe. These American forms, often called turtlebacks, are now generally classed as rejects when found on quarry or workshop sites. They show the early stages in the making of chipped knives and projectile points but were discarded owing to some flaw or imperfection which rendered them unsuitable for further chipping. A few rejects of primary form are illustrated in figure 62. They occur in abundance in the workshops of the more extensive quarries where material has been gathered for flintworking.

It is not, however, always easy to distinguish a reject from a similar crude form intended for further chipping unless we know the circumstances under which the specimen was found, for occasionally very crudely chipped forms were transported and cached. These undoubtedly were intended for further working. Two examples from a cache of thirty-one turtlebacks and nineteen finely chipped blades are shown at the left in e, of figure 63.

In the second stage of flint chipping the work was carried forward until most of the superfluous material was removed in the form of flakes or chips, and the implement approached the shape approximated in a, or c, of this figure. Occasionally during the secondary chipping one was broken, or it chipped erratically, in which case it was discarded. Comparatively few implements broken in the last stages of their making, however, are found in shop refuse. These crude leaf-shaped blades produced in the

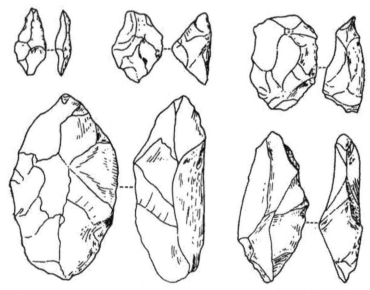

Figure 68. Rejects from Indian workshops at Mt. Kineo, Moosehead Lake, Me. Peabody Museum, Cambridge. (1/6.)

workshops at the quarries or other sources of supply were carefully packed and transported to the various villages, and are what are termed cache forms, for the reason that so many of them have been found by farmers and others cached in the ground where they were hidden by the Indians upon their return to the village from the distant quarry.

These cached blades were completed at leisure by their owners, their forms refined, the cutting edges improved, and notches made in some of them to aid in hafting. Much of the quarry work and the coarser chipping was done with stones of various sizes used as

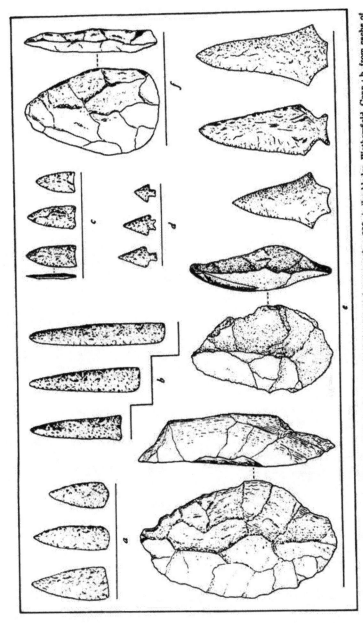

Figure 63. Cache Forms of Chipped Implements. a, From cache containing more than 200 similar blades, Wethersfield, Conn.; b, from cache of 36 blades, Meredith, N. H.; c, from cache containing 19 or more, Watertown, Mass.; d, from cache containing 112 similar points, Billerica, Mass.; e, from cache containing 31 unfinished and 19 finished blades, Arsenal grounds, Watertown, Mass.; f, from cache containing "a bushel" of red jasper blades, Dennysville, Me. (1/4.)

121

hammers. An antler punch (figure 122, m-o), and hand hammer were doubtless employed in the final stages of this preliminary work, and the more delicate chipping done with a smaller antler flaker by pressure.

By far the greater portion of the material used by our New England tribes in the manufacture of chipped implements is of local origin. There are numerous outcrops of felsite, rhyolite, and other varieties of "flint" that break with a concordal fracture, and erratic boulders of these materials are found in many sections. In Maine especially occur boulders of red and variegated jasper which were highly prized by the ancient flint chipper.

In central and southern New England, felsite, rhyolite, argillite, quartzite, and white quartz were used extensively. We may be sure that whenever a stone of suitable texture and attractive color was found it was appropriated for this work. There is a small outcrop of jaspar and chalcedony at Saugus Center which has been quite extensively worked by the Indians. This is probably the source of much of this material used for knives and projectile points in eastern Massachusetts.

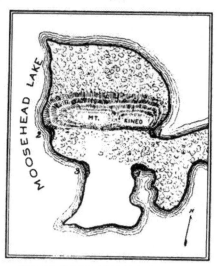

Figure 64. Map showing location of Indian workshops near Mt. Kineo, Maine.

Many knives and projectile points, however, may be seen in our local collections, the materials of which are apparently foreign to our states. A notable example of these importations are the blades shown in figure 31. These are chipped from a variety of quartz apparently native to Labrador and the implements were probably made there and brought to New England in pre-Algonquian times. In 1895 the writer examined the Indian workshops at Mount Kineo, Moosehead Lake.[47] This mountain is a solid outcrop of

[47] C. C. Willoughby, *Prehistoric Workshops at Mt. Kineo*, Maine. The American Naturalist, vol. XXXV, pp. 213-219.

porphyritic felsite. The talus slope at the foot of the great cliff which extends the full length of the southern side of the mountain is two hundred to three hundred feet in width. Patches of evergreens interspersed with deciduous trees were growing near its base, but its surface was practically free from soil. The slope of the talus is composed of comparatively small fragments intermixed with larger pieces. This talus is constantly forming and colored patches along the face of the great cliff mark the places from which masses of felsite have recently fallen. These are shattered as they strike the rocks below, and the larger pieces rolling down the slope are broken and chipped into innumerable forms. The recently fractured pieces are easily distinguished from those which have been long exposed to the action of the atmosphere. The fresh fracture presents a green surface sprinkled with small dots and squares of gray feldspar crystals. Upon long exposure the surface becomes a uniform dull gray. Upon this talus slope one can gather bushels of chips, flakes, and pseudo-implements showing the green fractures of recently fallen stone, which are wholly the work of nature. These, if placed unlabelled on the shelves of a museum, would be accepted without question as the work of man.

At points at the lower edge of the talus slope and at several places on the low peninsula south of the mountain are the old Indian workshops. Chips and rejectage occur in many places but the principal sites were located at points indicated on the plan, figure 64.

Workshops 1 and 2, near the eastern and western ends of the cliff, were evidently the principal blocking-out shops. A large amount of flakes, and general shop refuse were found. Large discarded worked pieces lay in beds of chips and ashes and charcoal occurred at intervals. Workshops 3 and 4 differed principally from those near the ends of the talus in the size of the rejectage. Both had been somewhat disturbed by the damming of the outlet of the lake and the consequent washing away of portions of the shore. Workshop 4 had been nearly obliterated, but the abundance of refuse along the beach showed the types of implements manufactured there. In both these workshops small and medium turtlebacks predominated.

I could find no evidence that the rock used was detached from the main mass by the Indians. There was no need of this, for freshly fractured pieces of proper size for easy transportation to the workshop camps were scattered over the slope of the talus in great number.

That most of the products of the Kineo workshops were intended for transportation is evident not only from the workshop refuse itself but from the chips, and specialized forms of this material both broken and perfect, which are found in nearly all of the burial places, village and camp sites which I have examined in central and southern Maine. Small chips of Kineo felsite are common in nearly all the village sites in the valleys of the Kennebec and Penobscot rivers and their tributaries and also in the sites and shellheaps of the inlets, small rivers, and islands between these rivers, and for some distance east of the Penobscot, and west of the Kennebec. The broken and discarded implements found in company with the chips in these places are commonly small knives and projectile points, scrapers, and perforators probably mostly made in the home camps from cache forms brought from Kineo. Numerous knife blades of this material have been taken from pre-Algonquian graves.

Boulders of Kineo felsite transported by glacial action are found in the region south of Moosehead Lake. Some of these were doubtless also used by the Indians as raw material. Boulders and smaller stones of red and variegated jasper are often found in central and eastern Maine. Cached blades of this attractive mineral will be referred to later. Mount Kineo was one of the most extensive sources for raw material in New England.

Outcrops of felsite in various colors and other rocks of this class, however, occur in many sections, and a large percentage of the knives, scrapers, arrow and spear points recovered are made from this class of minerals. Workshops occur at Marblehead, Wakefield, Blackman's Point, Marshfield, and many other places. In Rhode Island and the region of Cape Cod white quartz was extensively employed. This material, while hard and serviceable, does not flake readily and implements made from it usually have a clumsy appearance.

The term flint, as commonly used by American archaeologists, is broadly applied not only to flint proper but to other silicious stones of great hardness and of various colors, including chert, jasper, and chalcedony. These minerals show a smooth concoidal fracture and some of our most attractive implements were made from them. These varieties, however, are not common in New

Figure 65. Unfinished Blades of Jasper. A selection from a cache on Twin Sisters Island, Grand Lake, Me. Peabody Museum, Cambridge. (3/7.)

England and many of the artifacts made of such material were probably imported.

The above paragraphs refer principally to the materials used in making chipped implements, to the sources of supply, and to

125

the preliminary blocking out at the quarry workshops. We have reason to believe that the better work of this nature was done largely by professional flint workers whose chief occupation was the finding of suitable material, the reducing for ease of transportation the selected stone to the smallest sizes conformable to the types of implements to be later produced, and the transportation of these blanks to the home village, where the tools were finished at leisure.

For the safe keeping both of partially finished implements, and those which had been completed and were intended for barter, they were cached in the ground. Many of these hoards have been brought to light in recent years.

Probably the largest number of prospective implements taken from a single cache in New England were found in North Hadley. The hoard consisted of three hundred and nineteen blades averaging about four to five inches in length, most of them being leaf-shaped, without side notches. They are now in the Haffenreffer Museum at Mt. Hope, Rhode Island. In the collection of the Connecticut Historical Society at Hartford more than two hundred similar though smaller blades may be seen which were unearthed in Wethersfield, near Hartford, many years ago, three typical examples being shown in figure 63, a.

A cache of thirty-six finely chipped and slender blades of felsite apparently completed, was discovered in Meredith, New Hampshire, about fifty years ago. Three of these appear in b, of the above figure. In East Watertown, adjoining Boston another cache of well finished felsite knife blades or points was plowed out in a field of a market garden, nineteen of which are in the Peabody Museum at Cambridge; examples are shown in c.

On the arsenal grounds at Watertown, Mr. S. J. Guernsey of the above Museum discovered a very unusual cache. About thirty inches beneath the surface were thirty-one felsite turtlebacks of various sizes, much like the ordinary rejects common on quarry sites, and nineteen finished knives or spearpoints. Typical examples of both forms appear in figure 63, e. There was also in this cache a felsite adze blade which had been chipped into form and the cutting edge ground and polished. The knives had been placed in the pit first and the turtlebacks placed over them. The combined weight of the latter and the superimposed earth apparently caused the breakage of a few of the knives.

126

I have previously referred to the attractive red and variegated jasper which is more or less common in Maine and the adjacent territory to the east. A cache of large blanks of red jasper was found in Dennysville, eastern Maine, many years ago. A medium sized example of these is illustrated in figure 63, f. There were about a bushel in all. Several are in the National Museum at Washington and also in the Peabody Musuem at Cambridge. Others have become scattered. Some show traces of red ocher which had been placed with them in the cache.

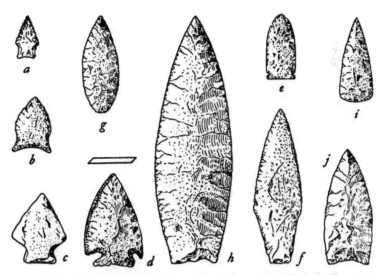

Figure 66. Chipped Knife Blades from various sections of New England. Those were probably hafted in short handles of wood, bone, or antler. (1/3.) See figure 144.

In the Peabody Museum at Cambridge is also an interesting group of about fifty blanks, and a few scrapers and chips, of variegated jasper, found by Dr. S. J. Mixter of Boston in 1904 between two boulders on Twin Sisters Island in Grand Lake, some thirty miles west of Calais. Two of the blanks were found on the surface, having been exposed probably by erosion. Most of the others were within a space of about three feet in diameter and one foot in depth. A selection is shown in figure 65. A very similar cache of artifacts of variegated jasper was found at the outlet of Moosehead Lake. In d, of figure 63 are three representative points

127

from a cache containing 112, found in Billerica, Massachusetts, in 1924. This cache is now in the collection of the Society for the Preservation of New England Antiquities, in Boston.

The chipped implements of New England fall naturally into the following five groups: knives, spearpoints, arrowpoints, drills, and scrapers.

Knives. The largest group probably consists of knives of various sizes and forms. The chipped blades were normally attached to short handles, usually of wood, but sometimes of antler or bone, to which they were securely fastened with gum or with gum and wrappings of cord, sinew, or thong. It is probable that every adult individual possessed a knife of flint or other stone.

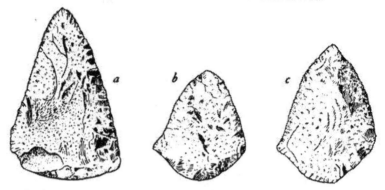

Figure 67. Chipped Scraper and Knives. The lower edge of the scraper, a, is worn smooth through long use. The implement was probably hafted in the end of a handle three to four feet long and used for scraping and softening deer and other large skins, New Haven, Conn. b, c, Knives of unusual form, probably used without a haft. The sharp projection at the left of each is an unusual feature. Bremen, Me., Peabody Museum, Cambridge. (1/3.)

Stone knives in their original wooden handles have probably never been found in New England, the climatic and other conditions being such as to favor the rapid disintegration of the hafts. The blades, however, are often found with burials.

Both sides of an antler handle with a piece of brass inserted for a blade are shown in figure 129, d. This knife was found with an Indian skeleton on Hermon Street, Winthrop, near Boston. The handle was preserved by contact with the metal and is undoubtedly of a type formerly used for flint blades. On one side of the handle are two holes drilled diagonally till they meet. This is for the passage of a suspending cord.

Numerous fine examples of prehistoric flint knives in their original handles have been obtained from caves and cliff houses in various sections of Mexico and the Southwest, and from a few graves and village sites in other parts of the United States. A few also have been obtained by early travelers from our historic Indians. Figure 144 shows various types of these prehistoric knives. The drawings are all from sketches made by the present writer over a period of many years and every specimen shown can be relied upon as authentic. It will be seen that nearly all these

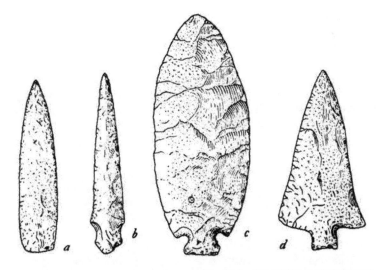

Figure 68. Spearpoints. The narrow stems of c, and d, seem to show conclusively that they were so used; a, and b, were probably also hafted as spear points although the evidence of such use is less marked. a, Shellheap, Tafts Point, Me.; b, Massachusetts; c, North Andover, Mass.; d, Westerly, R. I. (1/3.)

hafted blades can be duplicated by specimens from almost any of our larger local collections.

Several chipped blades from pre-Algonquian graves in Maine have already been described and illustrated, figures 30 and 31. There seems to be no difference between these and similar forms used by their Algonquian successors. We have but few authentic records, however, of chipped knife blades from Algonquian graves in New England, most of those which can be identified as Algonquian having been taken from the shellheaps of this people, in which are found nearly all the types of chipped implements in these states.

The principal types which can be quite definitely identified as knives are illustrated one third their natural size in figure 66. In the four examples, a-d, the shank is relatively broad for the attachment of the handle, which was secured in place with gum reinforced with wrappings of cord or sinew. The cutting edges of a, and d, are bevelled by fine chipping from one side of the edge only. This chipping appears along the left edge in the drawings, the opposite edge being bevelled upon the side not appearing in the illustrations. The diagram accompanying d, shows a cross-section through the center and illustrates the relative positions of the bevels. These bevelled blades are rare in New England.

In using a steel knife the unsophisticated Indian draws the blade toward his body. In these ancient flint knives the bevel is nearly always upon the upper side toward the body when in use. Sometimes, though rarely, a knife of this type is found made apparently for a left handed man. In such specimens the bevelling is reversed.

The bases of the specimens with outside notches in this figure were doubtless inserted in slits in the ends of wooden handles where they were secured with gum, probably of the spruce tree, prepared and hardened by boiling. In figure 67, b, and c, are two blades of unusual form that may well have been used without a haft. They are chipped from a variety of rhyolite. There is a sharp, carefully finished projection upon the left side of each which may have added materially to the cutting qualities of the implements, which seem to have been made for special work. They were both found in Bremen, Maine.

Spears. There is little data to guide us in identifying the chipped flint blades used as points for spears. Flint pointed spears and lances from historic tribes are rarely found in our museums, and their use seems to have been less common than is generally supposed. The majority of blades usually classed as spearpoints were probably knives; still many of these forms may have been used as points for spears which were employed both for securing game and as combined weapons and badges of office.

In figure 68 are shown four blades one third natural size, three of which, b, c, d, may be confidently classed as points for spears owing to their narrow shanks. The fourth specimen, a, may possibly be a knife, but its length and its relative narrowness would seem to place it in the same category as the other specimens. That the same form of blades was sometimes used both for knives and spearpoints is, however, probable. Wood says that our Indians

use no other weapons in warre than bowes and arrowes, saving that their Captaines have long speares, on which if they returne conquerors they carrie the heads of their chiefe enemies that they slay in the wars: it being the custome to cut off their heads, hands, and feete, to beare home to their wives and children, as true tokens of their renowned victorie.[48]

In the region of eastern New England spears or lances were also used for hunting deer on snowshoes in the deep snow. The animal was pursued till exhausted when, according to Champlain, he was dispatched by shooting with bow and arrows or by means of a "dagger" attached to the end of a short spike. Most of the spears used in New England for taking fish, lobsters, etc., were headed with bone.

Arrowpoints. The more common stone arrowpoints are illustrated in figure 69, two thirds their natural size. They are found on old village and camp sites and also in the shellheaps, but are rarely recovered from graves. The forms shown in h-n, sometimes occur in our older museums attached to very old arrows obtained many years ago from tribes in the central and western portions of the United States, and which were the forerunners of the iron points of the same general form made by traders to barter with the Indians in the old pioneer days of the West.

The Points figured in a, b, are of white quartz. This refractory material does not chip readily, and the points made from it are usually quite thick and have a clumsy appearance. It was a substance extensively used, however, in eastern Massachusetts and Rhode Island and large numbers of quartz points may be seen in the local collections of this region. The earliest account (1524) of the Indians of this immediate section tells us that their arrows were tipped with "jasper stone, and hard marble and other sharp stones."[49] The hard marble was doubtless this milk-white quartz.

Triangular stone arrowpoints are especially common in Massachusetts and some other sections of southern New England, and typical examples are illustrated two thirds natural size in a-g. These are the work of the later Algonquians and the form was

[48] William Wood. *New England's Prospect*, Boynton edition, p. 89.
[49] John Verarzanus, in The Relation of Hakluyt's Divers Voyages (1582). Hakluyt Soc. reprint.

perpetuated in the brass points of the proto-historic tribes of the same section (see figure 126, b-f). They are usually made of felsite or white quartz.

Various early writers have left us good descriptions of the arrows

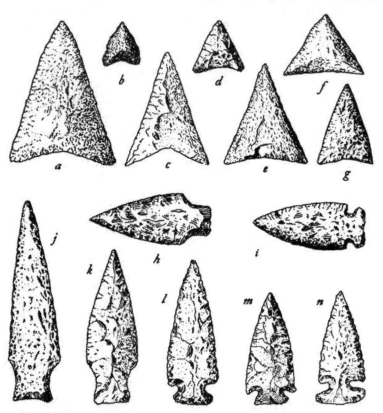

Figure 69. Arrowpoints. b, h, i, l, m, n, Maine; a, c, f, g, j, Massachusetts; d, Vermont; e, k, Rhode Island. (2/3.)

used by our New England tribes, but I find but one first hand account of stone points being used. This is by Verarzanus as above quoted. When the Pilgrims landed at Cape Cod they had an encounter with the natives. After the brief skirmish they picked up eighteen arrows which were afterwards sent to England by Master Jones. "Some of them were headed with brass, others with hartshorn [deer antler tips, see figure 122, a, e,] and others with eagle claws." Wood says:

Their bowes they make of handsome shape, strung commonly with the sinnewes of Mooses; their arrowes are made of young Elderne, feathered with feathers of Eagles wings and tailes, headed with brasse in shape of a heart or triangle, fastened in a slender peece of wood sixe or 8 inches long, which is framed to put loose in the pithie Elderne, that is bound fast for riving: their arrowes be made in this manner because the arrow might shake from his head and be left behind for their finding, and the pile onely remaine to gaule the wounded beast.[50]

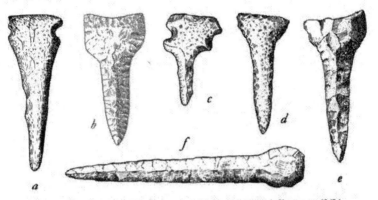

Figure 70. Drill Points. a, Maine; b, c, d, Massachusetts; e, f, Vermont. (2/3.)

Another interesting account is by Martin Pring, who visited Plymouth Harbor in 1603.

Their weapons are Bowes of five or sixe foot long of Wich-hasell, painted blacke and yellow, the strings of three twists of sinewes, bigger than our Bow-strings. Their Arrowes are of a yard and an handfull long not made of Reeds, but of a fine light wood very smooth and round with three long and deepe black feathers of some Eagle, Vulture, or Kite, as closely fastened with some binding matter, as any Fletcher of ours can glue them on.[31]

From these and other early accounts we learn that various kinds of points were used for arrows including those made of stone, eagle claws, bone, and antler. The tail of the horseshoe crab made an admirable arrowpoint. This is recorded by Champlain. He says:

[50] William Wood, *New England's Prospect*, Boynton edition, p. 95.
[31] G. P. Winship, editor, *Sailor's Narratives of Voyages Along the New England Coast*, pp. 56, 57.

Their weapons are pikes, clubs, bows and arrows, at the end of which they attach the tail of a fish called the signoc [horseshoe crab], others bones, while the arrows of others are entirely of wood.

Stone points seem to have gone out of use before the last quarter of the sixteenth century, triangular points made of sheet brass or broken brass kettles being often substituted.

Drills. Chipped stone drills are usually found in nearly every local collection, the more common types being illustrated in figure 70. Some of these seem to have been made of an arrowpoint or knife rejected in the process of making, as in a. Most drills were probably hafted in handles of wood, and rotated between the

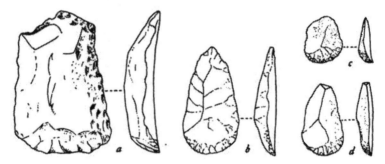

Figure 71. Snub-nose Scrapers. All from Maine. (About 2/3.)

palms, or used in some similar way. I have seen a prehistoric drill from the Southwest, of much the same form as c, hafted as follows: a stick about five inches long and one half inch in diameter was split through the middle. The upper wide portion of the stone point was placed between the two halves of the split stick midway between their ends with its point projecting at right angles to the length of the stick. It was then firmly bound in place with cords, and the two halves of the stick lashed together. By grasping this handle with the point of the drill projecting between the fingers, this mode of hafting was found to be very efficient. These implements were probably used in drilling both wood and the softer stones.

Scrapers. The specialized flint scraper is widely distributed in America, and in New England it occurs in most of our larger collections. While any sharp flake of flinty stone large enough to be grasped firmly will answer as a makeshift, the edge soon crumbles, producing scratches and an uneven surface. To prevent this crumbling and to produce a lasting and fairly even working edge, a secondary chipping along one side only of the edge was necessary, and in time the typical flint scraper, shown in figure 71, was evolved. The illustrations are two thirds natural size and show both the upper and side view.

The cutting edge appears at the lower part of each drawing. These implements are usually made from a large chip, the nearly flat side of its inner face being used for the under side of the tool. The cutting edge is rounded and finished by fine chipping. The side view in the illustrations shows the wide angle of the cutting edge, which is responsible for the implement's popular name, "snubnose scraper."

Implements of the above type, especially the larger ones, were used by the Eskimo in skin dressing, and were often hafted in short handles of wood or ivory elaborately fashioned to fit the hand. More southern tribes used similar blades fastened to handles of varying length in scraping and softening skins of deer and other animals. Our New England examples were doubtless also used in skin dressing as well as for other purposes. South of Cape Ann in the vicinity of Massachusetts Bay, Champlain found them employed in scraping away charred wood in making dugout canoes. He says:

The canoes of those who live there are made of a single piece, and are very liable to turn over if one is not skilful in managing them. We had not before seen any of this kind. They are made in the following manner. After cutting down at the cost of much labor and time, the largest and tallest tree they can find, by means of stone hatchets (for they have no others except some few which they received from the savages on the coasts of La Cadie, who obtained them in exchange for furs), they remove the bark, and round off the tree except on one side, where they apply fire gradually along its entire length; and sometimes they put red hot pebble-stones on top.

When the fire is too fierce, they extinguish it with a little water, not entirely, but so that the edge of the boat may not be burnt. It being hollowed out as much as they wish, they scrape it all over with stones, which they use instead of knives. These stones resemble our musket flints.[52]

Among the European collections in the Peabody Museum at Cambridge are two, which illustrate the very last of the chipped flint industries in England and France. These consist of two groups of gun flints and tools used in their making. The English flints are

[52] Champlain's *Voyages*, Prince Soc. reprint, vol. II, pp. 73, 74.

more angular in outline and are less carefully finished than those from the continent. The striking edges of the French flints are more rounded, the chipping is finer, and they bear a very close resemblance to c, and d, in figure 71. We may be fairly sure, therefore, that Champlain actually saw this type of scraper in use in eastern Massachusetts.

Our Indians were excellent workers of wood as their bowls and other dishes testify. In producing these utensils, scrapers of the above type, used in conjunction with fire, would be almost indispensable.

A large and very old chipped felsite scraper, somewhat similar to the above forms, but proportionally thinner, is shown one third natural size in figure 67, a. Its lower edge shows traces of the original fine chipping, which has been nearly obliterated by continued use probably for scraping and breaking the grain of large skins. The working edge is much worn and polished. It was probably a woman's tool and was hafted in a handle three to four feet long.

Scrapers of various sizes and shapes were often made by taking a random flake and chipping one edge. This secondary chipping is usually very neatly done, and such tools are easily indentified.

When searching old camp sites, especially in eastern Massachusetts, one is apt to find an occasional gun flint of the peculiar gray color so characteristic of English flint. These undoubtedly belonged to guns sold to the Indians in early colonial days and should not be confused with native flint scrapers which they resemble. An occasional English flint, formerly a part of a flint-and-steel fire lighter sometimes occurs, also nodules of this material said to have been brought to this country as ballast in trading ships and sold to colonial armorers.

Axe and Adze Blades. *The grooved axe.* This is quite common throughout the alluvial valleys and other portions of New England which had been brought under cultivation by the Indians. Few, however, have been found in the Maritime Provinces.

In the eastern woodland area of the United States and a part of the adjacent territory to the south and west it was an important implement among agricultural tribes. The principal purpose of this tool seems to have been felling trees in clearing land for maize fields. After the land was once cleared it was comparatively easy to keep it free from new growth by the annual or semi-annual burning of the weeds and stubble. Another use of this implement in the southern half of New England was doubtless for felling large trees for making dugout canoes which were used almost exclusively for water transportation in this section. Large numbers of small logs were also needed for building stockades, and planks of considerable width were employed to some extent for beds, platforms, and other purposes. The grooved axe, properly hafted, must have been a most effective tool in this work. In felling the larger trees, fire, of course was an important adjunct.

Various kinds of stone were used in making these axes, including quartzite, sienite, diorite, argillite, schist, granite, various porphyritic stones, and altered slates. Many were made of waterworn stones of a form which required a minimum of artificial shaping.

In a considerable portion of the specimens the cutting edge is well preserved. Many, however, have been blunted by use, and some are battered and broken. These implements may be broadly divided into three groups, each group being distinguished by the probable method of attaching the haft.

In the first group are included those axes having one, or rarely two grooves, completely encircling the blade, figure 72, a, h, i. In the second group the groove is on three sides only. The narrow back side from which the handle projects is thin and grooveless, figure 72, d, g. The third group consists of blades with grooves on three sides only but with a wide grooveless back, as in figure 73, a.

In addition to the above groups, axes are sometimes found notched at their narrow sides and without grooves. These are usually quite crude, the artificial shaping being confined principally to the notching and the grinding near the edge.

So far as is known there is no prehistoric example of a hafted grooved axe extant from the eastern woodland area. A careful study, however, of the grooved axes and mauls in their original handles which have been obtained from existing tribes and from prehistoric burial caves and ruins in different sections of America gives us a good idea of the methods probably followed in New England.

The axes of the first group above referred to were doubtless hafted as in a, of figure 74. A pliable withe, perhaps sometimes more than one, was placed in the groove and bent twice around the blade and secured as shown. In the double grooved axe a withe was probably prepared for each groove and the four projecting ends firmly lashed together for the handle.

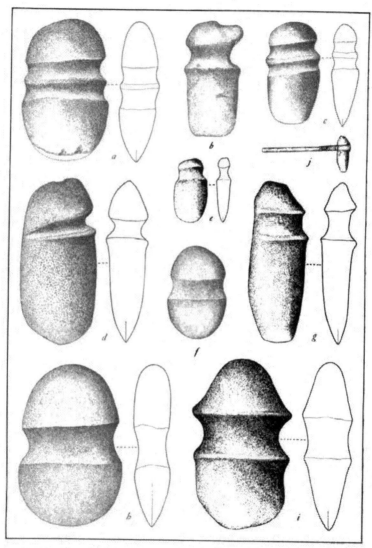

Figure 70. Grooved Axes. a–g, i, Massachusetts: a, near Concord, H. D. Thoreau Coll.; b, Marshfield; c, Middleboro; e, Cape Cod; f, Cambridge; g, Manchester; i, Salisbury; h, Ellsworth, Me. j, Probable method of hafting blade g. (1/5.)

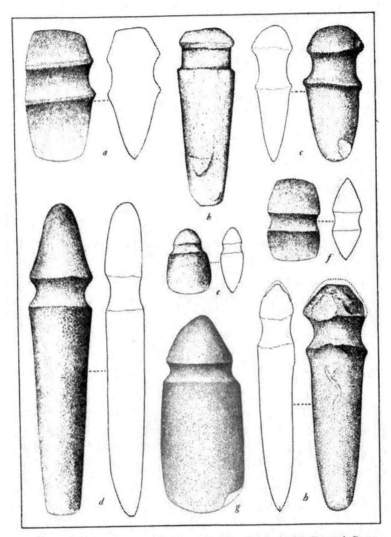

Figure 75. Grooved Axes. a, b, d, g, h, Maine: a, from near Portland; b, Togus; d, Dover; h, Damariscotta. c, e, f, Massachusetts: f, West Newbury. (1/5.)

This would make a very rigid haft. In the second group, a somewhat flattened withe was bent once around the blade and lashed as indicated in b, of the above figure. In the third group, a branch and a part of the limb was cut into the shape of the letter T and the flattened upper side of the crossbar fitted to the back of the blade and fastened as in c.

The majority of the grooved axe blades are made from more or less flattened oval waterworn stones of the proper size. One end of the stone was thinned by pecking and then ground to a cutting edge. A groove of the proper width and depth was pecked around the stone at its center or toward its upper end. The shape of the blade closely approached the original form of the stone, only a small portion of the surface being modified. Figure 72, f, and h, will serve as illustrations.

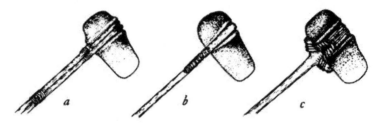

Figure 74. Probable method of hafting axe blades shown in figure 72 i, d, and figure 73, a.

In other examples the entire surface of the blade is artificial and upon either side of the groove are ridges of more or less prominence, as illustrated in figure 72, i. This axe, by the way, was originally much longer, the lower portion having been shortened by repeated sharpening, a feature noticeable in many of the older implements. The bordering ridge at either side of the groove adds materially to the strength of the axe. Most of the axes having a wholly artificial surface have these ridges more or less pronounced. Double bitted axes, figure 73, f, are rare. The interesting specimen shown in figure 72, b, has the upper portion wrought into the form of an animal's head, the only example of its kind that I have seen from New England, although adze blades and pestles are sometimes so ornamented.

Both Champlain and Wood say that large trees felled for making dugout canoes in this section were cut down by means of stone axes. Adair, who studied the customs of the Cherokee and Delaware tells us that the former Indians

twisted two or three tough hickory slips of about two feet long around the notched head of the axe [for a handle], and by means of this simple and obvious invention they deadened the trees by cutting through the bark, and burned them, when they either fell by decay, or became thoroughly dry. ... By the aforesaid difficult method of deadening the trees, and clearing the woods the contented natives got convenient fields in process of time.

Trees up to about six inches in diameter could have been felled without the aid of fire. So far as known, grooved axes have not been found in New England graves. A few have been recovered from shellheaps, but most of them are surface finds.

Grooveless Axes. In New England the grooveless axe or hatchet, like the grooved axe, may be assigned to the Algonquian occupation; it was apparently unknown to the pre-Algonquian people. I have examined many hundred adze blades from pre-Algonquian graves but have never seen a grooveless axe among them. This combined implement and weapon was used by the Algonquians, the Iroquoians, and other tribes to the south. The blade varies greatly in size, its length ranging from about two to ten inches, the greater number being four to six inches long. Figure 75 shows typical examples. They are wrought from a great variety of hard stones, some of them being exceedingly well made and highly polished.

The larger examples were doubtless used as implements, in connection with fire, in cutting and working wood, and the medium and smaller sizes as both implements and weapons.

Several prehistoric grooveless axes with more or less of their original wooden handles still attached have been found in the Algonquian and Iroquoian areas. These show conclusively the method of hafting. It is well known that wood is preserved for a long time if kept submerged, and most if not all of these were recovered from beneath the water. The finest example is illustrated in figure 76. This was found about eight miles from New Bedford, Massachusetts, under salt water in sand, and is now in the Museum of the American Indian, New York. Length of haft, twenty-seven and one half inches; length of blade seven and three fourths inches. In most of the hafted examples above mentioned the upper portion of the blade protrudes through the haft. In one specimen taken from the bed of the Ohio River opposite Elizabeth-

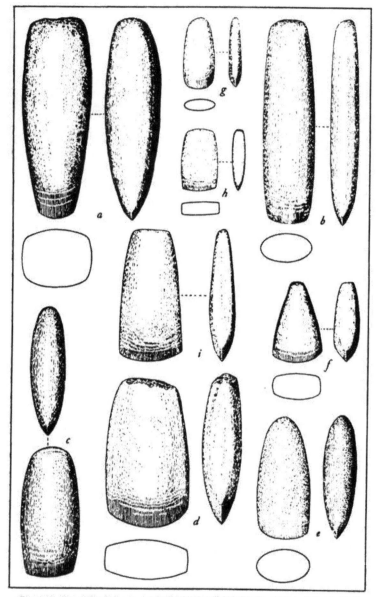

Figure 75. Grooveless Axes. a–c, f–h, Massachusetts; d, Swanton, Vt.; e, Walpole, N. H.; i, Connecticut. All Peabody Museum, Cambridge. (About 1/3.)

town, Illinois, in 1889, the short blade is fitted snugly into the hole which does not perforate the handle. The shorter and smaller New England blades were doubtless hafted in this manner.

The hafted grooveless axe or hatchet is probably the weapon referred to by Gookin in the following words: "tomahawks made of wood like a pole axe with a sharpened stone fastened therein."[83]

Williams says trees were felled with a "stone set in a wooden staff," which seems to refer to the grooveless axe rather than to the grooved variety.

A proper distinction is seldom observed by archaeologists between the blade of the grooveless axe and that of the adze. Both are often referred to as "celts," a word which should be relegated to the limbo where certain other European archaeological terms

Figure 76. Prehistoric Grooveless Axe in its original handle, found in sand beneath salt water about eight miles from New Bedford. Museum of the American Indian, New York. (1/7.)

are long since due. When hafted the edge of the axe is parallel to its handle, while the edge of the adze is at right angles to its haft. When the axe is viewed with its narrow side toward the observer as in the right-hand drawings of figure 75, a, b, etc., the two halves are symmetrical. On the contrary, when the adze is viewed with the narrow side toward the observer, the two halves are unsymmetrical. The adze was used by certain tribes among whom the axe was unknown.

Grooveless axe blades occur less frequently in New England than the grooved variety. They are less common than adze blades. Most of them are surface finds, although they are sometimes found in shellheaps.

From our standpoint it would seem that a wedge shaped stone blade set into a hole or perforation in a comparatively narrow handle would not prove a very serviceable implement. The pres-

---

[83] Daniel Gookin, *Historical Collections*, Mass. Hist. Coll., 1st series, (reprint 1859), vol. I p. 152.

sure of the blade in use would seem to have a tendency to split the haft. It should be borne in mind, however, that in the choice and use of wood, the Indians had acquired the highest knowledge of its natural properties and its adaptability to their simple needs. Handles of this form doubtless served their purpose well. Of course axes of the grooveless variety were less serviceable in heavy work than those with grooves, the hafting of the latter being better suited to the greater strain demanded.

Adze Blades. The simpler forms of adze blades were in general use over a large portion of America. Typical Algonquian blades from shellheaps and graves are illustrated in figure 77. I have

Figure 77. Algonquian Adze Blades. a–d, From Maine shellheaps: a, Hog Island, off Naskeag Point, Blue Hill; b, Whaleback shellheap, Damariscotta; c, Hog Island, Gouldsboro Bay; d, Garrison Island, Friendship. e, Grave at Beverly, Mass. (1/3.)

been unable to find any conclusive evidence that the more specialized gouge shaped forms, or those having dorsal grooves or knobs, were used by the Algonquians. They are, however, more efficient tools for certain kinds of work than the ordinary straight edged type such as we know the Algonquians possessed.

It seems certain that the Algonquians adopted from their predecessors the use of iron pyrites for fire-making. May they not also have taken over some of the more effective forms of the adze?

I know, however, of but three gouge shaped blades that may have come from shellheaps. One was picked up on the beach below an eroded Maine heap and may have fallen from the shells or from an ancient grave beneath them. Another was found by Dr.

J. W. Goldthwait six inches below the surface at the base of a shallow shell layer on the shore of Salt Bay, Damariscotta River. I have been unable to obtain a satisfactory history of the third. There is some evidence that the pre-Algonquian tribes were the originators of the lower layers of some of the New England refuse piles. Most of the adze blades known to be Algonquian are from the shell-heaps. They are perhaps the most common of the larger stone artifacts from these heaps. Their cutting edges are straight or nearly so, that is, approximately parallel to the line of their

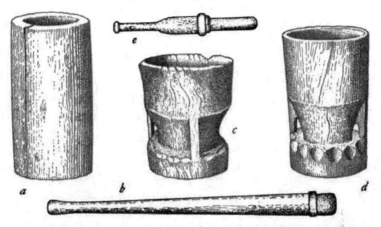

Figure 78. Historic Mortars and Pestles. a, b. From Nantucket Island; c, d. Mohegan Indians, Connecticut, after F. G. Speck; e. Wampanoag Indians, Old Dartmouth Hist. Soc. collection, New Bedford. a, b, Peabody Museum, Cambridge; c, d, Museum of the American Indian, New York. (1/12.)

greatest width. We find, also, in the graves of this people a few blades of this type, one of which is illustrated in e, of the above figure.

In this specimen, from a grave in Beverly, one side near its upper end has been used as an abrading tool, this part having the appearance of the left side of e; in figure 98.

Mortars and Pestles. The mortar and pestle or the metate and muller were implements very essential to all maize growing tribes. In the Northeast, the mortar and pestle were very generally employed although the rudimentary metate and muller in the form of a stone a foot or so in diameter with a flat upper surface, and a field stone of a size to fit the hand conveniently, were sometimes used and are frequently found on old village sites.

The mortars were of both wood and stone. But a few of the former have been preserved. In preparing corn foods, the early colonists adopted the Indian type of wooden mortar and examples may be seen in most colonial museums.

Wooden pestles were used in these colonial mortars and the only modification from what is probably the Indian pattern seems to have been the addition of a horizontal handle two feet or so in length and about an inch in diameter set into the side of the pestle at right angle to its length. The whole affair resembles a huge hammer with a long tapering head, the pestle proper being usually longer than the handle. The wooden mortars and pestles of the Algonquians of the Great Lakes region and also of the Iroquoians are well known to ethnologists, but little is recorded regarding those of the New England tribes.

In the Peabody Museum at Cambridge is an old wooden mortar obtained many years ago from an Indian family at Nantucket which is probably typical of many in common use in ancient times. It is made from a section of an oak tree trunk, and is twenty inches in height, eleven and one half inches in diameter, and has a cavity about twelve inches deep. This is illustrated in figure 78, a. As in most wooden mortars of Indian origin, the lower portion of the cavity is somewhat funnel shaped, which when in use allows the uncrushed kernels and coarser particles of corn to gravitate automatically to the center where they receive the full force of the pestle's stroke, while the finer particles gradually rise around the circumference of the cavity. With this in mind one can understand the efficiency of the ordinary stone pestle which upon first thought seems too small in diameter to be used to advantage in these mortars.

In the Museum of the American Indian are two well made mortars of pepperidge wood which Dr. Frank Speck has described and figured in his paper on the *Decorative Art of Indian Tribes of Connecticut.*[54]

Sketches of these appear in figure 78, c, d. He says:

Practically all of the large mortars for grinding corn in the household, among the Mohegans, were of this type. Their sides were tapered toward the pedestal, and there were from two to three handles on the sides near the bottom. Hollowed scallop work ornamented the edge of the pedestal. The mortars average about seventeen inches in height; and their cavity, narrow-

[54] F. G. Speck, Department of Mines, Geological Survey Canada, Memoir 75, p. 9.

ing towards the bottom, is very deep. The stone pestle is eighteen inches long. Until lately a few of these heirlooms were cherished in several Mohegan families.

While the greater number of wooden mortars used by the New England natives were probably plain sections cut from trunks of hardwood trees, with cavities formed by burning and scraping,

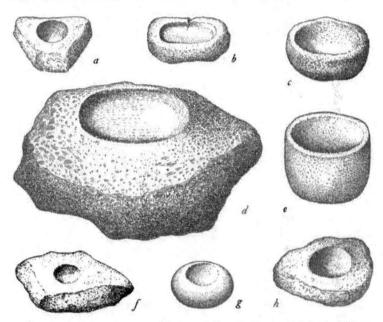

Figure 79. Stone Mortars. a–e, g, h, Massachusetts: a, East Bridgewater; b, Taunton; c, Agawam, near Springfield; d, Essex Co.; e, Plymouth; g, Newburyport; h, Springfield. f, Putnam, Conn. a, b, g, Peabody Museum, Cambridge; c, f, h, Amherst College Coll.; d, Peabody Museum, Salem; e, Pilgrim Hall coll., Plymouth. (About 1/10.)

others were doubtless ornamented to a greater or less degree as the Mohegan examples testify. The pestle belonging with the Nantucket mortar above referred to is of heavy oak. It is forty inches long, three inches in diameter at the larger end and gradually tapers to one and one fourth inches just below the upper extremity which is somewhat enlarged as shown in the drawing, b. The end of a broken stone pestle has been very neatly inserted into a cavity in its lower end where it is tightly bound with an iron band. The stone projects about three inches.

This implement is doubtless much like the more primitive wooden pestles, excluding, of course, the stone inset. It also resembles the wooden corn pestles whose form was probably adopted by the early colonists. It is unlike the typical double ended implement of the Iroquois and the Algonquians of the Great Lakes region.

Another example made of a part of a broken stone pestle inserted into the end of an oak handle and bound with a bone ferrule probably made of a section of the leg bone of a horse or ox is illustrated in e, of the above figure. It is in the collection of the Old Dartmouth Historical Society at New Bedford. The label tells us that it belonged to old Pashaie, an Indian of King Philip's tribe, who was allowed to remain on the farm at Smith's Neck as long as he lived.

In the preparation of maize and acorn foods wooden mortars were probably most commonly employed. Stone mortars, however, were often used, and many of them are found in our larger collections. These were frequently fashioned from field stones, no artificial shaping being attempted except in forming the cavity. Sometimes an example is found with the entire surface more or less carefully and symmetrically worked. Typical specimens are illustrated in figure 79. Those shown in a, d, f, and h, are of natural form, except the artificial cavities which vary from about four to seventeen inches in diameter. The smaller stone pestles would naturally be used with the smaller mortars. In g, the form is also natural excepting the cavity which is very shallow. A short muller similar to figure 82, i, may have been employed with this in preparing paint, or in bruising various barks and herbs in making poultices and other medicines which were much more common among our eastern Indians than is generally known; c, is of hard impure soapstone, its form being wholly artificial; an unusual example, b, has a shallow cavity upon either side. The largest mortar in the illustration is a granite boulder three feet in length. The artificial cavity measures seventeen inches in length and three in depth. It is now in the Peabody Museum at Salem and was found on a former Indian village site near the Ipswich River at Middleton. This probably was used in common by several families, hand stones or mullers being employed in crushing the corn and other food substances instead of pestles which would have been of little practical use in such a shallow mortar.

Larger communal mortars are not uncommon. A good example is illustrated in figure 80. It stands on the shore of Lake Alamoosook in Orland, Maine. Another is near an old village site in Concord, Massachusetts, a few hundred yards from the Old Manse. A fine example may be seen in a field in Sandwich on the Cape, where it is carefully preserved by the owner of the estate. Moorehead tells us that some twenty of these larger mortars occur in the valley of the Merrimack and its tributaries.[55]

Figure 80. Large Communal Mortar. Shore of Lake Alamoosook, Orland, Maine.

In some stationary mortars the depression or bowl is largely artificial. In others a natural depression has been artificially enlarged. Caution should be exercised, however, in identifying these objects. I have seen several so-called stationary mortars that were probably never so used. They were three to five feet in diameter with a saucer shaped depression which shows a more or less rough or uneven natural surface. Each of these was apparently a part of a boulder which had been fractured by glacial ice pressure and which broke with a concoidal fracture. The depressed surface of the mortar-like fragment was quite rough and unfitted for corn grinding. Sometimes, however, one of these would be chosen and

[55] W. K. Moorehead, *The Merrimack Archaeological Survey.* Peabody Museum, Salem, p. 20.

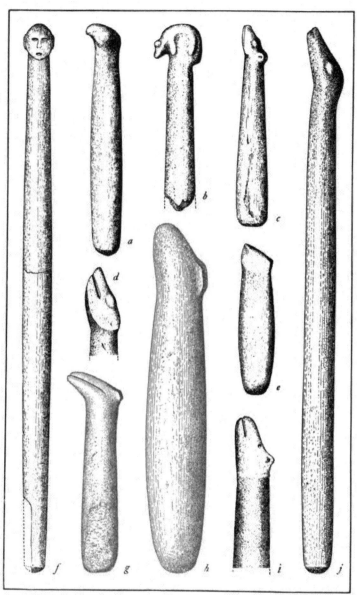

Figure 81. Stone Pestles. a, b, e, g, h, i, j, Massachusetts; a, Concord River Valley; b.
Middleboro; e, from grave at Revere; g, from grave at Winthrop; j, Essex Co. c, f, Maine:
c, Damariscotta; f, Vassalboro. d, Vermont, after Perkins. a, c, g, h, j, Peabody Museum, Cambridge; e, Peabody Museum, Salem; f, Kennebec Hist. Soc., Augusta; b, National Museum.
(About 1/5.)

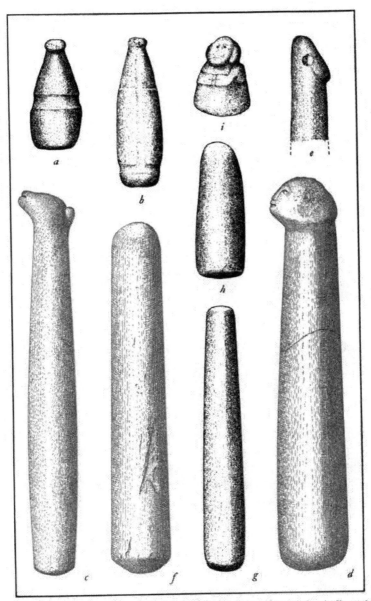

Figure 82. Stone Pestles. a, b, d, g, h, i, Massachusetts: a, Plymouth Co.; b, Harvard; d, Taunton; h, Belmont; i, Plymouth. c, e, f, Rhode Island: c, From grave at Burrs Hill; f, Warwick. b, f, g, h, i, Peabody Museum, Cambridge; a, Pilgrim Hall, Plymouth; c, Museum of the American Indian, New York; d, Old South Meeting House Coll., Boston; e, Mt. Hope Museum. (About 1/5.)

the depression smoothed by pecking and an excellent metate-like mortar produced.

Most of the stone pestles in our collections show no attempt at ornamentation. Some are quite crude though many are symmetrical and well finished. They vary in length from six or eight inches to about twenty-eight inches, the majority measuring ten to twenty inches. The longest one that I have seen measures thirty and three fourths inches and is less than two inches in diameter; the upper end, which is somewhat chisel-shape, is shown in figure 83, c. It is in the collection of the Framingham Historical Society.

Stone pestles are usually made of a compact fine grained slate or some variety of schist. The color is usually greenish-gray though some are nearly black. Probably ninety to ninety-five per cent of these implements are without knobs or ornamental heads such as are shown in figures 81-83. They were probably used principally in wooden mortars with conical cavities, in the preparation of corn foods. In the East they are confined principally to New England and the contiguous maize growing regions.

Schoolcraft figures on plate 21 of the fourth volume of his work a pestle with a knob or head at its upper end. On the same plate he gives a sketch of how this implement was supposed to have been used. The following is his reference (page 175).

The mode of pounding maize by suspending a stone pestle from the limb of a tree as practised by the ancient Pennacooks of the Merrimack Valley in New Hampshire is represented on plate 21. The pestle is commonly ornamented by the head of a man or quadruped, neatly carved from greywacke, or compact sandstone, the mortar also being of the same material.

Referring previously to the use of the spring-pole in connection with the mortar and pestle Schoolcraft says: (Vol. III, p. 467:)

After the introduction of the iron axe consequent on the discovery, stumps of trees were excavated to serve the purpose of the mortar, a practice which commended itself to the early back settlers, who improved on the idea by attaching a wooden pestle to a spring-pole loaded in such a manner as to lift the pestle from the block with but little effort.

These two paragraphs are somewhat contradictory. In one, Schoolcraft attributes the use of the spring-pole to the ancient Pennacooks, at least by inference. In the other he states that it was an improvement of the early colonists.

The knobs and carved heads on the pestles illustrated are primarily ornamental as seems to be proven by the occurrence of similar ornaments upon certain wooden bowls and dishes. Still it is not improbable that some of these ornaments and knobs may have served the purpose mentioned by Schoolcraft.

The two specimens illustrated in figure 82, a, and b, are of interest in this connection. These are undoubtedly pestles. The lower ends of both show this conclusively. They are both knobbed at the upper end, and while they superficially resemble large "sinkers" they belong to a very different class of objects. In b, there is a

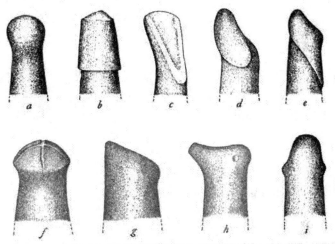

Figure 83. Stone Pestles, showing various ways of finishing the upper ends. All from Massachusetts with the exception of f, which is probably from New Hampshire. (About 1/5.)

vertical groove upon opposite sides which joins a horizontal groove encircling the pestle near its lower end, and which intersects a second encircling groove toward the upper end. It is very evident that these grooves were for holding lashings in place, of a material, probably sinew or thong, which upon drying would shrink tightly into the grooves. These lashings and the knob at the top were doubtless for securing the suspending cord which may have connected the pestle with a spring-pole of some kind, perhaps the limb of a tree. In a, there are no vertical grooves, a deeper horizontal groove serving to hold the lashings. Another pestle, nine and one fourth inches in length, the upper end of which is shown in figure 83, f, has cross-grooves on the upper portion of the knob, apparently for holding in place the bindings which secured the suspending cord.

The long snake-like pestle illustrated in figure 81, j, now in the Peabody Museum at Cambridge, has an interesting history. In 1780 there was incorporated in Boston the American Academy of Arts and Sciences. In the first volume of the Memoirs of this Society, opposite page 256, is a folded plate, at the bottom of which are introduced drawings of four stone specimens of Indian workmanship, one of which represents this pestle. In the list of gifts made to the Academy with the names of donors is the following.

"Mr. D. Watson. An emblematical stone found two feet below the surface of the earth, supposed to be wrought by aboriginals." Unfortunately the locality where it was found is not given, but it was undoubtedly somewhere in Essex County, eastern Massachusetts. This specimen was transferred by the Academy to the Boston Athenaeum where it remained till 1867, when it found a permanent home in the Peabody Museum at Cambridge. It is described and the head figured by Abbott [44] who says

This pestle is not cylindrical. Its surface is formed by a series of flat planes of uniform width, extending the entire length of the implement. Some of them are quite highly polished, while others are merely smooth.

This description must have been based upon a very superficial examination of the specimen. The pestle was originally nearly cylindrical, the flat planes mentioned by Abbott are neither continuous nor regular, they are evidently largely the result of the recent use of the specimen as a whetstone for sharpening steel knives and other tools.

The finest example of these long pestles that has come to the notice of the writer is shown in f, of the same figure. It is made of a greenish slate and the upper end terminates in a well carved human head. Its length is twenty-eight and one half inches.

It has been broken in two. The lower half was discovered near Seven Mile Brook, about that distance above Augusta, Maine. The upper portion was found about four years later a few miles from where the lower part was recovered. The two pieces fitted perfectly together. The implement must have been intentionally broken by a heavy blow across a tree trunk or some such object. It is now in the cabinet of the Kennebec Historical Society at

[44] C. C. Abbott. *Primitive Industry*, pp. 159, 160.

Augusta. The locality where a part of this pestle was found was not far from the site of the Mission of the Assumption founded by Father Druillettes about the middle of the seventeenth century. Could the teachings of this priest have had anything to do with the breaking of this "idol?"

Another much heavier pestle terminating in an effigy of a human head is shown in d, figure 82. It is of a fine grained black stone and has also been intentionally broken. It was found near Taunton and is now in the cabinet of the Old South Meeting House, Boston.

The well wrought pestle terminating in the head of a bird, a, figure 81, from the vicinity of Concord, belongs to the Henry D. Thoreau collection now in the Peabody Museum at Cambridge. Thoreau was much interested in local Indian antiquities and brought together a very creditable collection. The example shown in c, of the same figure is from the edge of the stream connecting Biscay and Damariscotta ponds, and was presented to the Peabody Museum by Mr. Albert J. Phelps of Damariscotta, Maine. It is an especially good example of Indian sculpture.

The specimen with the grotesque head, g, was taken from the grave of a child at Winthrop just across the bay from Boston. With this burial were two small pottery vessels, an antler spoon, a small elongated pebble, one end of which somewhat resembled the head of an animal, and the pestle illustrated. It seems evident that the latter had been used as a plaything by the child whose fondness for it determined its final resting place. This pestle is of special interest as it conclusively shows that these implements were in use as late as the latter half of the sixteenth century, the approximate date of the cemetery in which the burial occurred.

A pestle of unusual symmetry and finish is illustrated in figure 82, c. It is from a grave at Burr's Hill, Rhode Island, and is in the Museum of the American Indian, New York.

The short pestle or muller represented in i, of the above figure is sculptured to represent a portion of the human form. Its base is slightly rounded and is worn smooth by long use as a muller. The original label still attached to it reads "Indian Stone Image, found at Plymouth. Gift of I. Thaw, Aug. 17, 1795." This forms a part of the Lowell collection in the Peabody Museum at Cambridge.

The ordinary, every day pestles in common use throughout this

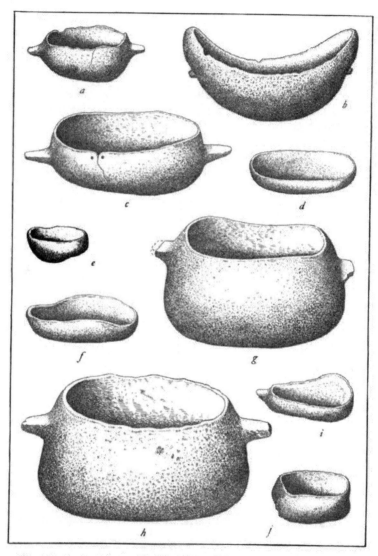

Figure 84. Soapstone Pots and Dishes. All from Massachusetts with the exception of *i*, which is from Cranston, R. I.: a, Tewksbury; c. Lawrence; d, Hadley; e, Worcester Co.; f, Millbury; g, Lynnfield; h, South Hadley Falls; j, Hadley. a, b, e, f, i, Peabody Museum of Cambridge; d, h, j, Amherst College Museum; c, Andover Archaeological Museum; g, Society for the Preservation of New England Antiquities, Boston. (About 1/7.)

region, such as occur by the score in most of the larger collections of Indian antiquities are rarely found in graves. Many of them are carefully fashioned, others are crudely made. In figure 82, f, g, are shown two of the better class. In h, of this figure is one of natural form, the only modification being at the lower end.

Soapstone Pots and Dishes. In addition to wooden bowls, bark receptacles, and pottery vessels, the New England Algonquians used cooking pots and other dishes made from steatite, or soapstone as it is commonly called. Good examples are shown in figures 84, 85. They were quite extensively used, especially in the southern half of this area, where several prehistoric quarries occur which furnished the raw material. Soapstone vessels of the types illustrated are by no means confined to New England but are found also in the Middle States and as far south as Virginia. I have seen a few examples with typical side handles from the Labrador Eskimo, but these seem to be not very old.

Fragments of these vessels occur on old camp sites in all of our New England states and occasionally an unbroken pot is unearthed.

Sometimes a fragment will show one or two perforations near its edge, which indicates that the vessel had become cracked or broken and afterward mended by binding the broken edges together with a cord which passed through two or more perforations. By stopping the crack with some substance not easily affected by heat, the vessel again became useful. Figure 84, c, shows a pot with a crack through the side and with two holes for the lashing, a good illustration of this method of repairing.

It seems evident that at least the larger examples which are usually supplied with handles were used principally in cooking, for many fragments are found with the convex side blackened by contact with fire. The well-known heat retaining property of soapstone added much to the value of these utensils as food containers. The largest example, h, in the above figure has a capacity of about sixteen quarts. All the specimens shown in this illustration are from Massachusetts, with the exception of i, which is from Rhode Island.

Figure 85 illustrates an unusually fine example with four handles, found at Dickey Plain, Manchester, New Hampshire. It is now in the collection of the Historical Society of that city.

The better known prehistoric sources of supply of this material, in New England are the quarries at Wilbraham, Westfield, and

Millbury, Massachusetts, the one at Providence, Rhode Island (figure 86), and also at Portland, Middlesex County, and at Bristol, Connecticut. Soon after the discovery of the one at Providence, it was visited by Professor Putnam who has given us the following interesting description.[57]

The seam of soapstone was completely covered by the soil that had accumulated over the ancient chippings, and was discovered by the workmen after removing many cart-loads of the pulverized rock. In clearing out the

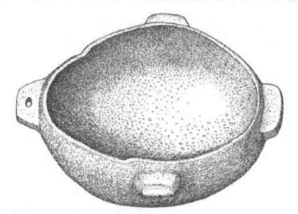

Figure 85. Soapstone Pot. An unusually fine example. From Dickey Plain, Manchester, N. H., Manchester Historical Association Collection. (1/4.)

ancient quarry, over three hundred cart-loads of débris of the manufactory were taken away, and this débris consisted almost entirely of the fine particles of soapstone which had been chipped off in the process of taking out the pot-forms from the mother rock. When this material had been cleared away the peculiar character of the surface of the rock at once attracted attention, and then notice was taken of the fragments of pots and the large number of roughly pointed stones that were lying about and bearing evidence of having been used.

At the time of my visit, many of these rude chisels had been carted a few hundred yards distant to fill up a low piece of land, and others had been thrown in a pile on the ledge. A careful estimate of the number convinced me that at least two thousand of these rude stone chisels had been found on the ledge, or in the immediate vicinity. They were all of nearly the same size, rudely chipped to a blunt point at one end, and roughly rounded to fit the hand at the other. Those brought to the Museum vary in length from five to eight and one-half inches, and in weight from one to four pounds; the majority being of about seven inches in length and from two to three pounds in weight.

[57] F. W. Putnam, Reports of the Peabody Museum of Archaeology and Ethnology, vol. II, pp. 274-276.

These chisels were made from the hard stone of adjoining ledges, and their manufacture must have required considerable labor. A short trial of the chisels upon the soapstone showed the facility with which the steatite could be pecked by these rough implements, and what patience combined with muscle would accomplish.

Associated with the stone picks, or chisels, were between seventy-five and a hundred large rounded stones, weighing from twenty-five to a hundred or more pounds each, which might have been used as hammers for the purpose of breaking off large masses of the soapstone.

Figure 86. Prehistoric Soapstone Quarry, Providence, R. I. Most of the debris left by the workers has been cleared away, exposing the bottom of the excavation and showing numerous depressions and light colored rings where partially finished pots have been detached.

The bed of steatite had been excavated its full width, and nearly all its length and depth as far as at present exposed. The remains of the circular and oval masses, that had been broken off from the sides of the ledge, showed that the seam of steatite was formerly from six to twelve feet deep; the whole of this mass of rock having been worked out and probably made into utensils.

Several fragments of pots were found in the débris of the ledge, evidently broken during manufacture, and also several unfinished pot-forms just as detached from the matrix; while on the ledge itself the pot-forms could be followed out through their various stages of development.

The method of procedure in getting out the mass from which the utensil was to be made was identical with that described by Mr. Schumacher, as

159

followed by the California Indians. The outside of the vessel being roughly shaped and the stone cut away to the required depth, the mass was broken off, the detached surface hollowed out and the outside more carefully finished. In the eastern specimens, however, we do not usually find such a smooth and perfect finish as noticed in the Californian pots.

In one part of the ledge, where an impure seam of harder material has divided the workable steatite, a limited area is formed, which enables an estimate to be made of the number of pot-forms taken out. These forms, as shown by the remaining portions, were from six to twenty-one inches in diameter. On the walls and floor of this limited space, fifteen feet long, eight

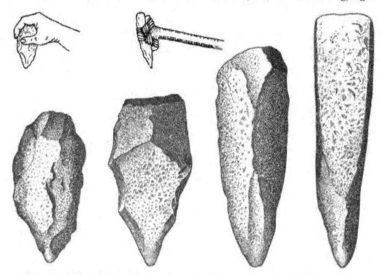

Figure 87. Picks used in making soapstone vessels. From quarry at Bristol, Conn. Similar implements are found in the debris of all our soapstone quarries. (1/3, except insets.)

wide, and six deep, were evidences of the removal of sixty pot-forms. As many as three or four hundred pots had probably been made from the material taken from this part of the ledge alone, and several thousand must have been taken from the whole ledge, which suggests that these vessels were in considerable demand, or that the place had been long used.

The reader will be glad to know that this quarry is now surrounded by a small park. An appropriately worded bronze tablet informs the visitor of its origin and purpose.

In general the above account would apply also to other soapstone quarries as far south as Virginia.

The crudely fashioned pot-forms seem to have been rarely finished at the quarry, but like the roughly made blades from the flint quarries, were transported to camps or villages to be finished at leisure. There is a close resemblance between the picks used in working soapstone throughout the northeastern section of the United States. They are found in large numbers in the refuse of all these sites. Figure 87, shows typical forms. They were easily and quickly fashioned, and while the smaller ones were probably used without handles, most of them were doubtless furnished with hafts, which rendered them most serviceable in blocking out and excavating the utensils. The surface of the better made vessels seems to have been finished with flint scrapers.

In New England soapstone pots and dishes had apparently gone out of use before the arrival of Europeans, for I find no mention of them in the accounts of early writers; nor so far as I am aware have they been found in proto-historic graves. They appear to be of old Algonquian origin. One of medium size with handles, and two smaller ones without handles were taken from graves in the old Algonquian cemetery at Holyoke, an account of which is given on page 83. These are now in the museum at Amherst College.

Soapstone pots seem to have been in use among the Delawares as late as 1748, and are mentioned by Peter Kalm. He says they were

made sometimes of a greenish and sometimes of a grey pot-stone, and some are made of another species of apyrous stone; the bottom and the margin are frequently above an inch thick. The Indians, notwithstanding their being unacquainted with iron, steel and other metals, have learnt to hollow out very ingeniously these pots or kettles of pot-stone.

The better New England examples are often neatly made and are sometimes ornamented along the edge with a series of notches.

Sculptured Life Forms and Petroglyphs. Lescarbot, writing early in the seventeenth century tells us that the Armouchiquois, a term applied to New England tribes south of the Abnaki, practiced painting and sculpture and made images of beasts, birds and men of stone and wood as handsomely as good workmen in France. This statement may be somewhat exaggerated, but the well carved heads appearing on stone pestles and other implements which we have illustrated and which also ornament the wooden bowls of southern New England, as well as the stone effigies which we are about to describe, indicate that these tribes were proficient in such work.

161

Most of the effigies produced were probably of wood, and few of these have survived. Those of stone were doubtless less common. The human head seems to have been a favorite subject. Large ones are rare. Figure 88 is an interesting example, now in the Peabody Museum at Salem, which was found in 1811 while excavating for a cellar for the house of John Boyd at Essex, Massachusetts. It is thirteen inches in height. It is sculptured from a granite boulder, the features of the face, the ear, and the chin being formed by cutting away the surface. Most of the remaining portion is natural. The line shown behind the ear is a natural seam.

Smaller stone heads, evidently intended to be worn as gorgets or as pendants for necklaces, are frequently found in Massachusetts and other sections of southern New England. Figure 89, shows several drawn natural size. Each specimen is perforated for suspension, or has a groove encircling it for the same purpose. In d, the groove does not show clearly in the drawing but it occupies the same relative position as in c, of the same figure.

These effigy heads may be regarded as symbolizing manitos. Dr. Brinton, writing of the Delawares, says:

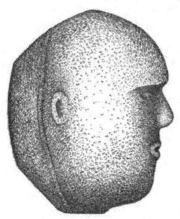

Figure 88. Sculptured Head made from a small boulder. Found while excavating cellar for the house of John Boyd, Essex, Mass., in 1811. Peabody Museum, Salem. (1/6.)

They rarely attempted to set forth the divinity in image. The rude representation of a human head, cut in wood, small enough to be carried on the person, or life size on a post, was their only idol. This was called *wsinkhoalican.*[58]

Dr. F. G. Speck writing of the Delaware Big House Ceremony mentions twelve carved face images which were hung in the interior of the Big House, "those on the center pole being visible symbols of the Supreme Power, those on the upright posts, three on the north wall and three on the south, the manitu of these respective zones; those on the eastern and western door posts, those of the east and west."

[58] D. G. Brinton. *The Lenâpe and Their Legends,* p. 68.

162

The larger of the crudely sculptured heads illustrated in the lower half of figure 90, were probably used in ceremonies. The one shown in g, is about ten inches in length and has a maximum thickness of two inches. It is made of sandstone. Its natural smooth surface was used for the face, and the rougher fractured surface of the back was smoothed by pecking. On either side of the back, at points corresponding to the position of the ears is an irregular funnel-shaped cavity about an inch across and half an inch deep. Traces of red pigment appear upon the face and a small amount of yellow pigment is noticeable on the back. The

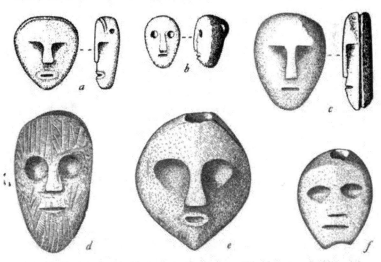

Figure 89. Sculptured Heads, worn as personal ornaments or talismans. b, Groton, Conn. All others, Massachusetts: a, Belchertown; c, Hadley; d, Ribley's Hill, Concord; e, f, Wellfleet. a, c, Amherst College Museum; b, Slater Museum; d, Tolman coll.; e, Peabody Museum, Cambridge; f, G. L. Kittredge coll. (About 1/1.)

yellow color may have been the result of contact with a disintegrating firestone. This interesting effigy was found while digging potatoes in Albion, Maine, and probably came from a grave. The two examples illustrated in d–e, and f, are made of oval waterworn stones, the only modification being the cavities for the eyes and mouth, and the alteration of the back of the head of the former specimen, as shown in d. The larger of the two, f, came from a grave in Warren, Rhode Island, and is in the cabinet of the Rhode Island Historical Society at Providence. The head i, was found in a potato field in North Lisbon, New Hampshire, sometime previous to 1884. The form is wholly artificial, and is an unusually good example of this type of work; j, came from a farm in Mechanic Falls, Maine; and the highly conventionalized example, h, was found in Newton, Massachusetts.

What is perhaps the most interesting sculpture thus far brought to light in this section is shown in a, b, c, of this figure. It is made of a piece of sandy limestone about a foot in length, a considerable portion of which still retains its natural surface. It represents the upper portion of an Indian woman carrying upon her back her child. What is probably a part of the upper extremity of the cradle board appears above the child's head and a part of the carrying strap seems to be indicated passing across the forehead of the mother. The right arm is much out of place, and the left arm is less clearly shown. The child seems to be clinging to the back of its mother in a position reversed from what we should expect if fastened to a cradle board. This was found about eighteen inches below the surface on the northwestern shore of Lobster Cove, Annisquam, Massachusetts, in 1922.

A very good representation of a seated bear appears in figure 91. It is made of a hard dark colored stone and was found in 1830 near the corner of Essex and Boston Streets, Salem. It is now in the Peabody Museum of that city.

A somewhat different class of objects appears in figure 92. In a, we have a nondescript animal which suggests the seal. It is made of steatite and is ornamented with a zigzag pattern very neatly executed. It was found near the outlet of Lake Alamoosook in Orland, Maine, but apparently does not belong to the pre-Algonquian group of artifacts so abundant in that general region.

We have in d, a symmetrical oval pebble about one half of an inch in thickness. A groove has been cut upon either side near the upper end, apparently for receiving a suspending cord or for fastening some object to it. Upon the side illustrated is a central groove with two crossbars, very neatly ground into the surface. This is combined with a lightly incised figure probably representing an insect. This is undoubtedly a fetish. It was found with potsherds in clear sand about eighteen inches beneath the surface on a village site in Pembroke, Massachusetts, by Mr. L. W. Jones, who presented it to the Peabody Museum at Cambridge.

It is well known to ethnologists that material objects, especially

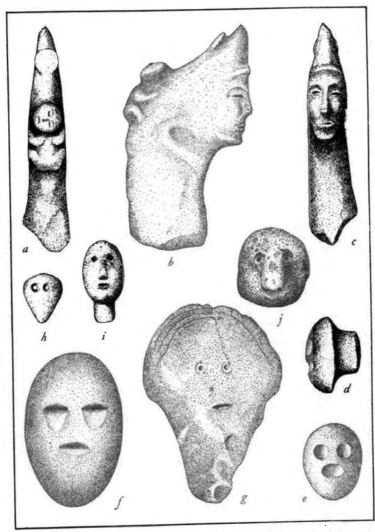

Figure 90. Sculptured Heads. a, b, c, Three views of effigy of upper portion of a woman with cradle (?) and child at her back, sculptured from limestone, Annisquam, Mass.; d, e, two views of head wrought from an oval pebble, Fall River, Mass.; f, oval stone with artificial depressions representing eyes and mouth, Warren, R. I.; g, sandstone effigy from Albion, Me.; h, conventionalized head, Newton, Mass.; i, North Lisbon; j, Mechanic Falls, Me. a–e, h, Peabody Museum, Cambridge; f, Rhode Island Hist. Soc. (1/5.)

stones or concretions resembling human or animal forms, or any of their parts, were supposed to possess supernatural powers and were highly valued as fetishes by those who found them. Such objects were often used with no modification. Others show slight alterations. If, for instance, a stone was found resembling the head of a bird or animal, eyes or a mouth might be added to render the object more realistic, but such changes are usually slight. In many instances it is surprising to see how closely some of these stones resemble animate forms.

An excellent example of this type of fetish is illustrated in c. This is a clay-stone concretion. The bottom or side not shown in the drawing is flat. The object resembles an animal curled up, in repose. The lower three fourths of the body is formed of light clay. The upper portion is of brown clay colored by infiltration of dark material while the body was forming. The three bosses of light clay were deposited after the main part of the concretion was complete.

Figure 91. Effigy of Seated Bear. Found near corner of Boston and Essex Streets, Salem, about 1830. Peabody Museum of Salem. (1/3.)

We can imagine the excitement of the Indian who found this curious stone. It did not, however, quite satisfy him, so he added a mouth, with short crosslines to represent teeth, (which do not show in the drawing) and drilled two holes for nostrils. He then made a number of ornamental incised lines on the dark portion of the back, perhaps in imitation of the markings on the body of the animal he thought it represented. With the exception of the mouth, nostrils, and lines on the back, the form is wholly natural.

This specimen was found in sand, about three feet from the surface at Windsor, Connecticut, and is probably from an old Algonquian grave. It is now the property of the Peabody Museum at New Haven.

Petroglyphs. Pictographs on rocks are not very numerous in New England, although Massachusetts possesses in the Dighton Rock inscription one of the most noted examples in America. This rock is situated on the eastern bank of the Taunton River near the northwestern corner of Assonet Neck, about eight miles below Taunton, and on the opposite side of the river. The rock is a silicious conglomerate. Its sloping western face is about twelve feet in length, and its height about five feet. This face is nearly covered with inscriptions which are wholly revealed only at low tide.

Dr. E. B. Delabarre of Brown University has made an exhaustive study of the inscriptions and the extensive literature pertaining to them which is set forth in his fully illustrated book, *Dighton*

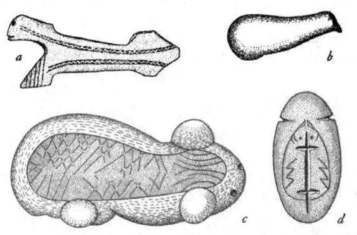

Figure 92. Life Forms, probably fetishes. a, Steatite effigy somewhat resembling a seal; from near outlet of Lake Alamoosook, Orland, Me. b, Chalcedony concretion from village site, Vassalboro, Me. c, Clay concretion resembling an animal in repose; form natural except nostrils, teeth, cross-hatch and short curved lines on back; Windsor, Conn. d, Pebble notched near upper end, and having an incised design probably representing an insect; Pembroke, Mass. a, d, Peabody Museum, Cambridge; c, Peabody Museum, New Haven; b, Kennebec Hist. Soc., Augusta. (2/3.)

Rock, to which the reader is referred for an excellent detailed account of this and other New England petroglyphs.

Dr. Delabarre has listed under forty-three headings the different drawings, engravings, and photographs which he has been able to find in Europe and America relating to Dighton Rock. These range from John Danforth's delineation of 1680 to the excellent flashlight photographs recently made by him. More than a hundred pages are devoted to theories advanced by various writers concerning the probable meaning of the inscription and the people to whom its origin has been attributed, which include Phoenicians, Scythians, Trojans, Jews, Egyptians, Libyans, Japanese, Chinese, Norse, Portuguese, English, and the American Indian. The bibliography of the subject numbers 596 items. Many of these theories were, of course, advanced before knowledge of the wide distribution of Indian pictographs became general.

The inscriptions as they appear today are a jumble of designs including Indian pictographs, Roman letters and figures, and other markings. It should be remembered that the inscriptions are under water at high tide and have been subject to erosion for many years.

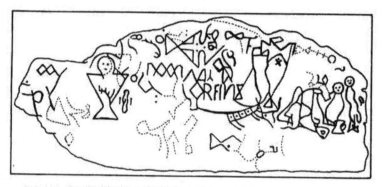

Figure 93. The Dighton Rock Inscription. This is a copy of Mallery's reproduction of the drawing made for the Rhode Island Historical Society about 1834. It probably shows as well as any the pictographs of Indian origin without an excessive admixture of characters which may be attributed to Europeans; portions, however, of the group shown near the center are obviously of European derivation. (1/36.)

As our interest is primarily in the inscriptions which are of native origin, I have selected the drawing prepared for the Rhode Island Historical Society, figure 93, as probably showing as well as any the principal Indian designs without an excessive admixture of European characters. Dr. Delabarre has made an exhaustive study of the many letters and numbers which he attributes to Europeans, and those interested in the subject are referred to his book.

Of the principal Indian figures shown in the above illustration, there are three of human form, the large one at the left and two smaller ones at the right. Other prominent designs made up largely of connected triangles, also some of the less conspicuous

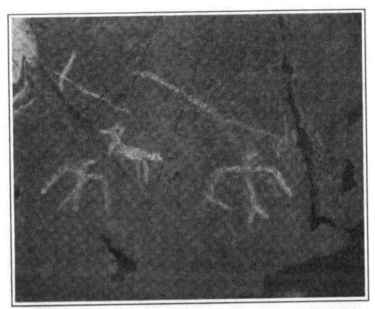

Figure 94. A portion of a group of Pictographs consisting of five or six thunderbirds, a small quadruped, and a few seemingly casual lines, on a large boulder now under water, near Brattleboro, Vt. This photograph was made in 1866.

Figure 95. Pictographs at Bellows Falls, Vt. This photograph was made in 1866.

markings, may doubtless be accepted as Indian, including the long tailed animal with lines across the body and intervening dots, a method of delineation also appearing in some of the human figures on Mark Rock, Warwick, Rhode Island, which are probably of the same period. Other rock writings in the vicinity of Narragansett Bay have been found at Tiverton, Portsmouth, and Mount Hope.

In the Connecticut Valley are two quite noted inscriptions. One is on Indian Rock, which is situated on the south side of West River, near Brattleboro. It is now under water having been flooded by the building of a dam in the Connecticut River. The inscription shows five or six thunderbirds, a small quadruped, and a few seemingly casual lines. A portion of these is illustrated in figure 94 from a photograph taken in 1866.

Farther north at Bellows Falls are other petroglyphs consisting of crude faces and cup shaped depressions, which are shown in figure 95. This picture was also taken in 1866.

When a small boy I remember searching for and finding these "Indian heads" during a Sunday School excursion to Bellows Falls, at that time the terminus of the Cheshire railroad. Searching unsuccessfully for these pictographs in 1927, Dr. Delabarre concluded that they were covered with filling or had been destroyed as a consequence of recent industrial developments.

There are interesting groups of pictographs at Machias, Maine, consisting largely of well executed pictures of many deer and human figures, apparently of both men and women. Similar figures appear upon a rock in the upper Kennebec River at Bingham, Maine.

Numerous inscribed stones of small size have come to light from time to time, upon which appear various designs. Some of these are undoubtedly of Indian origin, but I have seen so many obvious fakes of this nature, that great care should be exercised in accepting as genuine any such object without first carefully checking its history.

Miscellaneous Implements and Ornaments of Stone. *Stone Hoes.* In planting and cultivating their gardens the Algonquians of this section used various implements. Wood speaks of clamshell hoes and Champlain saw the shells of the horse shoe crab used as hoes, but neither of these writers tells us whether or not they were hafted. The Stockbridge Indians, and doubtless others also, used the shoulder blade of the bear, moose, or deer fastened to a wooden handle, and Roger Williams says that stone hoes were formerly employed.

In figure 96 are shown several hoe blades from various parts of the Connecticut Valley made of a fine grained trap rock. They

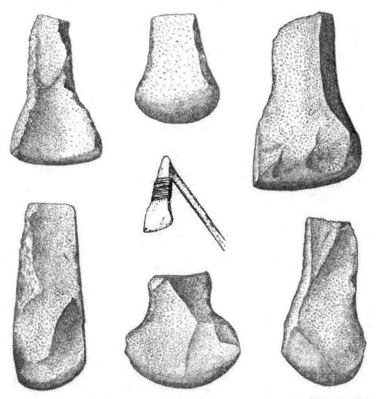

Figure 96. Hoe Blades, made of trap rock, Connecticut Valley, Mass. The central drawing shows probable method of hafting. Peabody Museum, Cambridge. (1/3.)

have been roughly chipped into shape and the lower portion ground to a blunt edge. There is a peculiar luster to the ground part which often extends over a portion of the adjacent chipped surface. This luster or patina is supposed to be caused by contact with the soil during use. It seems to be more than a polish. Many of the large leaf shaped agricultural implements of the Middle West show in a more marked degree this peculiar luster. I have also seen it near the edge of a very large grooved axe from Massachusetts which may have been used for grubbing up roots in clearing land. Stone hoe blades are found in various sections of New England, especially in the southern portions. A good many, crudely chipped, have been obtained in the vicinity of Narragansett Pier.

Stone Clubs. In figure 97 we have an interesting stone club drawn about one third natural size. It is in the Mt. Hope Memorial Museum at Bristol, Rhode Island, and was found on the Elery Wilmouth Farm, Rehoboth, Massachusetts. I have seen three or four similar though larger stone clubs apparently not of Indian make, said to be from the vicinity of Taunton, which should not be confused with this specimen which has every appearance of being

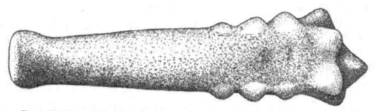

Figure 97. Stone Club, from the Elery Wilmouth Farm, Rehoboth, Mass. King Philip Museum, Mount Hope, R. I. (About 1/3.)

old and authentic. It is a reproduction in reduced size of an ancient type of wooden club such as I have seen offered for sale by Penobscot Indians, with their baskets, bark boxes, etc., at summer resorts. In making these wooden clubs, a small tree with a proper development of roots was selected and cut off about thirty inches from the ground. The stub was then uprooted and the roots cut off an inch or so from the trunk. The short stubs of these roots were then rounded or pointed much as shown in the stone copy.

Abrading Stones. There is a type of implement often overlooked by students, examples of which are shown in figure 98. They usually consist of a compact fine grained silicious pebble of a size to be conveniently grasped in the hand. The peculiar artificially shaped portions of these tools are produced wholly by use.

One of the narrower edges is usually worn away to a considerable depth, the apparent result of use as an abrading tool, probably in shaping or sharpening implements of slate or other stones of similar hardness. Typical specimens of this group are figured in d, e, f.

172

Each of these examples shows marks on the lower end of use as a hammer. In b, the abrasions appear upon both sides. In a, and c, in addition to the broad abrading notches at the lower part of each, there is a series of long narrow grooves upon the upper part which recall the grooves in the smaller tools of figure 58. They may have been useful in preparing sinew thread or softening and stripping fiber for cordage. I find that pebbles apparently of

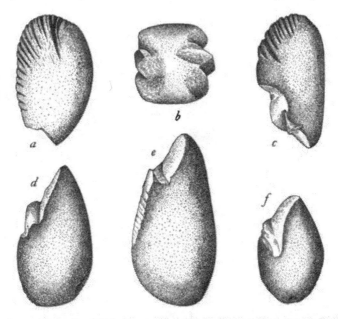

Figure 98. Abrading Implements. a, Rhode Island; all others Massachusetts. Peabody Museum, Cambridge. (1/3.)

similar composition to these abrading stones are of little use in working wood but they are very effective in working shell, slate, and other stones which are not too hard.

In figure 99, a, is a stone about two inches in thickness showing several grooves. Judging by the fragmentary grooves appearing at the left it must have been originally somewhat larger. The grooves are deeper and wider in their centers than at their ends. This was apparently a grinding stone for the shaping and sharpening of tools of bone and other material such as awls, bodkins, and points for darts, harpoons, etc., which were common among all of our tribes.

Mr. F. P. Orchard has called my attention to a flat rock of gritty structure about six feet across lying on the shore of Nauset Harbor at Eastham, Cape Cod, which has twenty-one similar grooves ranging from about six to sixteen inches in length and about one half inch in diameter across the center. There are also several shallow oval basins a foot or more in length where imple-

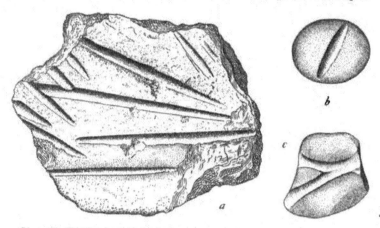

Figure 99. Grinding Stones for finishing bone implements, arrow-shafts, etc. All from Massachusetts: a, North Eastham, Cape Cod, collection of Densmore Green; b. Yarmouth-port; c, Newton. (1/3.)

ments of various kinds have apparently been finished by grinding. Other portions of the rock also show the effects of abrasion. This seems to have been a favorite workshop for finishing axes, adzes, bone implements, bodkins, and other tools. Dr. Delabarre has described similar finishing shops upon certain ledges near Purgatory, Sachuest Beach, Middleton, Rhode Island. Some of the grooves are larger than the ones at Eastham.

Most collections show one or more grooved pebbles or fragments of stone similar to b, or c, of the above figure, of a size to be conveniently grasped in the hand. Such stones are thought to have been employed in smoothing and polishing arrowshafts, but they would also be useful in other work, such as the fashioning of bone and antler implements; b, is a quartzite pebble unmodified except for the groove; c, of sandstone, has similar grooving on both sides, and the greater part of the remaining surface has apparently been used in abrading.

Net Sinkers. Seine fishing was followed both by the Iroquoian and Algonquian people of the woodland area, not only in the warmer seasons when streams and lakes were open but also in the winter when they were ice-bound.

Seines are but casually mentioned by the early New England writers. Williams says the Indian nets, which are called ashóp, are set across some little river or cove, wherein as the tide falls

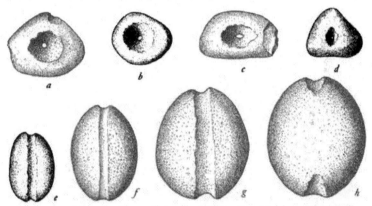

Figure 100. Perforated and Grooved Stones, probably used as net sinkers. All from Massachusetts: c, West Medford; d, Barnstable; e, Salem Neck; f, Beverly; g, Lowell; h, Ipswich. Peabody Museum, Cambridge. (1/3.)

they take bass with their arrows. He also says that sturgeons were sometimes taken in nets which were made of strong hemp. Wood is more explicit,

their Sturgeon netts be not deepe, not above 30. or 40. foote long, which in ebbing low waters they stake fast to the ground, where they are sure the Sturgeon will come, never looking more at it, till the next low water.[59]

Not only did our local tribes use seines of various sizes but also purse-nets, for Josselyn says that alewives were taken "with nets like a purse net put upon a round hooped stick with a handle." [60]

While I find no explicit mention of gill-nets being used by the New England tribes it is evident that fish were also taken in this manner. The size of the mesh in gill-nets varies according to the

[59] William Wood, *New England's Prospect*, Boynton edition, p. 95.
[60] John Josselyn, *Two Voyages to New England*, Veazie reprint, pp. 109, 110.

size of the fish to be taken. In the summer the seine was set across some stream or in a lake. To the lower edge were attached net weights of stone and to the upper edge were fastened wooden or bark floats. This arrangement kept the seine stretched in an upright position in the water. When fish attempted to pass through the net their gills were caught in the lines of the meshes where they were securely held.

I find no mention of seine fishing through the ice in New England but as it was known to the Hurons, to the Algonquians of the Great Lakes, and is today practised by the Montagnais of Labrador, it seems quite certain that in New England, with its innumerable lakes and streams, this effective way of taking fish was not unknown.

The procedure was as follows: an opening was cut in the ice about three by four feet in size, or large enough to allow the net to be drawn through readily. Several smaller holes were then cut six or eight feet apart, in a line from the large opening, the number of smaller holes being determined by the length of the seine. The net was then spread out and to one end of the cord forming its upper edge and which carried the floats, was fastened a line somewhat longer than the seine itself. The other end of this long line was attached to one end of a pole which was then pushed into the water of the largest opening and slid from hole to hole under the ice, carrying the attached cord. This cord was then drawn through the last hole, thus carrying the net under the ice. By securing the opposite end of the net at the large opening the seine could be drawn back through this opening, the captured fish removed, and the net reset at will.

Williams says the seines of our Indians were made of hemp (Apocynum). Probably other fibers were also used, especially that of the linden, but whatever material was chosen, a well made seine required an immense amount of labor, involving the gathering and preparation of the fiber, the twisting of the cordage, and the spacing and knotting of the meshes. From what we know of the excellency of New England textiles we may be sure that these nets must have shown admirable workmanship. We should expect, therefore, to find the stone weights or sinkers which were attached to the lower portion of these seines to be well made and in keeping with the rest of the equipment.

In figure 100, e, f, g, are shown three oval water worn pebbles which may be classed as weights for seines. They are usually unmodified except for the groove which encircles them, although sometimes the stone chosen was not quite symmetrical and a part of its surface was pecked away to improve its contour. Occasionally one is found, the shape of which is wholly artificial. A marked uniformity in the contour of these objects is often noticeable. The grooves are formed by pecking and are quite rough, a feature which added to the security of the binding cords which undoubtedly fastened them to the lower edge of the net.

This form of sinker is quite widely distributed in New England and is especially abundant in the southern portions. They vary in length from about two to seven inches, the majority measuring three to five inches. The meshes of gill-nets varied in size according to the bigness of the fish sort, and it is natural to infer that the larger seines were supplied with the larger weights.

In h, of the above figure is an oval pebble notched at either end, apparently for holding in place the binding cord, although it may be an unfinished sinker of the grooved type. This form is less common. Ordinary flattish pebbles are sometimes found roughly notched on opposite edges which were doubtless also used as net sinkers. Indeed, this cruder form has been employed in recent times by White fishermen.

The small pebbles shown in a-d, are perforated by pecking from either side. They are not drilled. While not very common they are quite widely distributed in New England. They probably served as weights for small seines. Symmetrical pebbles of a larger size, which may also have served as weights, are occasionally found perforated at the center or near one end. (See figure 143, f.)

In figure 101, a, we have a notched stone shaped by pecking over most of its surface, which represents a group quite common in certain parts of southern New England. They are not very uniform in shape but are quite free from roughness which might catch or fray the cordage of a fishing net. They may also be provisionally classed as sinkers for seines.

Mauls, Hammerstones, Pitted Stones. The grooved stone b, in figure 101, is much like those in e-g, of the preceding figure, except that the groove is at right angles to its longest diameter. Some of these may also be net weights but as a class they impress one as having other functions. The smaller examples resemble certain club heads used by the plains tribes. Many of the larger ones, however, are battered or more or less flattened upon either end

177

which was undoubtedly brought about by use as mauls. Such implements were probably hafted after the manner of grooved axes. The material culture of the Virginia Algonquians was much like that of our southern New England tribes. Hariot says that each Virginia household had stones for cracking nuts and for grinding shell and other material. These were undoubtedly like the hand hammers, anvils, pitted stones, and grinding stones common on most of the old village sites in New England.

Many of the hand hammers are waterworn pebbles of a size to be conveniently grasped in the hand, which show more or less

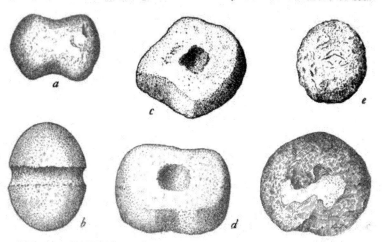

Figure 101. a, Notched stone, probably net sinker. b, Grooved stone. c, d, Pitted stones. e, f, Hammerstones. a, b, d, Massachusetts: a, d, Swansea. c, Plainville, Conn.; e, Rhode Island; f, Maine shellheap. All Peabody Museum, Cambridge. (1/3.)

battering or wear. Large cobblestones are common, having one side worn smooth or more or less pitted through use, on which roots and seeds were ground or bruised, and the larger bones of deer and other food animals crushed in preparing stews. Grinding stones of proper texture for working bone and stone are also common, and chipped knives, drills, and scrapers for working wood and other material are by no means rare. Burnt cobblestones of a reddish color, from the ancient fire hearths, are perhaps the most common indications of the presence of old camp sites.

In e, and f, of figure 101, are two well worn examples of a variety of hammerstone common in the shellheaps and often occurring on village sites. They are usually made of felsite or some variety of flinty stone which chips with a concoidal fracture. They are formed by chipping and a freshly made tool of this type has many sharp points or projections scattered over its surface. When newly fashioned these hammerstones were undoubtedly used very largely in pecking into shape adze blades, axes, and many other implements which were first roughly formed by chipping. After the tool had acquired nearly the desired shape through the use of these hand hammers, its surface was often finished with the aid of a grinding stone containing silica, and then polished.

Most of the surface of adze blades and axes was finished by pecking, the lower portion near the cutting edge only being ground. Many hammerstones of this type show much wear and the older

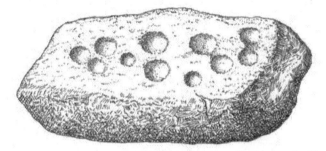

Figure 102. Stone with pits upon both sides, probably used for holding nuts and acorns while being cracked. Putnam, Conn., Amherst College Museum. (About 1/4.)

ones were probably employed for general domestic purposes in addition to what seems to have been their original function.

Two examples of that group of artifacts known as pitted stones, pitted hammers, anvils, nut crackers, etc., are pictured in c, d, of the above figure. Many are made from a somewhat flattened, rounded pebble, three or four inches in diameter, such as may be picked up in almost any field. A slight depression is pecked in the center of each side. These depressions are thought by some to be for receiving the thumb and finger when the stone was being used as a hand hammer, the periphery usually being battered by use. Should a properly shaped pebble not be at hand almost any stone could be quickly chipped and pecked into the desired shape. The depressions may also have been used for holding walnuts, acorns, and other nuts while cracking them. Large quantities of acorns

179

were used in making acorn meal, and walnuts were especially prized, both for the meat and the oil which they contained. These pitted pebbles are sometimes notched upon opposite sides as in d. Larger stones having several pits as in figure 102, are occasionally found in southern New England. It seems evident that these were used with hand hammers for cracking nuts and acorns.

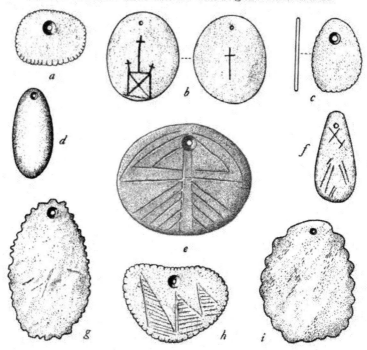

Figure 103. Pendants for the neck or ears. e, Tiverton, R. I. All others Massachusetts; a, f, Concord River Valley; b, Attleboro; c, Holliston; d, Burial Hill, Plymouth; g, Rowley; h, Sudbury; i, Connecticut Valley. a, f, Tolman coll., Concord; c. L. K. Gahn coll.; d, Pilgrim Hall, Plymouth; e, Nat. Museum; g, Peabody Museum, Salem; h, Peabody Museum, Cambridge; i, Amherst College Museum. (2/3.)

Neck and Ear Pendants. We know but little regarding the neck and ear pendants and other personal ornaments of our prehistoric tribes for most of them were probably of perishable material and have long since disappeared. Wood speaks of the longing desire of the Indians of his day for many kinds of ornaments. They wore "pendants in their ears as forms of birds, beasts, and fishes, carved out of bone, shells, and stone."

Probably the most numerous groups of prehistoric pendent ornaments which have survived are the small effigy heads shown in figure 89, and the trinkets made of very thin pebbles, or occasionally of thin pieces of schist which are illustrated in figure 103. The form of the pebbles is unmodified except for the perforation, and the notching of the edge, or the incised decoration which appears on some of them. In specimens made of shale the outline is usually artificial.

While most of the pendants illustrated are probably prehistoric, the example shown in b, found near Attleboro, Massachusetts, is obviously of a later date. It has the Christian cross incised upon one side, and what appears to be a church surmounted by three crosses upon the other. This is, evidently, a Catholic emblem, and is probably the work of an Indian neophyte, perhaps from the French missions of the Kennebec River. It will be remembered that Samoset, who met the Pilgrims at Plymouth, was from that region.

The specimen shown in d, is a pebble unmodified excepting for the perforation. It is relatively thicker than the average. It was found with an implement, a near duplicate of figure 58, a, while excavating on Burial Hill, Plymouth, and probably came from an ancient grave. The largest of these illustrated, e, from Tiverton, Rhode Island, is decorated by a pattern in incised lines as is also the heart shaped one below it, found in Sudbury, Massachusetts. In the collection at Amherst College are six of these thin flat pebbles, wholly natural except the perforations, which were taken from a grave at Springfield. They probably formed a part of a necklace, or other personal ornament.

Tobacco Pipes. The platform tobacco pipe which is doubtless the oldest New England form, we have already described. The types illustrated in the accompanying drawings are mostly of later origin although some of them are apparently quite old.

The use of tobacco by the New England tribes was doubtless confined to the Algonquian groups who have occupied the land since the expulsion of their predecessors, who, we have reason to believe, had never acquired the tobacco habit.

Perhaps there is no group of artifacts more clearly showing the trade relations of our Indians than tobacco pipes. The majority of these were the product of local artificers, while others were obtained through trade with the Iroquois and other people to the west and south. Roger Williams says:

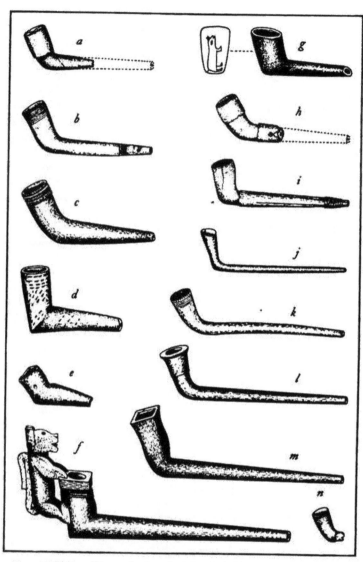

Figure 104. Tobacco Pipes. a, f, g, l, m, stone; b, c, d, e, h, i, n, terra-cotta; j, sheet copper; k, sheet lead. a, b, c, e, g, h, i, k, l, m, n, Massachusetts: a, k, l, n, graves, Revere; b, grave, Ipswich; c, Hadley Falls; e, Barnstable; g, Wilbraham; h, grave, Chelsea; i, grave, Winthrop; m, grave, North Plymouth. d, Shellheap, Waldoboro, Me.; f, grave, Warren, R. I.; j, Stratford, Conn. a, b, d, h, i, k, n, Peabody Museum, Cambridge; l, Peabody Museum, Salem; c, Springfield Natural History Museum; f, Museum of the American Indian; g, Amherst College Museum; j, N. L. Bull Coll.; e, H. A. Jones Coll.; m, Pilgrim Hall, Plymouth. (1/3.)

Generally all the Men throughout the Countrey have a Tobacco-bag with a pipe in it, hanging at their back, sometimes they make such great pipes both of wood and stone, that they are too foot long, with men or beasts carved, so big or massie, that a Man may be hurt mortally by one of them; but these commonly come from the Mauquáuwogs [Mohawks], or the men eaters, three or foure hundred miles from us: They have excellent Art to cast our Pewter and Brass into very neate and artificiall Pipes.[61]

Williams wrote the above about the year 1643, some twelve years after his arrival in New England. He was a very keen observer of Indian customs. It should be remembered, however, that the English clay pipes of the period were very small, and that in comparison some of the larger Indian pipes seemed quite massive, especially those made of wood with pewter or lead lining for the bowl, an example of which, four inches in height, from Rhode Island, Williams's own province, is shown in c, of figure 106. This must have had a stem about two feet long. Old wooden pipes of Indian make are now very rare in New England. I know of but two examples that have come down to us, the one above referred to and another, from Maine, which is of a much later date. This is ornamented with a carved representation of a dog and a human face, and is doubtless Abnaki work.

When near Monhegan Island in 1605, Captain Waymouth saw the small claw of a lobster used as a pipe. This he says "will hold ten of our pipes full."

Some of the more southern New England tribes were proficient in casting buttons and small ornaments in one-piece moulds such as are shown in figure 131, but I have never seen a pipe wholly cast of pewter or brass from this section. There is, however, a cast pewter pipe from Pennsylvania in the Peabody Museum at Cambridge which seems to be of Indian origin.

Figure 104, j, shows a pipe made of European sheet copper from a burial at Stamford, Connecticut, and k, one of sheet lead, from a grave at Revere. This has the usual ornamental dots and lines around the upper part of the bowl which appear on many pottery pipes of Indian make. In the stone pipe, a, from a grave at Revere Beach, the bowl is bound with sheet brass, and the part of the stem which has been lost was probably also of this metal. The bowl of h, from a grave at Chelsea, was also bound with sheet brass, and a small portion only of the sheet copper stem remains.

[61] Roger Williams, *Key Into the Language of America*, Coll. Rhode Island Hist. Soc., vol. I, p. 55.

183

From a grave at Winthrop, across the bay from Boston, came the pottery pipe figured in i. This has a stem of sheet brass, bound near the smaller end with sinew. With this pipe, and preserved by contact with the brass, were fragments of the coiled netted bag of native make, figure 132, d, which probably contained both pipe and tobacco. Most of the original stem of the small pottery pipe, n, has been broken off. What remains has been trimmed down, evidently to fit a stem of sheet copper or brass. In each of the above, the bowl and stem were doubtless originally made in a

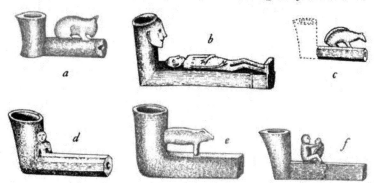

Figure 105. Tobacco Pipes made by the Cherokee Indians and imported into New England. a, b, c, Connecticut: a, Stamford; b, Waterbury; c, New Preston. d, e, Rhode Island. f, Gill, Mass. c, f, Mattatuck Hist. Soc., Waterbury; d, e, King Philip Museum, Mt. Hope, R. I. (1/3.)

single piece as in b-e. Upon becoming broken the metal stems and bands were added, both for use and for ornament.

The small pottery pipes appear to have been in common use from the later prehistoric period down to Colonial times, and were probably all of local manufacture. European sheet brass and copper appear to have been common among the New England coast tribes throughout the greater part of the sixteenth century. When Gosnold visited Buzzards Bay in 1602 he found the natives using "pipes steeled with copper." Brereton's account is more explicit. He says:

the necks of their pipes are made of clay hard dried . . . the other part is a piece of hollow copper, very finely closed and cemented together.[62]

This native terra-cotta pipe with small bowl may well have been the model for the diminutive clay pipes of European make

[62] Brereton, *Account of Gosnold's Voyage*, Mass. Hist. Coll., 3d series, vol. VIII. p. 88.

common during the early colonial period. Most of the native pottery pipes have been taken from graves. Fragments are sometimes found on old village sites, and occasionally one is recovered from a shellheap. Figure 104, d, was obtained from one of these refuse piles at Waldoboro, Maine, by Arlo Bates, and e, came from a shellheap at Barnstable, Mass. It is now in the collection of Howard A. Jones, of Wakefield.

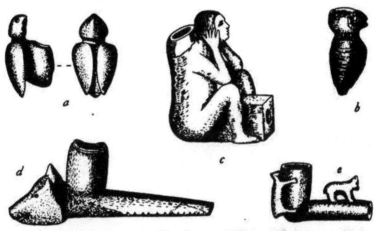

Figure 106. Tobacco Pipes. a, d, e, Massachusetts: a, Wellfleet; d, Newburyport; e, Marshfield. b, c, Rhode Island. c, Is a very old wooden pipe with bowl of pewter or lead, probably Narragansett Indians. a, Torrey coll.; b, Norris L. Bull coll.; c, National Museum; d, Peabody Museum, Cambridge; e, J. H. Campbell coll. (1/3.)

The finely modeled soapstone pipe represented in figure 104, l, was found with a skeleton in Revere. Fowke figures a similar one of soapstone from Caldwell County, North Carolina. Another long pipe of the same material, m, with the upper portion of the bowl square instead of circular is from a burial place on the line of the Old Colony Railroad at North Plymouth. It is now in Pilgrim Hall, Plymouth. The effigy pipe, f, is from a burial on Burr's Hill, Warren, Rhode Island, and is in the Museum of the American Indian, New York. It is nine and one fourth inches long and may be assigned to about the first half of the seventeenth century. It will be noticed that all the angles of this pipe are such as would probably be produced only with steel tools. The three last mentioned examples, l, m, and f, doubtless belong to the historic period.

185

In figure 105 are illustrated several pipes from various sites in southern New England, which were undoubtedly made by the Cherokee Indians, and which found their way north through trade, probably in the eighteenth or latter part of the seventeenth centuries. Referring to pipes among the more southern Indians of his day Adair writes:

They make beautiful stone pipes, and the Cherokees the best of any of the Indians, for their mountainous country contains many different sorts and colors of soils proper for such uses. They easily form them with their toma-

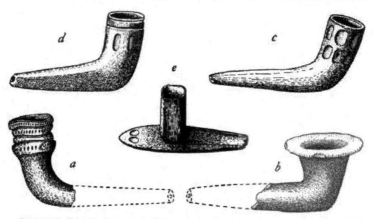

Figure 107. Tobacco Pipes. a, b, Terra-cotta; c, d, e, stone. a, Hadley, Mass.; b, South Hadley Falls; c, northwestern Vermont, after Perkins; d, Hartford Co., Conn.; e, Brooklin, Me. a, Amherst College Museum; b, from sketch by W. J. Howes; d, Connecticut Hist. Soc. e, E. E. Tyzzer coll. c, d, e, Were probably inlaid with oval pieces of shell. (1/3.)

hawks, and afterwards finish them in any desired form with their knives, the pipes being of a very soft quality till they are smoked with and used with the fire, when they become quite hard.[63]

Zeisberger informs us that

The Cherokees, who through the years have had much intercourse with the Delawares, brought with them many tobacco pipes for trade. . . . When completed they blackened the pipes and in such a way that they retained their color. These pipes are made so neatly that they are no heavier than the European pipes.[64]

The following is from Myer's Indian Trails of the Southeast:

The Cherokee region of the Appalachians yielded steatite admirably suited

[63] Adair, History of the North American Indians, p. 423.

[64] David Zeisberger, History of the Northern American Indians, Ohio State Arch. and Hist. Soc. reprint, p. 54.

to the manufacture of fine pipes. There are many authentic records of Cherokee carrying quantities of pipes to distant regions for sale or barter, and these are found at many points in the middle and southern United States.[65]

That numbers of these Cherokee pipes were obtained by the Indians of southern New England is proved by the examples illustrated in this figure. One from Gill, northwestern Massachusetts, is shown in f. The broken example, c, is from New Preston, Connecticut. Both of these are in the collection of the Mattatuck Historical Society at Waterbury. From Stamford came the one shown in a. There are also two fine specimens, d, and e,

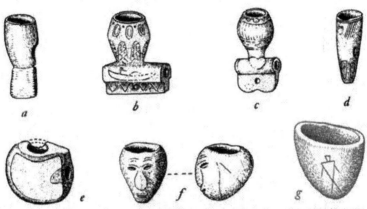

Figure 108. Tobacco Pipes. a, b, c, Maine; b, c, Abnaki Indians. e, f, g, Massachusetts; e, Harvard; f, Connecticut Valley; g, Agawam, near Springfield. a-e, Peabody Museum, Cambridge; f, g, Amherst College Museum. (1/3.)

in the Haffenreffer collection, at Mt. Hope, Rhode Island, from graves in southern New England.

In b, we have a somewhat different type from others in the group, but doubtless also of Cherokee make. It was found while excavating for Trinity Church parish house at Waterbury, Connecticut.

The pipe illustrated in figure 106, e, is somewhat similar in conception to the Cherokee specimens, but is probably of local origin, though the design may have been inspired by the latter. It is of soapstone and was found near Brant Rock, Marshfield.

The pottery pipe, figure 107, a, shows Iroquoian characteristics and was probably made by this people. It was found in Hadley

[65] W. E. Myer, Forty-second Report, Bureau of Am. Ethnology, p. 736.

and is now in the Amherst Museum. The specimen of the same material illustrated in b, is from a drawing kindly made for the writer by Mr. William J. Howes of Holyoke. Fragments of others of this form have been found in the Connecticut Valley, and Mr. R. P. Bolton has reported similar ones from northwestern Vermont.

In c, and d, of the above figure are shown two pipes of a widely distributed form. The feature which especially distinguishes them is the oval depressions surrounding the bowl; c, is of gypsum and is from western Vermont; d, is of steatite and was found in Hartford County, Connecticut. A similar pipe, somewhat disintegrated and broken, found by E. M. Wheelock, at Vinalhaven, Maine, has similar depressions. The top of the bowl, however, instead of being cut square across, is curved upward, the side next to the stem being higher than its opposite, a characteristic of certain Iroquoian pipes. The oval depressions are also a noticeable feature in many of the finer stone effigy pipes of these Indians. These depressions may once have contained shell inlay. As pipes having these oval depressions were much more common among the Iroquoians than among the New England Algonquians, the specimens illustrated may well have been the product of the former people, although shell inlaying was practiced by our southern New England tribes as late as the seventeenth century, as shown by certain old wooden bowls and clubs.

In figure 106, a, are shown two views of a steatite pipe found while digging clams at Wellfleet, Cape Cod. It is now in the collection of Howard Torrey of Reading, Massachusetts. It was, of course, used with a wooden stem. While it has characteristics of the Iroquoian pipes, it is probably of local origin. This also applies to b, of the same figure, which is from Rhode Island and is now in the famous Bull collection at Hartford.

The pipe illustrated in figure 106, d, has an interesting history. It is made of a gray steatite somewhat mottled with different shades of brown in places, and its form at once recalls to mind certain specimens from Tennessee and North Carolina. The modeling of the head and certain other features, however, seem to indicate its local origin. It was found in 1783 with human bones by Gen. Jon. Titcomb in a woodland which he owned a mile from Newburyport. It was presented to the American Academy of Arts and Sciences, incorporated in Boston in 1780, and was illustrated with three other archæological specimens from Massachusetts in the first volume of the *Memoirs* of the society in 1785.

The three other specimens were an adze blade (gouge), a grooved axe, and the long snake-like pestle shown in figure 81, j. Marshall H. Saville has called attention to these illustrations in *Indian Notes and Monographs*, vol. V, no. 1,[66] and goes on to say

In searching through the volume for some description of the objects, reference was found to them on pages XXXI and XXXII, in a list of gifts to the Academy, with the names of the donors as follows: Rev. Dan Fuller. Indian utensils, viz. a stone-ax and gouge, see plate III, fig. A and C.

Jon. Titcomb, Esq. An Indian stone pipe, having 13 notches on one, and 11 notches on the other side of the stem. Those on one side according to tradition, express the number of enemies slain; and those on the other side denote the number of prisoners actually taken by the proprietor. See plate III, fig. 13.

Mr. D. Watson. An emblematical stone [pestle] found two feet below the surface of the earth, supposed to be wrought by the aborigines. See plate III, fig. E.

There can be no doubt as to the New England origin of these specimens but it is unfortunate that it was not deemed of sufficient importance to indicate the location from whence they came.

The above extract is from Saville's note published in 1919. Ten years later he gives us additional information about the pipe from which the following is taken.

Now I am able to determine the provenience of the most interesting specimen to which attention was called, namely, a stone pipe. . . . A recent important publication of the Hispanic Society of America bears the title: *The Diary of Francisco de Miranda Tour of the United States 1783–1784.* . . . Late in the year 1784 Miranda made a trip by stage from Boston to Portsmouth, passing en route through the towns of Salem, Ipswich, and Newburyport. . . . In an entry in the diary recording his return visit to Newburyport, under date of Sunday, October 24, he writes that after having listened to a sermon by the Rev. J. Murray, a Presbyterian minister, a discourse which lasted for two and a half hours, he was taken to dinner by a prominent merchant, John Tracy, who lived in one of the best houses in the town. After dinner was concluded, he says, " there was brought there an *espada* (sword), and a stone pipe, work of the Indians, which had been found the year before with human bones by General Titcomb in a woodland which he owned, a mile from Newburyport. It was worthy of admiration for the patience and ingenuity which was required to execute it without metal tools, as it appeared."[67]

Now this pipe was of course the one which General Titcomb afterward presented to the American Academy. At least three of the four specimens illustrated in the Academy's plate were sub-

[66] Publications of the Museum of the American Indian, New York.

[67] Indian Notes, vol. VI. no. 3, pp. 300–302, Mus. Am. Ind., New York.

sequently transferred to the Boston Athenaeum. Upon the establishment of the Peabody Museum at Harvard University in 1866, they were, in the year following, again transferred to that institution, and are among the first hundred specimens catalogued, but no data accompanied them, and the Museum is indebted to Saville for their interesting history.

In figure 108 are illustrated several pipe bowls originally furnished with wooden stems. Such pipes are not uncommon and most of them were probably made by individuals for their own use.

They are usually of steatite, sandstone, or slate; a, is from Maine and has a thin flat handle projecting from the bottom of the bowl, an arrangement sometimes found on pipes of various periods, and the forerunner of the basal projections upon our modern clay pipes, the use of which is obvious. On the front of pipe g, opposite the stem perforation, is incised a very characteristic figure of a man. This pipe is of reddish sandstone, and was found at Agawam, Massachusetts, in the Connecticut Valley.

In b, and c, of this figure are shown two Abnaki pipes from Maine. This general type was and is widely used among the northern Algonquians, from the Blackfoot of the Northwest to the Nascapee of the Northeast. It is popularly known as the Micmac type. It probably entered New England from the North within historic times. In this section it is usually small, and is sometimes quite elaborately ornamented with pleasing incised patterns. Among the Blackfoot and some other northern Algonquians it is often of large size and without elaborate ornamentation.

Pottery. It seems evident from a study of the ceramics of our New England tribes that the art of potterymaking was introduced into these states by that group of people whose culture centered in the region south of the Great Lakes, and who succeeded in driving eastward and expelling from our territory the non-pottery making people whose artifacts we have described in the early pages of this book. Moreover this art seems to have undergone little change during the long period which must have elapsed between its introduction and the later arrival of the Iroquois in the valleys of Lakes Erie and Ontario and the St. Lawrence River, and who in turn expelled most of the older Algonquians from that territory.

Our most prolific sources for obtaining sherds of this native ware are the shellheaps scattered along our entire coast. Whole vessels are rarely found except occasionally in graves, but pots of various sizes were in common use in most of the camps of the

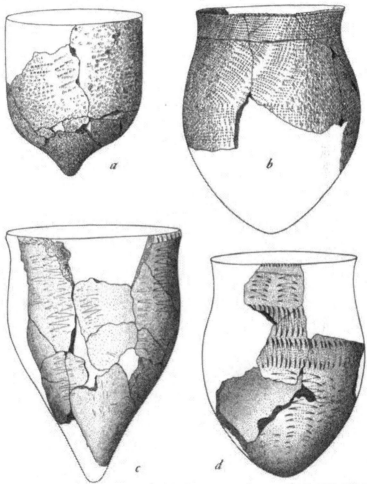

Figure 109. Pottery Vessels, old Algonquian type. a, From grave at Revere, Mass.; b, c, from four feet below surface of Whaleback Shellheap, Damariscotta, Me.; d, from grave at Waterville, Me. All Peabody Museum, Cambridge. (About 1/3.)

gatherers of clams, oysters, and other bivalves, and they could be quickly and easily made in the immediate vicinity if suitable clay was procurable. Potsherds are also found on inland village sites but they are less common than in the shellheaps and are often less well preserved.

In some of the larger shellheaps one would expect to find cruder pottery in the lower layers than in the upper. This may perhaps occur in a few heaps, but it does not seem to be true in general, as sherds of various degrees of fineness in both texture and ornament are commonly found at all depths. There are, however, quite marked differences between the few examples of pottery from graves known to be proto-historic and the greater part of the older ware from the shellheaps. As a rule the later ware is of somewhat finer quality, and the bodies of the vessels are more globular, approaching in these respects the pottery of the Iroquois.

Most of our earlier ware has more or less pointed bases, although in some instances they are well rounded. This early pottery seems not to have been suspended

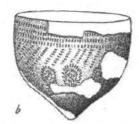

Figure 110. Pottery Vessels, old Algonquian type. a, Vicinity of Groton, Mass., Samuel A. Green coll.; b, Shellheap, Penobscot Bay, Bates coll., Peabody Museum, Cambridge. (1/3.)

over the fire but was probably set into a small heap of earth or ashes, or supported by hearth stones, and the fire kindled about the base. Among John White's noted water color drawings of Indian Life (Roanoke Colony, 1585–1588) is one entitled "The seething of their meete in Potts of earth"[68] which shows a close duplicate of figure 109, a. The vessel in White's drawing is slightly higher in proportion to its width and its basal point is a little longer. Otherwise the pot shown in a, would have served

[68] Reproduced in pl. II of Holmes's Aboriginal Pottery, Twentieth Rpt. Bureau of Am. Eth.

as a perfect model for the drawing. In the picture burning sticks are arranged about the base of the pot, care being taken that its basal point shows clearly. This is but one of several instances of the marked similarity of certain phases of the culture of the two regions. Hariot tells us that the Virginia Indians set their

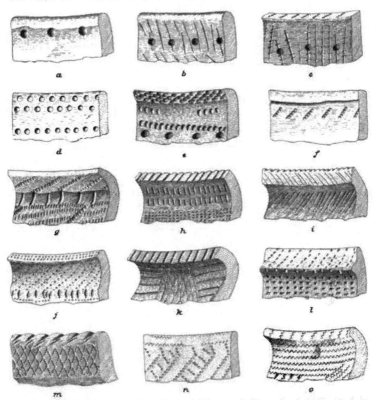

Figure 111. Sections of Pot Rims. From shellheaps and village sites in Maine. Peabody Museum, Cambridge.

cooking-pots upon a "heape of erthe to stay them from falling" and "putt wood under which being kyndled one of them taketh great care that the fyre burn equally rounde about."[69]

We may assume that the older Algonquian cooking-pots of New England were rarely suspended over the fire, but were used

[69] Thomas Hariot, *A Brief and True Report of the New Found Land of Virginia*, Holbein edition. p. xv.

principally if not wholly as above described. Typical examples
are shown in figures 109 and 110. Some have a moderately flaring
rim which seems to have been evolved for esthetic or utilitarian
qualities other than for holding a ligature for the attachment of a
suspending cord.

A selection of typical pot rims is shown in figure 111. In many
of the vessels the decorations are confined to one or more zones

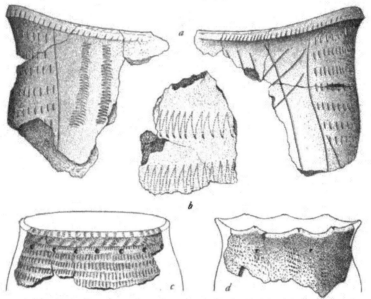

Figure 112. Pot Sherds, old Algonquian. a, From fourteen feet beneath surface of Whaleback Shellheap, Damariscotta, Me.; c, from shellheap, Keenes Point, Muscongus Bay, Me.;
d, from shellheap, Tafts Point, Me. Peabody Museum, Cambridge. (About 1/4.)

just below the rim while in others they cover the greater portion
of the body also. Incised lines, dots, and impressions made with
simple stamps of various patterns, make up the bulk of the decorations. These stamps were often a flat stick with the end notched,
or a chip or similar object wound with a string. In n, and o, the
wavy lines are produced with the edge of the common cockle shell.
The circular raised portion in the center of sherd o, is produced by
placing the finger against the outer side of the rim, and pressing
the end of a stick against the inner side. No two vessels are alike,
and the decorative patterns occur in endless variety. The bodies

of some of the pots are cord marked, indicating the use of the cord wrapped paddle in shaping them.

One of the most persistent patterns and one which might almost be called the hall mark of the old Algonquian potter is the zigzag design shown on each of the four vessels in figure 109, and on the

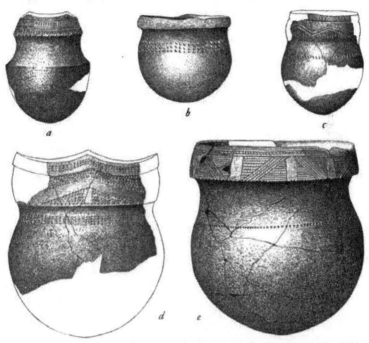

Figure 113. Pottery Vessels, protohistoric Algonquian. From Massachusetts graves: a, Revere; b, Hingham; c, d, e, Winthrop. Peabody Museum, Cambridge. (About 1/3.)

sherds a, b, of figure 112. This is produced with the aid of a chisel-like tool having a slightly curved and notched edge. This is placed against the clay and carried forward with a rocking motion, each opposite corner being raised and slightly advanced, alternately, the tool not being wholly lifted from the clay. This has been incorrectly called the roulette pattern. It was not, however, made with a roulette. This is also a common pattern on the pottery from the Hopewell, Turner, and other mound groups of the Ohio region, and is another indication of the probable ethnic connection of the two people.

I have seen no specimens which show conclusive evidence of having been built up wholly by coiling, and it is doubtful if this process as we know it in the Southwest was followed by our Indians. It would be natural of course in forming a pot by any primitive process occasionally to add one or more strips or coils of clay, and sometimes a sherd will show evidence of this. I am inclined to accept the following process followed by certain Canadian tribes, and described in Sagard's History of Canada, written in 1636, as being much like that in vogue in New England:

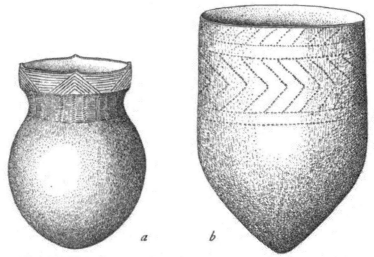

a *b*

Figure 114. Pottery Vessels. a, East Windsor, Conn., American Museum, New York; b, South Windsor, Conn., Wadsworth Athenaeum, Hartford. (About 1/6.)

They are skilful in making good earthen pots which they harden very well on the hearth, and which are so strong that they do not, like our own, break over the fire when having no water in them. But they cannot sustain dampness nor cold water so long as our own, since they become brittle and break at the least shock given them; otherwise they last very well. The savages make them by taking some earth of the right kind, which they clean and knead well in their hands, mixing with it, on what principle I know not, a small quantity of grease. Then making the mass into the shape of a ball, they make an indentation in the middle of it with the fist, which they make continually larger by striking repeatedly on the outside with a little wooden paddle as much as is necessary to complete it. These vessels are of different sizes, without feet or handles, completely round like a ball, excepting the mouth, which projects a little.

Our pottery was restricted to cooking vessels and tobacco pipes. The ornamentation consisted largely of lines, dots and indentations often arranged in pleasing patterns, usually in zones.

Ornamental knobs, figures of men or animals modelled from the body of the vessel or luted to its surface, were of very rare occurrence. A pot from Wakefield, Rhode Island, showing a crude human-like figure in relief, is in the Museum of the American Indian in New York. Mr. William J. Howes of Holyoke reports simple luted bosses on a few sherds from the Connecticut valley. He also reports sherds from vessels upon which a plumbago slip had been used. This mineral probably was obtained from the old mine at Sturbridge. Such instances, however, are rare.

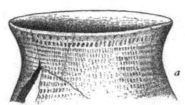 

Figure 115. Pot Rims, East Windsor, Conn. American Museum, New York. (About 1/3.)

The clay from which our pottery is made varies considerably in quality and texture. It was usually tempered by adding crushed stone containing considerable quartz and feldspar. Crushed burnt shell was also used for this purpose.

We have but few accounts by early writers of the use of native pottery in New England. Gookin in 1674 says:

> The pots they seeth their food in, which were heretofore, and yet are, in use among some of them, are made of clay or earth, almost in the form of an egg, with the top taken off, but now they generally get kettles of brass, copper, or iron. These they find more lasting than those of clay, which were subject to be broken; and the clay or earth they were made of, was very scarce and dear.[70]

Morton writes:

> They have earthen potts of divers sizes, from a quarte to a gallon, 2. or 3. to boyle their vitels in; very stronge though they be thin like our Iron Potts.[71]

[70] Daniel Gookin, *Historical Collections,* Mass. Hist. Coll., 1st series (reprint 1859), vol. I, p. 151.

[71] Thomas Morton, *New English Canaan,* Prince Soc., reprint, p. 159.

Champlain found pottery in use along the Massachusetts coast, and says that "when the natives eat Indian corn they boil it in earthern pots which they make in a different way from ours."[72]

A few examples of this later pottery, unquestionably proto-historic or early historic have been taken from graves which also contained glass beads and objects made of European sheet copper and brass. Three of these are shown in figure 113 c, d, e. A few others undoubtedly of this period may be seen in various collections, but the accompanying data is usually insufficient to throw much light on the history of their discovery. Like the vessels of the Iroquois this later Algonquian pottery was doubtless commonly suspended over the fire. The bodies became more globular than in the older ware, and the necks more constricted for the purpose of applying a thong to which suspending cords could be fastened, the more globular body exposing a greater surface directly to the heat when raised above the coals. From the account of the first landing of the Pilgrims at Cape Cod we learn that the mat-covered wigwam which they found contained a fireplace with

foure little trunches [crotched sticks] knockt into the ground, and small sticks laid over, on which they hung their Pots, and what they had to seeth.[73]

In this later Algonquian pottery we find certain Iroquoian characteristics which are at once apparent upon comparing the illustrations, figure 113, with those of figure 116, which are distinctly Iroquoian types; a, of the latter figure, is from a grave in Putnam, Connecticut; b, from a historic grave in Deerfield; and c, d, e, are from northwestern Vermont.

There does not seem to be as yet conclusive evidence of extended occupation of any portion of New England by the Iroquois with the possible exception of the eastern Champlain Valley. Professor Perkins, who has studied that section extensively, reports that the artifacts found "appear to be more characteristically Iroquoian than Algonquian"[74] but that there is a mixture of the work of both of these people. At one time the Iroquois seem to have claimed a considerable portion of the territory west of the Connecticut River and every year two old Mohawks might be seen going from village to village collecting tribute from our Indians and haughtily issuing orders from the great council at

[72] Champlain's *Voyages*, Prince Soc. reprint, vol. II, p. 86.
[73] *Journal of the Pilgrims at Plymouth*, Cheever's reprint, p. 39.
[74] G. H. Perkins, Am. Anthropologist, n.s., vol. 11, p. 607.

Onondaga.[75] War parties were constantly making raids, but we are inclined to think that a peaceful or extended occupation of western New England by the Iroquois was unknown with the possible exception of the northern Champlain Valley.

In addition to the few unbroken Iroquoian pots that have been recovered in New England, occasional fragments have been found either of Iroquoian origin or showing strong Iroquoian character-

Figure 116. Pottery Vessels, probably Iroquoian. a, From grave, Putnam, Conn.; b, from protohistoric grave, Deerfield, Mass.; c, Colchester, Vt.; d, New Burlington, Vt.; e, Bolton, Vt. a, Amherst College Museum; b, Memorial Hall, Deerfield; c, d, e, Museum of the University of Vermont, Burlington. (1/6.)

istics. Several of the latter are in the Peabody Museum at New Haven, from the Fort Shantok site, Mohegan, Connecticut.

Figure 114, a, shows a partially restored pot from East Windsor, now in the American Museum, New York. An excellent example from the eastern section of South Windsor appears in b. It is about eighteen inches high and is in the collection of the Wadsworth Athenaeum at Hartford. The two rims shown in

[75] J. W. De Forest, *History of the Indians of Connecticut*, p. 66.

figure 115 are also from East Windsor. Mr. W. C. Orchard has figured and described in *Indian Notes* (Museum of the American Indian) vol. VII, no. 2, a pot with a globular body having a neck nearly an exact duplicate of b, of this figure, which was found in Middleboro, Massachusetts. Christopher Wren also illustrates the same type from eastern Pennsylvania.

Native pottery went out of use in New England at an early date for good kettles were sold to the Indians by Dutch and French traders. Governor Bradford, in a letter dated September 8, 1623, says the natives could obtain of these traders

not toys and trifles but good substantial commodities as ketkels, hatchets, and clothes of all sorts; yea the French do store them with Biskay shalops, fitted both with sails and ores, with which they can either row or saile as well as we; also with peeces, powder and shot, for fowling and other services. . . Also I know upon my own knowledge many of the Endians to be as well furnished with good ketkels, both strong and of a large size as many farmers in England.[76]

That the Indians sometimes copied European table crockery in their native clay is shown by the finding of a typical flat-bottomed mug with looped handle in a grave near Springfield. This is now in the Peabody Museum at Cambridge. There is also in the above Museum a small section of a plate about twelve to fourteen inches in diameter with a plain raised edge also of Indian pottery, from one of the shellheaps at Damariscotta. This is probably from near the surface but its depth is unrecorded.

Shellheaps. Nearly the entire coast of New England is dotted with shellheaps which are most numerous between Bar Harbor and Portland. Southward to Cape Cod others are found, although many have been destroyed by cultivation and grading. To the west of this cape these refuse piles are made up largely of the shells of the oyster with a mixture of those of the quahog, or hard shell clam. Heaps consisting principally of the soft shell clam are found more commonly to the north and east. Oyster shellheaps occur in various sections, those of the Damariscotta River in Maine being the most extensive in New England.

As shellheaps or middens as they are sometimes called, are the accumulation of food refuse, mixed with ashes, soil, and leaf mould, the composition of any one depends, of course, upon the kind of food available in the immediate vicinity. Near the old oyster beds

---

[76] American Hist. Review, vol. VIII, p. 295. (Quoted by Mary C. Crawford in *Days of the Pilgrim Fathers*, p. 234.)

they are almost wholly of oyster shells, while in other sections they are composed principally of the shells of the clam or a mixture of those of the oyster, clam, scallop, and mussel, with a few of other species, together with bones of various quadrupeds, birds, and fishes. Fragments of pottery, and bone and stone implements, of kinds more commonly used in obtaining or preparing food, occur in most of the heaps. Sometimes human burials are found, but they are rare.

In some of the more recent deposits to the south and west of Massachusetts Bay, many of the quahog shells which make up a part of the heaps are broken into fragments. This was done to obtain the purple portion for the manufacture of wampum, which became of great trade value to the Wampanoag, Narraganset, Pequot, and other tribes of southern New England in the seventeenth century. Small heaps, a few feet in diameter, are sometimes found at a distance from the water. In such instances the unshelled fish had been transported, probably in baskets, but the larger heaps are near the water's edge and often near existing beds of the bivalves.

Sometimes the fish have become extinct in the immediate neighborhood as have many of our native oysters within historic times.

There are numerous references to the gathering of shellfish by the Indians in colonial times. Roger Williams tells us that the Indians generally delight in clams, and in winter and summer

at low water the women dig for them: this fish and the naturall liquors of it, they boile and it makes their broth and their Nasaúmp (which is a kind of thickened broth), and their bread seasonable and savoury in stead of Salt.[77]

The Pilgrims were given baskets of roasted crabs and other dried shellfish by the Wampanoag, and at one of Massasoit's villages they were regaled with oysters. Wood says that in the winter the women "are their husbands' Caterers trudging to the clamme banks for their bellytimber."[78]

Among the important animal foods of the Indians Josselyn includes dried oysters.

Lobsters the *Indians* dry as they do *Lampres* and *Oysters*. . . . the *Oysters* are long shell'd, I have had of them nine inches long from the joynt to the toe, containing *Oysters* . . . that were to be cut into three pieces before they could get them into their mouths.[79]

[77] Roger Williams, *Key Into the Language of America*, Coll. Rhode Island Hist. Soc., vol. I, p. 104.
[78] William Wood. *New England's Prospect*, Boynton edition, p. 101.
[79] John Josselyn, *Two Voyages to New England*, Veazie reprint, p. 86.

The Penobscot Indians still remember their former visits to the seashore to gather clams, which were dried and packed in birchbark boxes for winter use. Champlain speaks of the abundance of oysters along the shores of Cape Cod and there were also large beds near the mouth of the Charles River. Governor Winthrop tells of two man-servants of one Moodye of Roxbury, returning in a boat from the windmill at Boston, who stopped at the oyster bank to gather oysters. They neglected to fasten their boat which floated away as the tide rose and they were both drowned.

The building up of these refuse piles has covered a long period of time. While many have been explored, and excellent collections of implements made, little attention has been given to their stratification, or to the positions in which the artifacts were found in relation to the different strata. A few of the heaps were evidently begun by the pre-Algonquian people, and afterward continued by the early pottery-making Algonquians. We seem to have some evidence of this in Maine at Tafts Point, West Gouldsboro; Golden Cove, Vinalhaven; and Turner's Farm, North Haven; where certain artifacts common among the pre-Algonquian people, and not known to have been used by the later Algonquians, were found at or near the bottom of the heaps. For this data we are indebted to the notes of the late Professor Arlo Bates, who for a period of some ten years spent his summers exploring the Maine shellheaps, and whose collection is now in the Peabody Museum at Cambridge. Similar evidence has also been found at Perkins Island, Ipswich.

In addition to the shells of clams, oysters, and other mollusks which make up the great bulk of these heaps, bones of mammals, birds, and fishes occur occasionally, but they form a very small fraction of the deposits. The long bones of the larger mammals are usually broken for the purpose of extracting the marrow and rendering them more usable in making stews, which formed so important a part of the Indians' diet.

From a shellheap at York River, Maine, Mercer obtained pieces of the femur and humerus of a young person, broken in a similar manner, which he considered evidence of cannibalism.[30]

The bones of the deer and turkey seem to be most numerous in many heaps. Bones of the Indian dog occur, while those of the

[30] H. C. Mercer, *Exploration of Aboriginal Shell Heaps, York River, Me.* Publications of the Univ. of Pennsylvania, vol. VI.

Great Auk were found by Jeffries Wyman at Mount Desert; Goose Island, Casco Bay; and at East Wareham, Massachusetts, which is near the head of Buzzards Bay.[81]

The Great Auk, now extinct, miscalled Penguin by early voyagers to New England, was found in this section till well into the seventeenth century. It was known to Josselyn as the "Wobble" and is described by him in that quaint book *New England's Rarities* as "an ill shaped *Fowl* having no long Feathers in its Pinions which is the reason they cannot fly, not much unlike the *Penguin*."

Jeffries Wyman seems to have been the first to recognize the importance of a scientific examination of the shellheaps of our section, and in 1867 he published a short paper on the results of his work in Maine and Massachusetts. A brief description of three of the more important deposits examined by him follows:

Gouldsboro, Maine. The deposit extended along the shore of a small island for about two hundred and fifty feet, and thirty to forty feet inland. Its thickness varied from a few inches to about three feet. A section through its thickest part showed two layers of shells separated by six to eight inches of vegetable mould mixed with earth and gravel. The lowest layer was made up of the shells of the clam, whelk, and mussel, all much decomposed and mixed with earth. The upper layer, consisting of shells of the same species as the lower, was in a much better state of preservation. Remains of an old fireplace, bones of animals, and various kinds of implements were found.

Cronch's Cove, Goose Island, Casco Bay. The largest heap examined was about one hundred and fifty feet long, forty feet wide, and from a few inches to three feet in depth. The shells were deposited in two layers very much as at Gouldsboro. The heap was composed mostly of clam shells but those of the quahog were not uncommon, while shells of the mussel, whelk, cockle, and scallop also occurred with the usual mixture of earth, charcoal, animal bones, and a few artifacts.

Cotuit Port, Barnstable, Cape Cod. Within the distance of a few miles, a large number of shellheaps are met with, estimated to cover many acres. Some of them have a thickness of one to two feet, others only a few inches. Examinations were confined chiefly

---

[81] Jeffries Wyman, Am. Naturalist, vol. I, p. 574; Second Rpt., Peabody Museum of Am. Arch. and Eth., p. 17.

to one of the larger deposits. Shells of the oyster, clam, quahog, and scallop were found in large numbers but were unequally distributed. Bones of the deer were most abundant, but those of the seal, fox, and mink were collected, also bones of the wild turkey, duck, turtle, and fish. Very few artifacts were recovered.

The publication of Wyman's report aroused considerable interest among local societies and collectors, with the result that many of the heaps known only locally were brought to the attention of various institutions, and many of the larger deposits were more or less thoroughly explored. Messrs. Albert I. Phelps and A. T. Gammage, both of Damariscotta, carried on work under the direction of Professor Putnam, for the Peabody Museum at Cambridge, in the many heaps scattered over the coastal area between the Kennebec and Penobscot rivers. Some fifty-eight of these refuse piles were plotted by Mr. Phelps during this work.

In addition to these Professor Bates examined and located on coast charts upward of seventy-seven additional heaps, mostly in the region east of Rockland, and Dr. Moorehead has added others to his published archæological maps of this section. The following extract from the unpublished notes of Professor Bates relating to one of the largest heaps explored by him is of special interest:

Golden Cove, Vinalhaven, Maine. Of the two heaps at the entrance of the Basin, Vinalhaven, the outside one, that of Golden Cove, is considerably the larger. It is on a bank sloping upward from the shore. At the outer edge it is from two to five or six feet at its base above tidewater. On the shore it measures perhaps a hundred feet, and in its widest part extends back for sixty or seventy. It has been much dug and muddled over by amateurs, and with Oric, I tried to do systematic work here in 1905. During that summer we camped here for six weeks, and dug at the heap all of that time. We found the deposit about eight feet at its deepest point; but at that time we made no sections. It is now not possible to make sections which would represent anything but the lower layers of the deposit except in a few of the shallower parts. The only one I took was on a slope which showed no signs of having been disturbed.

Surface turf; 20 inches of shells, clams, with a few snails and mussels; 3 inches of loam; 6 inches of clam-shells, with a considerable number of sea-urchins; 5 inches of clam-shells, with some ashes; loam.

This heap at Golden Cove is interesting in many ways. In the parts near the middle of the shore line, the lower stratum is composed at the bottom exclusively of surface shells — mussels, sea-urchins, and winkles. The mussels largely predominate, although the shells are disintegrated into shining dust and scales. Gradually clam-shells begin to appear, and once they assert themselves they dominate. For the most part, indeed, the bulk of the deposit is unmixed clam-shells. The mussels and winkles with an occasional quahog, appear here and there, and occasionally bunches of the crumbled remains of sea-urchins. The fishermen assert that when the sea-urchin carries its eggs the spawn makes a bunch of pleasantly edible material, and these spots of shell may mark repasts in the spawning season. I have found the lowest layer of other of the Penobscot Bay heaps made up exclusively of surface shells, and the impression one gets is that at first in coming to the shore the Indians knew only of the shellfish in sight. The occupancy of the site at Golden Cove was evidently long continued. I should like to be able to say that the different layers displayed a well defined gradation in workmanship of findings, but this is by no means the case. It is true that in the layers of mussel-shells it is here as elsewhere, so far as my experience goes, extremely rare to find anything, and my impression would be — I am unable to refer to absolute records — that what — if anything — is found is of rude workmanship. It is also true that the most elaborate findings at Golden Cove [h, and i, figure 123,] came from the very top of the heap. The fact remains, however, that from the very bottom of the deepest part of the midden came excellent pottery and stone work of marked skill.

In the Sawyer's Island shellheap in Sheepscot Bay, Mr. Gammage found a similar condition as that recorded by Professor Bates at Golden Cove. The heap extended along the shore for about seven hundred and fifty feet and covered about two acres to a depth of six inches to approximately four feet. It was composed mostly of clam shells with a considerable number of mussels and very few of quahog. In some places for a lower layer there were very old deposits of mussel shells, three or four inches in depth, in which no artifacts were found, although potsherds and chipped flint occurred in the later deposits above them.

The shellheaps at York River, southwestern Maine, have been mapped and described by Mercer. To the south in the vicinity of Ipswich River, Massachusetts, are numerous middens composed largely of oyster shells while others are principally of the clam. These have been mapped by the late Curtis Sears. This map, together with many of the artifacts secured, is preserved in the Peabody Museum at Salem. The Pine Grove shellheap, located on the Marblehead shore, just east of the southern end of Salem Harbor is one of the earliest to be described. At that time, however, 1840, it was thought to be of natural formation.

There must have been numerous shellheaps in early colonial times in the vicinity of old Boston, for there were extensive oyster beds in the Back Bay and the lower Charles River. The only ones that I find recorded were in Back Bay, Cambridge, and Cambridgeport. Most, if not all of them, have been obliterated.

The many middens on Cape Cod have been mapped by Henry E. Chase.[82]

Mr. Norris L. Bull of West Hartford, whose excellent collection of Connecticut Indian antiquities we have frequently had occasion to mention, has done good work in the shellheaps of the southeastern section of that state.

Dr. George Grant MacCurdy of the Peabody Museum of New Haven writes me that in the central and western portions of Connecticut, these refuse piles consist principally of oyster shells with a mixture of those of the quahog and a few other species, the more notable deposits being at Beach Park, off Clinton; Mulberry Point, Guilford; Bradford Point; Double Beach and Short Beach, east of New Haven; Light House Point, New Haven; Milford, both sides of the harbor; Laurel Beach, mouth of the Housatonic River west shore; and off Compo Hill, Westport.

Shellheaps of the Damariscotta River. The most remarkable shellheaps in New England are situated upon either bank of the Damariscotta River in Maine, at the outlet of an expansion known as Salt Bay, at the head of tide, within the towns of Newcastle and Damariscotta. Salt Bay is fifteen miles from the mouth of the estuary. It is about two miles in length, and is fed by a small stream flowing from Damariscotta Pond, a long narrow body of fresh water lying a short distance to the northwest.

The principal heaps are indicated on the accompanying map, figure 117. In addition to these are numerous small, scattered masses of shells which may indicate nothing more than occasional camping places for a short period. The great middens are composed almost wholly of oyster shells although shells of the clam, quahog, and other varieties are sometimes found.

The Peninsular Mound lies along the west bank of the river for a distance of about four hundred feet. Its greatest width near its southern end is approximately seventy-five feet. The peninsula is nearly covered with a growth of spruce and other trees which encroach upon the mound making it difficult to determine the extent of the deposit to the westward. The river side of the mound, and the bank upon which it rests, have for many years been

[82] H. E. Chase, *Notes on the Wampanoag Indians*, Annual Rep. of Smithsonian Inst. for 1883 p. 905.

subject to erosion, and a considerable portion has been washed away leaving an irregular cross-section. This shows that the southern third of the eroded deposit rests upon the river beach and is only slightly elevated above the water. The northern two thirds of the eroded front of the heap rests upon land which gradually rises from the beach level to a height of nearly twenty-five feet at its northern end, the depth of the shells gradually diminishing as one goes northward. The greatest height of the shells as measured by the writer in 1910 was twenty-two feet at a point

Figure 117. Map showing location of the principal shellheaps of the upper Damariscotta River, Me.

about one hundred and fifty feet from its southern end. The mound was originally higher, for quantities of shells have been used for making lime in a nearby kiln, or have been carted away for other purposes. The mound was measured at about this point by Mr. Gammage in 1886, who found its height to be a few inches more than twenty-seven feet. Bordering the river a few hundred feet to the south is another large deposit now covered with grass and a few scattered trees.

The deposit which is of the greatest interest to the archæologist, however, stood upon the higher eastern bank of the river, and was locally known as the Whaleback Mound. This heap extended from the edge of the bank, which at this point rises to a height of fifteen feet, backward from the river for a distance of three hundred and forty-seven feet. Its greatest width was approximately one hundred and twenty-three feet, and its greatest height, sixteen feet.

The prospective commercial value of this great deposit of oyster shells being recognized, a large mill was built near its southern end, and practically its entire contents were ground up for fertilizer and hen food in 1886. Figure 118 shows a cross-section of the mound at the time of its destruction. Fortunately the project became known to Professor Putnam, who made arrangement with the owners for the competent local antiquarian, Mr. A. T. Gammage, to be present during the excavations to record such facts as might be of scientific value, and to secure all artifacts found, for the Peabody Museum at Cambridge.

The work was continued for four months, during which time practically all of the shells were removed with the exception of those of the lowest layer, which were too badly disintegrated to be of use. While the artifacts recovered were very few in comparison

Figure 118. Longitudinal Section of Whaleback Shellheap, Damariscotta, Me., looking northwest. This photograph was made in 1886 while the shells were being removed for commercial purposes.

with the yield of most of the shellheaps along the coast, especially as regards bone implements, the potsherds were fairly plentiful and of unusual interest, as they show that there was little, if any, advance made in the art of pottery making during the long period required for the accumulation of sixteen feet of shells. The sherds were found throughout the mound at various depths, and in a few instances in the lowest layers and once on the original surface beneath the mound. Two masses of clean blue clay were encountered; one at a depth of eight feet, the other, about a bucket full, nine feet deep in the shells. This had probably been collected by the Indians for making pottery. In most of the sherds the clay had been tempered with crushed stone, not with burnt shell. Pottery from this mound is illustrated in figures 109, b, c, and 112, a.

The reason for the scarcity of projectile points and other implements of bone and stone is doubtless owing to the fact that the
great oyster beds furnished an almost unlimited supply of food,
not only for immediate use but also for drying for future consumption. It was unnecessary to add fish and the usual results of the
chase to the bill of fare while gathering and drying these great
oysters, some of the shells of which measure twelve inches in
length. It is not probable that these beds were appropriated by a
single group of people to the exclusion of their neighbors. They
were doubtless visited by individuals from various distant villages,
who carried home the bulk of the oysters gathered.

In addition to the broken pottery there were found about a
dozen stone adze blades of various sizes, several hammerstones of
ordinary forms, a small lot of stone arrowpoints and rejects and
about forty bone and antler awls and handles. A number of
prongs of deer antler were secured, some of them broken, which
had evidently been used for prying open the valves of oysters, the
cuts on the body of these tools made by the sharp edges of the
shells being very noticeable. Some of these are shown in figure 119.

Portions of six human skeletons were found in the northeastern
half of the mound. The bones of five of these had been disturbed,
a part of them having been dug up by farmers while removing
shells, and afterward reinterred. With two of the reburied skeletons
were found six beads made of European sheet brass, two of which
appear in figure 127, d. A local tradition tells us that at this point
in the heap some years ago two skeletons were found with a large
number of these beads which were taken away and subsequently
lost. Near the center of the northeastern half of the heap, and
at a depth of four feet, a skeleton was unearthed lying at length,
with a clean and regular layer of shells above it. The skull was
missing. As our New England Indians sometimes cut off and
carried away the head of an enemy or rebellious subject, it seems
probable that this individual had been subjected to such treatment.

The heap was composed almost wholly of oyster shells although
those of the clam, quahog, mussel, razor, and periwinkle were
occasionally found but only in small quantities. Bones of various
quadrupeds and birds also occurred sparingly; the most common
seem to be those of the deer and Indian dog.

During the demolition of this mound several sectional drawings

209

were made by Mr. Gammage which show the alternate layers of shells and other accumulations, and the general process of the growth of the refuse pile. These cross-sections show irregular alternate layers of shells from a few inches to two or more feet in thickness interspersed with layers of ashes and leaf mould. Sometimes the beds of ashes were several inches in thickness and would gradually thin out at their edges.

Near the base of the heap one of the dark layers could be traced for nearly one hundred feet. In general the stratifications were such as would be expected from a long occupation of the site by

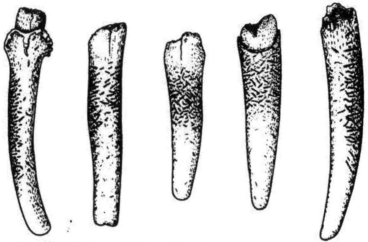

Figure 119. Antler Prongs probably used for opening oysters. From Whaleback Shellheap, Damariscotta, Me. (About 1/3.)

Indians who made a business of collecting and opening oysters, throwing the shells aside, building long continued fires beneath their drying scaffolds, and cooking their food in fragile pots at these same fires. Naturally these pots were sometimes broken and the fragments cast aside to become a part of the general refuse.

Drying racks were erected by setting crotched sticks in the ground, across which other sticks were laid forming a framework upon which the oysters were doubtless placed. Among the important foods of our Indians Josselyn mentions "dry'd Oysters, *Lobsters* roasted or dryed in the smoak."[83] Again he says the

[83] John Josselyn, *Two Voyages to New England*, Veazie reprint, p. 101.

Indians feed much upon the lobster, "some they dry as they do *Lampres* and *Oysters* which are delicate breakfast meat so ordered."[84]

We have no detailed account of the method followed by our Indians in drying clams and oysters. It was undoubtedly the same, however, as used in drying fish and lobsters, a good account of which is given by Wood, who says:

In the Summer these Indian women, when Lobsters be in their plenty and prime, they drie them to keepe for Winter, erecting scaffolds in the hot sunshine, making fires likewise underneath them, by whose smoake the flies are expelled, till the substance remain hard and drie. In this manner they drie Basse and other fishes without salt, cutting them very thinne to dry suddainely, before the flies spoile them, or the rain moist them, having a special care to hang them in their smoakie houses, in the night and dankish weather.[85]

To prepare oysters and clams for drying they were probably strung upon twigs for ease in handling and transportation. In the Peabody Museum at Cambridge is a specimen which illustrates in an interesting manner the method of stringing clams for drying and transportation by the coast Indians of British Columbia. Upon three sticks, the middle one of split cedar about one fourth of an inch in diameter, and the two outer, twigs of the thimbleberry, are very neatly and symmetrically strung fifty clams which form a package about twenty inches long and four inches wide. While the details of this method may differ somewhat from those followed by our eastern Indians, the same general scheme was probably prevalent in both regions, as may be inferred from the following extract from Peter Kalm's "Travels" written about the middle of the eighteenth century.

The *Indians* who inhabited the coast before the arrival of the *Europeans* have made oysters and other shellfish their chief food; and at present, whenever they come to a salt water, where oysters are to be got, they are very active in catching them, and sell them in great quantities to other *Indians*, who live higher up the country; . . . Among the numerous shells which are found on the sea shore, there are some, which by the *English* here are called *Clams*, and which bear some resemblance to the human ear. They have a considerable thickness, and are chiefly white, except the pointed end, which both without and within has a blue colour, between purple and violet. They are met with in vast numbers on the seashore of New York, *Long Island* and other places. The shells contain a large animal, which is eaten both by the *Indians* and *Europeans* settled here. A considerable commerce is carried on in this article,

84 Josselyn. Ibid., p. 86.
85 William Wood, *New England's Prospect*, Boynton edition, p. 101.

with such *Indians* as live further up the country. When these people inhabited the coast, they were able to catch their own clams, which at that time made a great part of their food, but at present this is the business of the *Dutch* and *English*, who live in *Long Island* and other maritime provinces. As soon as the shells are caught, the fish is taken out of them, drawn upon a wire, and hung up in the open air, in order to dry by the heat of the sun. When this is done, the flesh is put into proper vessels, and carried to *Albany* up the river *Hudson*; there the *Indians* buy them and reckon them one of their best dishes. Besides the *Europeans*, many of the native *Indians* come annually down to the sea shore, in order to catch clams, proceeding with them afterward in the manner I have just described.

It should be remembered that the Indians did not live continuously on the shellheap sites; they were visited at certain periods during the year when the people were not otherwise engaged in their agricultural pursuits, or in hunting, or gathering berries, acorns, and roots. This is why so few well made implements of stone are found in the refuse. Many of those which do occur are of a kind that can be easily and quickly made from stones picked up in the neighborhood. To this group belong most of the chipped flint arrowheads, knives, and scrapers, which though not very common, are found in many of the heaps, and the flakes thrown off in their making show conclusively that many of them were locally produced.

The ordinary hammerstone, about the size of one's fist seems to be the most numerous of any of the stone implements recovered. They are often much battered and well rounded, and were used for many purposes including, doubtless, the breaking up of the larger bones of mammals in preparing stews. The next numerous group of the larger stone artifacts is adze blades. These are often battered and broken. Probably the greater number, especially the better finished ones, were transported to the sites from the more permanent villages. Others are quite crude and may well have been of local make. They were probably used principally in gathering fire wood, for preparing the framework of lodges, and erecting scaffolds for drying clams and other sea food. Stone implements of other forms occur occasionally, but they are rare, and seem to have little connection with the principal activities which centered about these old sites.

Potsherds are found in considerable numbers in most of the larger heaps. This is a reliable indication that at least a part of the deposit is of Algonquian origin. The contour and general decoration of most of the sherds indicate that they belong to the older group of Algonquian pottery, characterized by a more or less pointed base.

Bone implements are fairly common, and owing to the comparative dryness of the interior of the heaps they are generally in a much better state of preservation than those accompanying burials, or found on village sites. As a rule they are such as may have been made between tides for securing fish and game in the immediate vicinity. These will be treated in the following section. Objects of European origin are rare and when found are but a few inches deep in the shells. Occasionally a coin, button, or an arrowpoint of sheet iron occurs, but this is not surprising, for we know that the Indians gathered shellfish for some years after the arrival of the Europeans.

Fresh water Unio mussels or clams were sometimes gathered for food by our Indians but their use was not extensive. Jeffries Wyman calls attention to a Unio shellheap near Concord, Massachusetts, in which Henry D. Thoreau used to dig for Indian artifacts. Thoreau was much interested in these objects and brought together a good collection from the vicinity of Concord which is now preserved in the Peabody Museum at Cambridge.

This heap was visited by the late Oric Bates and the following reference to it is taken from his manuscript in the Peabody Museum library. About two miles above Concord

at a sharp bend in the river on the north side rises a little plateau some 25 feet high. A half hour's scratching about revealed a meager deposit of shells (*Unio complanatus* and *Unio varidis*) in which were found an arrow-point, the butt of a [flint] knife and a few chippings. . . . The deposit is today about 30 feet long, and about 8 inches deep.

Few heaps of this nature in the east have been brought to the attention of archæologists. Some of them have been doubtless destroyed by cultivation.

Bone and Antler Implements. For the preservation of the various types of bone implements in common use among the Algonquians of this section we are indebted principally to the shellheaps. These refuse piles are usually situated on well-drained land suitable for camping, and the compact layers of shells had a tendency to protect from moisture the bone and antler implements lost or discarded during the periodical occupation of these sites.

On the contrary bone implements placed with ordinary burials in this climate soon became disintegrated and are rarely found. The few which have been recovered belong principally to the protohistoric period.

Bone and antler were extensively used in making many types of implements. These materials occupied an intermediate place between stone and wood. They were fairly easy to work, and were very serviceable. Bone was preferred for most of the smaller objects, antler being reserved for certain types which from their form or size made it preferable, and it was easier to work than bone especially after being boiled. Leg bones of the deer and moose were commonly used in making the larger bone implements, the metacarpal and metatarsal, commonly called cannon bones, being favorites. The bone was split lengthwise by cutting a deep groove upon opposite sides with sharp flints and breaking it apart. Suitable pieces for making harpoon points, awls, bodkins, etc., were obtained by again grooving and breaking off pieces and cutting and grinding them into the desired form. Excellent examples of grooved and split bones and antler showing the processes followed are found in most of the larger shellheaps.

Ivory was rarely used. I have never seen an implement or ornament made of it from our New England heaps. Arlo Bates found a piece of ivory in a heap at Golden Cove, Vinalhaven, Maine, in 1919. It consisted of about four inches of the lower end of a walrus tusk which had been cut across somewhat more than one third through on opposite sides and broken off from the main portion of the tusk. This had been grooved longitudinally, and a small piece removed for further working, the same processes being followed as in cutting bone and antler. This piece of ivory had doubtless found its way south through trade.

All of the points illustrated in figure 120 are apparently made from the leg bones of the deer or moose with the exception of the larger harpoon points o, and p, which are of antler. The largest of the bird spear points, g, is apparently wrought from the cannon bone of the moose. This interesting specimen, showing fine workmanship, was drawn up with the anchor of a fishing vessel at the mouth of Vinalhaven harbor in 1888 and presented to the Peabody Museum at Cambridge by Mr. S. M. Johnson. A similar though somewhat smaller point, h, of the same figure, was found in a shellheap on Calf Island, Blue Hill Bay, by Professor Bates. The finely made point, i, is from North Haven, Maine.

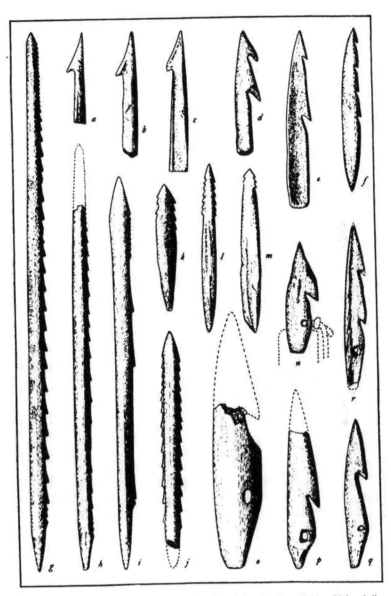

Figure 120. Spear and Harpoon Points. Made of bone and antler. All from Maine shell-heaps except g. which was drawn up with anchor in Vinalhaven Harbor: b, c, d, k, n, q, Damariscotta River; e, l, Deer Island; f, i, North Haven; a, Waldoboro; h, Blue Hill Bay; j, Georges River; m, Casco Bay; o, Friendship Bay; p, Birch Point; r, Penobscot Bay. All Peabody Museum, Cambridge, except i. (1/2.)

In order to acquire a clearer knowledge of the probable functions of the points shown in this figure, comparison should be made with those in use among historic tribes.

We have little data bearing on the subject from our northern Indians for their bone implements were discarded for those of iron at an early date. Many of the Algonquian forms from the shell-heaps, however, are nearly duplicated among the more remote Eskimo, especially in Alaska. By turning to the works of Nelson, Murdock, and other students of these northern people, much information can be gained regarding the function of our New England types.

The points shown in a–f, of figure 120, were doubtless for long-handled spears used in taking fish of a medium size. The long points, g–j, are probably for darts employed in taking waterfowl. While I know of no bone side prongs having been recovered from our shellheaps such as were commonly used by the Eskimo on the shafts for similar long points, we do know that slate side prongs were used in the Penobscot region by the pre-Algonquian people (see figure 36).

The type illustrated in k–m, seems to be a more local form. This would be effective in taking lobsters, large numbers of which were secured for food and for fish bait. Josselyn says they were taken in large bays

when it is low water, and the wind still, going out in their *Birchen-Canows* with a staff two or three yards long, made small and sharpen'd at one end, and nick'd with deep nicks to take hold. When they spye the *Lobster* crawling upon the Sand in two fathom water, more or less, they stick him towards the head and bring him up. I have known thirty *Lobsters* taken by an *Indian* lad in an hour and a half, thus they take *Flouke* and *Lumps*.

Several harpoon points are shown in n–r, of figure 120, and b, of figure 121. The latter which is made of antler is unusually large. It is from a shellheap at Niantic, Connecticut, and is in the collection of Norris L. Bull of Hartford. These points were for taking sea-bass, bluefish, sturgeon, etc., and possibly also for seal, although I recall no reference to our New England tribes taking seal in this manner. The larger points were, of course, used for the larger fish. The point was fastened to a long line and set into the socket in the end of the shaft. When the fish was struck the point became detached from the shaft and the fish was secured by hauling in the line. Josselyn gives a good description of the use of the harpoon.

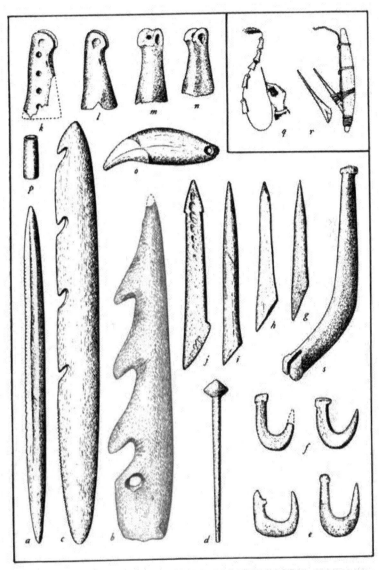

Figure 121. Artifacts of Bone and Antler. b, d, s, Are of antler, all the others are bone. a, c, Spear points; g–j, points for large fish-hooks; e, f, fish-hooks; d, pin probably for fastening garment; p, bead of bird bone; o, bear tooth pendant; k–n, worked toe bones of deer used in game; q, method of using k–n; r, method of using g–j; s, shank for fish-hook. a, f, g–i, o, p, r, Peabody Museum, Cambridge; k–n, Peabody Museum, Salem; b, e, N. L. Bull coll.; d, Springfield Nat. Hist. Museum; s, Torrey collection. (1/2 except inset.)

Bass and *Blew-fish* they take in harbours, and at the mouth of barr'd Rivers being in their *Canows*, striking them with a fisgig, a kind of dart or staff, to the lower end whereof they fasten a sharp jagged bone . . . with a string fastened to it, as soon as the fish is struck they pull away the staff, leaving the bony head in the fishes body and fasten the other end of the string to the *Canow*: Thus they will hale after them to shore half a dozen or half a score great fishes: this way they take *Sturgeon*; and in dark evenings when they are upon the fishing ground near a Bar of Sand where the *Sturgeon* feeds upon small fishes . . . the *Indian* lights a piece of dry *Birch-Bark* which breaks out into a flame & holds it over the side of his *Canow*, the *Sturgeon* seeing the glaring light mounts to the Surface of the water whare he is slain and taken with a fisgig.

The type of fishhook used over the greater portion of northeastern America is shown much reduced in size in r, of the inset in figure 121. This is one of several obtained many years ago by Professor Lee of Bowdoin College from the Nascapee Indians of Labrador. The shank is of wood, split near its lower end, into which is inserted the flat end of a fish spine, where it is securely bound with thong. This spine, detached from the shank, is also shown separately. If fish spines of the proper size were not available, splinters of bone properly pointed and shaped could be quickly substituted. In g, h, i, j, are illustrated four points for this class of fishhook with their lower ends beveled to fit into the slit in the extremity of the wooden shanks.

Champlain has given us a good description of a hook of this type which was given him by an Indian near Plymouth harbor in 1605.

There came to us two or three canoes, which had just been fishing for cod and other fish, which are found there in large numbers. These they catch with hooks made of a piece of wood, to which they attach a bone in the shape of a spear [point], and fasten it very securely. The whole has a fang-shape, and the line attached to it is made out of the bark of a tree. They gave me one of their hooks, which I took as a curiosity. In it, the bone was fastened on by hemp, like that in France, as it seemed to me, and they told me that they gathered this plant without being obliged to cultivate it; and indicated that it grew to the height of four or five feet.[86]

Sagard, in his *Histoire du Canada* (1636), writes that while among the Hurons

We found in the bellies of several large fishes hooks made of a piece of wood and a bone, so placed as to form a hook, and very neatly bound together with hemp; but the line being too weak for drawing on board such large fishes, the result was the loss of labor of the fisherman, and of the hooks thrown into the sea by them, for in verity, there are in this fresh-water sea sturgeon,

---

[86] Champlain's *Voyages*, Prince Soc. reprint, vol. II, p. 77.

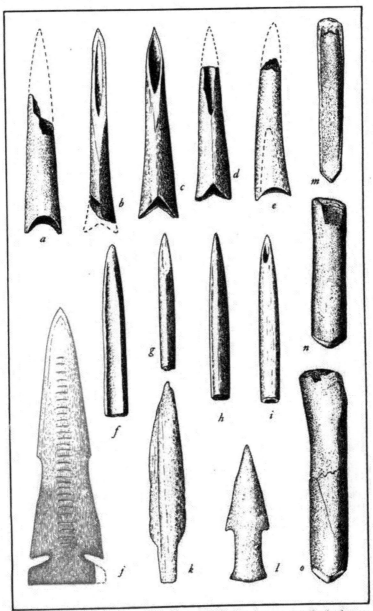

Figure 122. Artifacts of Bone and Antler. a–l, Projectile points; m–o, antler implements for stone chipping. b, From grave at Manchester, Mass.; f–i, from grave at Winthrop, Mass.; a, c–e, j–l, m–o, Maine shellheaps; j, Lamoine; l, Castine; m, Bar Harbor; n, Southport; o, Vinalhaven. (About 1/2.)

assihendos, trout, and pike of such monstrous size, that larger ones cannot be seen anywhere else.[87]

That this general form of hook was sometimes furnished with an antler shank is proved by the recent finding of an excellent example in a Cape Cod shellheap by Howard Torrey of Reading which is now in his collection. This is shown one half size in s, of figure 121. A bone point like g, but a little smaller, inserted in the cleft of this shank and lashed as in r, would complete the implement and make an excellent hook for taking large fish.

The points illustrated in figure 125, are representative of perhaps the most numerous group of bone artifacts from the shellheaps. They consist of splinters of bone about one and one half to three inches in length made more or less symmetrical by grinding. One end is pointed and the other extremity is usually flattened or brought to a blunt point. Occasionally both points are sharp as in b, and f. They were doubtless used for a variety of purposes, although their chief function may have been points for arrows and projectiles. An examination of almost any large collection of them shows examples which seem well fitted for points for the above type of hook. I know of no record of the use by our New England Indians of property marks such as often occur on the harpoon points of the Eskimo for proving ownership. The point illustrated in e, of this illustration, however, has incised upon it the figure of a man holding in his hand what appears to be a spear, which may have served some such purpose, although the absence of similar marks from the vast majority of such points renders it improbable. This point was obtained with many others from a shellheap near Blue Hill, Maine, by Dr. E. E. Tyzzer.

Small hooks made of a single piece of bone like those illustrated in figure 121, e, f, have been found principally in Rhode Island and the adjacent region. The two in e, were taken with one other from the archaic level of a shellheap at Niantic, Connecticut, and are in the Bull collection at Hartford. The two shown in f, are from a shellheap at Narragansett Pier, Rhode Island. These may be of the type known to the Narragansets, according to Williams, as peewâsicks — little hooks, to distinguish them from the large hooks which were called maúmacocks.

In figure 122, f – i, are shown four of two clusters of five bone arrowpoints from a grave at Winthrop, near the shore of Boston

[87] Charles Rau, *Prehistoric Fishing*, Smithsonian Cont. to Knowl., 1884, p. 269.

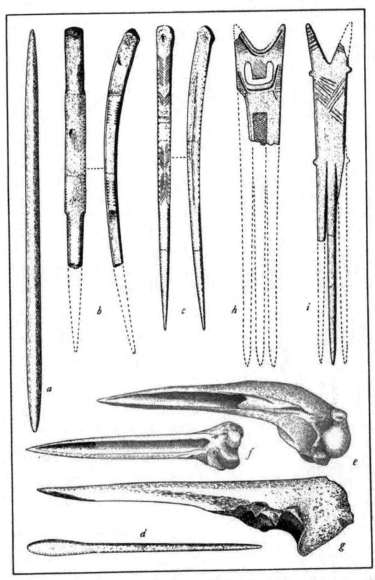

Figure 125. Artifacts of Bone and Antler. a–g, Bodkins and awls of bone; h, i, ornamental combs of antler. From Maine shellheaps: a, f, Damariscotta River; c, g, Bremen; b, Cushing; e, Kimballs Island; d, Deer Island; h, i, Vinalhaven. Peabody Museum, Cambridge. (About 1/2.)

Harbor. Antler arrowpoints are illustrated in a, and e; e being of a type common in the middle states and adjacent territory but rare in New England. They are made of the tips of deer antlers ground to a point and hollowed out at the larger end to fit the end of the wooden shaft. They are usually straighter than the example shown. The excellent points represented in b, c, d, are of bone and are furnished with a double barb. The natural cavity at the base is enlarged to receive the shaft. Specimen b, is from a grave at Manchester, Massachusetts, the other two from Maine shellheaps. The large spearpoint, j, is an unusually fine one. This is from a Maine shellheap and is in the Andover museum.

The three punch-like objects shown at the right in figure 122, m, n, o, are antler flint-flakers such as are found over a large portion of North America. These are somewhat larger than the average, and were doubtless used with a hammer of stone or hard wood, in the preliminary roughing out of blades and projectile points, which were afterward finished by pressure with a smaller though similar flaker of antler. In the various accounts of flint chipping by the Indians there are few references to the punch and hammer. It is apparent, however, that their use was wide-spread as a preliminary process to the final pressure flaking of the more delicately finished blades.

Catlin, in describing the process of arrowmaking among the Apache,[88] says that the flint to be worked was placed in the left hand where it was firmly held by two or more fingers. The punch was grasped between the thumb and two fingers of the right hand, and a cooperator sitting in front with a mallet of very hard wood struck the punch upon its upper end. Both the holder and the striker sang, and the strokes of the mallet were given in time with the music.

In his illuminating paper on Yahi archery[89] Dr. Pope gives an interesting description of Ishi's method of making arrowpoints.

A boulder of obsidian was shattered by throwing another rock on it. The chunks thus obtained were broken into smaller size by holding a short segment of deer horn or piece of bone against a projecting surface, and smartly striking it a glancing blow with a stone. The resulting flakes of obsidian best suited for arrowheads were roughly three inches long, an inch and a half wide and half an inch thick.

[88] George Catlin. *Last Rambles,* pp. 184, 185.

[89] S. T. Pope, *Yahi Archery.* Univ. Calif. Pub. Am. Arch. and Eth., vol. XIII, pp. 116, 117, pl. 27.

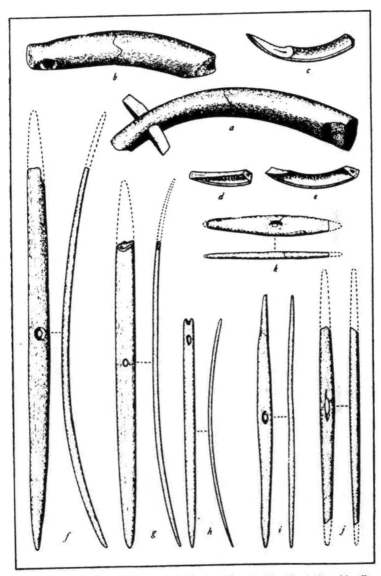

Figure 124. Artifacts of Bone and Antler. a–e, Beavertooth cutting tools and handles; f–j, needles for sewing flag leaf mats; k, shuttle for weaving snowshoe mesh. From Maine shellheaps: a, French's I., Casco Bay; b, Whaleback Shellheap, Damariscotta; c, d, Deer Island; e, Morse's I., Friendship Bay; f, Crotch I., Friendship; g, Kimball Island; h, Damariscotta; i, Birch Point; j, Hog Island; k, Vinalhaven. All Peabody Museum, Cambridge, excepting a, which is in the collection of E. S. Everett of Portland. (1/2.)

These were chipped into arrowpoints with the aid of the ordinary pressure flaker of antler. The pressure flakers, formerly widely distributed among the Indians, were very similar to m, of the above illustration except that they were usually smaller and frequently longer. The shorter ones were set firmly into a handle and the longer ones were either used without a separate handle or were bound to a stick which was sometimes long enough to be steadied by placing its opposite end between the arm and body of the manipulator.

Perhaps the most numerous artifacts from the shellheaps are awls and bodkins made from the bones of various quadrupeds and the larger birds. They are frequently made of splinters broken from the long bones of the deer, with one end ground to a point. Some of them were probably fitted to short handles, others had the upper portion wrapped with a piece of the skin of some animal. The ulna of the deer was much favored as it required little work to produce a serviceable tool (figure 123, g). The humerus and leg bones of the turkey were also favorites (e, f,), the large unworked upper ends serving as excellent handles, especially when wrapped with a piece of skin. While the functions of these implements were manifold, one of the principal uses was undoubtedly as an aid in basket-making.

Most of these tools were crude, but occasionally carefully formed and well finished specimens are found. Two of especial interest are illustrated in b, and c, made apparently from deer ribs and ornamented with notches and incised lines.

A well formed bone pin is shown in d, which seems better fitted for use as a garment fastener than as an ordinary tool. This came from a shellheap, on Deer Island, Maine. Another of similar nature is illustrated in figure 121, d. It is of antler, taken with two or three others from a grave at Bellows Falls, Vermont.

Portions of two comb-like head ornaments are shown in figure 123, h, i, from a shellheap at Golden Cove Basin, North Haven. They were found by Professor Bates during his long continued explorations of the shellheaps of Maine. They are of deer antler. Such ornaments are not common although several have recently been reported from New England shellheaps. Combs of this material, or bone, seem to have been more common among the Iroquois than among our New England Algonquians.

An interesting cutting tool consisting of an antler handle with a sharpened beaver incisor inserted through a perforation near one end is illustrated in a, of figure 124. This was found with the tooth in place in a shellheap by E. S. Everett on French's Island, Casco Bay, about 1922. It represents a type of tool evidently widely distributed, but of which only three or four perfect examples are known to the writer. Dr. W. C. Mills[90] has figured two from an intrusive burial in one of the mounds at Mound City, Ross County, Ohio, and he records a third from another mound in the vicinity. A fifth specimen minus the sharpened tooth, from Michigan, is in

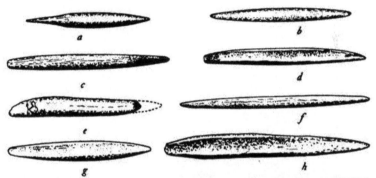

Figure 125. Typical Bone Points from the Maine shellheaps. They form, perhaps, the most numerous group of artifacts from these refuse piles. Many are doubtless points for arrows, others are probably points for fish-hooks of the type shown in figure 121, r. (2/3.)

the Peabody Museum at Cambridge, and in b, of this figure, is a drawing of another handle from the Whaleback shellheap at Damariscotta. Chisels and knives made from the incisors of the beaver were used for various purposes by the Indians throughout the habitat of this animal, the hard outer enamel of the tooth being ground to a sharp edge. Some were set into a hole at one end of a short handle of wood or antler, the tooth being nearly parallel to the length of the handle, others were set crosswise to the haft as in a, of the drawing. Sometimes the lower jaw of the animal was cut through its center between the incisors, one of which, ground to a cutting edge, remained embedded in the half-jaw, which served very well for a handle, especially if wound with a thong or a piece of skin. Beaver tooth knives and chisels with artificially

[90] W. C. Mills, *Exploration of the Mound City Group.* Certain Mounds and Village Sites in Ohio, vol. III, part 4, pp. 394, 397.

ground edges occur in most of the shellheaps. Both the lower and upper incisors were used, the lower being much more common. Good examples of these chisels are illustrated in d, and e, and a knife with a portion of the side ground for cutting is shown in c. References to the use of these implements are rare. Captain John Smith writes of the Virginia Indians:

to make the noch of his arrow he hath the tooth of a Beaver, set in a sticke, wherewith he grateth it by degrees.[91]

He also says that bone fish hooks were worked out in the same way — "grated as they noch their arrows." The remarkable wood cutting habits of the beaver undoubtedly had a marked influence in the choice of the incisors of this animal for cutting implements, for it would be in keeping with what we know of the workings of the Indian mind if supernatural powers were attributed to these tools.

Double-pointed needles for sewing flag (cat-o'-nine-tail) leaves together in making mats for covering wigwams are shown in f – j, of figure 124. One of these, h, has been broken through the perforation and re-drilled, thus converting it into an ordinary single pointed needle. The larger specimens are made from deer ribs. This type of needle is still used by the more primitive Algonquians of the Great Lakes area for mat making. A somewhat similar tool, but shorter and straighter, is illustrated in k. This is a shuttle or needle for weaving the mesh in snowshoes.

Several worked phalanges or toe-bones of the deer are illustrated in figure 121 k – n. The upper end of each is perforated. They have all been cut across near the base and the natural hollow enlarged to receive the end of its companion when strung upon a cord as in q, of the inset. One of them, k, has side perforations. These bones formed parts of three cup-and-pin games such as are still in use among the more primitive Algonquians and some of their neighbors. The game consists of a number of these bones strung upon a string or thong, to one end of which is fastened a pin of bone or wood several inches long, and to the other extremity the end of the tail of some small animal, or a piece of buckskin bearing one or more perforations.

In playing, the head of the pin is grasped in the hand and the bones swing upward as in q, the player endeavoring to catch one

[91] Capt. John Smith, *Works*, Arber edition, vol. I, pp. 364–365.

or more of them on the pin's point. The counting varies, but in general the bone which lies nearest the hand on the string counts the highest. When two or more bones are caught they count according to the number impaled. As the base of one bone usually fits over the top of the one below, it is possible for two or more to be caught at the same time. If the pin enters a side perforation as in k, the count is relatively high.

This bone, k, was taken from a grave in Saugus, Massachusetts, some fifty years ago; l, with a notched base, came from a shell-heap at Eagle Hill, Ipswich. A second one was found with it. The two shown in m, n, were dug up at the corner of La Grange and Harrison Streets, South Salem, in 1866. They probably came from a grave. All of the above are in the Peabody Museum at Salem.

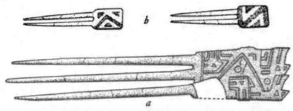

Antler Combs or Hair Pins from a Cape Cod shellheap. a, C. S. Crowell coll; b, H. Torrey coll. Both sides of b, are shown, and the incised designs were originally colored.

Naturally one would expect to find few personal ornaments in the shellheaps. The canine teeth of the bear perforated for suspension near the root end as in o, of figure 121, are occasionally found. These were favorite ornaments among Indians generally, and especially so among the Great Earthwork Builders of the Ohio region, who often wore them attached to their clothing and sometimes cut them into various forms, or set them with fresh water pearls. The perforated canine teeth of smaller mammals also occur.

A few beads consisting of sections cut from the larger bones of birds, like p, of the above figure, are sometimes recovered but one is more apt to find pieces of bone from which such beads have been cut.

THE LATER ALGONQUIAN GROUP

THE separation of the older Algonquians of New England from their western kindred by the Iroquoian invasion (see figure 3) is doubtless responsible in a measure for the marked changes in the material culture of the later tribes of these states. One of the most notable of these changes was the shape of the pottery vessels which acquired a more globular form, like those of the Iroquois, which were intended for suspension over the fire. The older Algonquian pots were supported by hearth-stones or by setting their pointed base into the earth.

We notice also a change in the form and material of many of the tobacco pipes, probably through Iroquoian contact, a large proportion of whose pipes were of terra-cotta. Many of the late New England pipes were of this material and were easily and quickly made.

The later Algonquians of New England continued the use of iron pyrites for fire-making, a method which their ancestors doubtless adopted from their predecessors, and which the first English settlers found in quite common use, especially in the more southern sections of New England. Our Algonquians seem to have preferred this method to the fire drill brought with them from the West, although both were in use.

At the time of the arrival of Europeans, that portion of New England approximately north and east of Massachusetts was occupied by the Abnaki tribes. These are usually classed linguistically with the Cree and Montagnais whose habitat lies north of the Great Lakes and the St. Lawrence River. The Abnaki probably entered New England by crossing the St. Lawrence. Both their social and material culture differed considerably from that of the tribes of southern New England. They used birch bark extensively in their arts. Wigwams were covered with it. Their canoes were made of it, and many of their household utensils such as boxes, dishes, kettles, etc., were fashioned from it. They probably introduced the snow-shoe. Their social organization was more like the hunter tribes of the north. Agriculture was followed to some extent. This, however, was probably adopted after their arrival in New England.

The tribes found by the colonists occupying the southern portions of our states, or at least the principal ones, seem to be rem-

228

nants of that older Algonquian group which entered New England from the southwest. Their culture, both social and material, was higher than that of their more northern neighbors. According to Cotton Mather, society among the Indians of eastern Massachusetts was composed of three classes, the highest being made up of people of royal blood (and those who had been formally adopted into a clan). From this group were drawn the chiefs, priests, and other tribal officers. The common people, called sanops, composed the second class. These possessed rights to tribal lands, and constituted the mass of the community. The third group consisted of outsiders who had joined the tribe but had not been formally adopted, together with their descendants, and others with no legal rights. Members of this group owned no land. They sometimes became attached to families as servants, or obtained their living as best they could. The office of sachem or head chief was hereditary. If male heirs were wanting the title descended to a female, and sometimes, though rarely, to the chief's widow. Wood says

It is custome for their Kings to inherite, the sonne alwayes taking the Kingdome after his fathers death. If their be no sonne, then the Queene rules; if no Queene, then the next to the blood-royall.[92]

The sachems or "Kings" were absolute masters of their people, whose fortunes and services were subject to their disposal.

Referring to Mayhew's account of the social structure of the Indians of southeastern Massachusetts, which is quoted by him in full, Dr. Speck says:

The class divisions of medieval European society could scarcely be better outlined in the same number of words than as we see them described here. It is, indeed, difficult to vision them as applying to the society of an Indian tribe on the Atlantic coast. Yet the evidence confronts us as a piece of positive testimony to the existence of a class subdivision in southern New England.[93]

This highly developed social organization, which must have existed among the mound-building people of the Ohio region, seems to have been brought into New England by their advancing outposts. It is highly probable that at least some of the later Algonquian tribes of the Atlantic seaboard from Virginia to central New England are the survivors of this ancient group. There are various strong cultural resemblances between the later tribes of southern New England and those of Virginia.

[92] William Wood. *New England's Prospect*. Boynton edition, p. 83.
[93] F. G. Speck in Indian Notes and Monographs, no. 44, pp. 24–28. Museum of the American Indian, New York.

The proto-historic tribes of the later Algonquian group are those encountered principally by the voyagers and traders of the sixteenth century. Following the discovery of Newfoundland by Cabot in 1497 ships from various nations of Europe visited the northeastern coast of America and had more or less communication with the natives. Verarzanus the Florentine visited New England in 1524. He gives an interesting account of the Indians, describing their habitations, dress, canoes, agriculture, etc. He spent fifteen days among them either in eastern Massachusetts or Rhode Island. He writes as follows of the copper found among them at that time.

We saw many plates of wrought copper which they esteem more than gold, which for the color [yellow] they make no account of, for that among all other is accounted the basest. They make most account of azure and red. The things they esteemed most of all those which we gave them were bells, crystals of azure color, and other toys to hang at their ears and about their necks.[94]

This copper must have been obtained from previous explorers of whom we have no definite account; for although an occasional implement and a few beads wrought from native copper have been found, nothing in way of metal plates has been recovered in New England which was not made of European copper or brass. Many objects of these foreign metals have been taken from graves belonging to the sixteenth century and will be described later. Cartier sailed up the St. Lawrence in 1535, and it appears that trade "out of England to Newfoundland was common and frequented" as early as 1548.

In 1578, Anthonie Parkhurst wrote a letter to Richard Hakluyt, a portion of which is as follows:

Now to answer some part of your letter touching the sundry navies that come to Newfoundland or Terra nova, for fish: you shal understand that some fish not neere the other by 200. leagues, and therefore the certaintie is not knowen; and some yeres come many more than other some, as I see the like among us: who since my first travell being but 4. yeeres, are increased from 30. sayle to 50. which commeth to passe chiefly by the imagination of the Westerne men, who thinke their neighbours have had greater gaines then in very deed they have, for that they see me to take such paines yeerely to go in proper person: they also suppose that I find some secret commoditie by reason that I doe search the harbors, creekes and havens, and also the land much more than ever any Englishman hath done. Surely I am glad that it so increaseth, whereof

[94] John Verarzanus, in The Relation of Hakluyts Divers Voyages (1582), Hakluyt Soc. reprint, p. 65.

soever it springeth. But to let this passe, you shall understand that I am informed that there are above 100. saile of Spaniards that come to take Cod ... besides 20. or 30. more that come from Biskaie to kill Whale for Traine. These be better appoynted for shipping and furniture of munition, then any nation saving the Englishmen, who commonly are lords of the harbors where they fish, and do use all strangers helpe in fishing if need require, according to an old custome of the countrey, which they do willingly, so that you take nothing from them more then a boat or twaine of salt, in respect of your protection of them against rovers or other violent intruders, who do often put them from good harbor, &c. As touching their tunnage, I thinke it may be neere five or sixe thousand tunne. But of Portugals there are not lightly above 50. saile ... whose tunnage may amount to three thousand tuns, and not upwarde. Of the French nation and Britons, are about one hundred and fiftie sailes, the most of their shipping is very small, not past fortie tunnes, among which some are great and reasonably well appointed, better then the Portugals, and not so well as the Spaniards, and the burden of them may be some 7000. tunne. Their shipping is from all parts of France and Britaine, and the Spaniards from most parts of Spaine, the Portugals from Aviero and Viana, and from 2. or 3. ports more. The trade that our nation hath to Island maketh, that the English are not there in such numbers as other nations.[95]

From the above we learn that at this date there were evidently nearly 400 European vessels engaged in taking fish or whales, and probably a portion of them incidentally trading for furs, in an area 600 miles in diameter in the vicinity of Newfoundland and Cape Breton. The New England coast was doubtless within this 600 mile area, and there seems to be no reasonable doubt that it was visited by many of these ships and that there was considerable intercourse between these vessels and the natives. This seems to be a plausible explanation of the origin of the quantities of copper and brass objects recorded by early writers as in possession of the Indians of this region, and it doubtless explains their presence in the sixteenth century graves.

It will be noted that in the many pre-Algonquian graves which have been opened practically no bones were discovered. In the few cemeteries of prehistoric Algonquian culture that have been found, many of the skeletons had entirely disappeared, and with few exceptions only minor fragments were recovered. In a protohistoric sixteenth century burial place on Indian Ridge, the estate of Dr. F. B. Harrington at Ipswich, one or two graves were uncovered in 1907 and in them were found the pottery pipe shown in b, figure 104; a bracelet of small beads of sheet brass strung

95 Hakluyt's Voyages, Glasgow edition 1904, vol. VIII, pp. 9-11.

alternately with beads of blue glass and mussel shell, the string
on which they were strung being perfectly preserved owing to
contact with the metal. There was also a necklace of small oval
white glass beads, and an old bronze brazier. Only a few fragments of bone were noticed. Obtaining permission from the owner
of the estate, investigations were carried on in behalf of the Peabody Museum for several days. A few additional graves were
opened, but no artifacts were found. In each of these additional
graves the skeleton had disintegrated, leaving nothing but a whitish paste in the damp soil in place of the larger bones. This, upon
drying turned to powder, not even a tooth was discovered. The
bodies had been interred in soil composed largely of clay, which
allowed the water to percolate but slowly; consequently the disintegration of the bones may have been more rapid than it would
have been had they been buried in sand or gravel. It is evident
that nearly all of the well preserved skeletal material which has been
recovered in New England is not older than the beginning of the
sixteenth century.

There is ample historical and archaeological evidence of the
occurrence of various objects of European sheet copper and brass
among our natives during the proto-historic period. Brereton
in 1602 saw among the Indians of Massachusetts:

... great store of copper, some very red, and some of a paler colour [brass]:
none of them but have chaines, ear-rings, or collars of this metal: they head
some of their arrows herewith much like our broad arrow heads, very work-
manly made. Their chaines are many hollow pieces cemented together, each
piece of the bigness of one of our reeds, a finger in length, ten or twelve of
them together on a string, which they wear about their necks: their collars
they wear about their bodies like bandeliers a handful broad, all hollow pieces,
like the other, but somewhat shorter, four hundred pieces in a collar, very
fine and evenly set together. Besides these they have large drinking cups
made like sculls and other thin plates of copper, made much like our boar
spear blades, all of which they so little esteem, as they offered their fairest
collars and chains for a knife or such like trifle, but we seemed little to regard it.[96]

"Scull" or skull as above used is a term applied to that part
of a headpiece or armor which covered the crown of the head; in
other words, a metal skullcap. A portion of one of these cups or
basins hammered from sheet copper was found with a burial at
Winthrop which will be later described.

One of the most interesting and widely known proto-historic

---

[96] Brereton, *Account of Gosnold's Voyage*, Mass. Hist. Coll., 3d series, vol. VIII. p. 91.

Indian burials found in New England is the "Skeleton in Armor" made famous by Longfellow's poetic and fanciful rendering of a very prosaic occurrence, namely the unearthing in 1831, at Fall River, from a sand bank near the line between Fall River and Tiverton, of an Indian skeleton accompanied by objects made of European metal. These objects were apparently identical with some of those described above by Brereton.

The skeleton was buried in a sitting posture, with legs flexed and the hands raised to the upper part of the chest. It was wrapped in several coverings of woven material of different textures, the finest innermost. Outside was a casing of cedar bark.

On the chest was a plate of sheet brass about fourteen inches long, five and one-half wide at one end and six at the other, both ends being broken and crumbled, as in figure 126, h. Lying across this plate were thirty to forty tubes or beads placed close together side by side, each about four and one half inches long and one fourth inch in diameter, made by bending sheet brass around what is probably a piece of elder wood with pith removed. These beads formed a portion of a belt or bandoleer which doubtless encircled the body. Through each of these long beads a thong was passed which fastened them to other thongs running transversely along the top and bottom of the belt, the method of attachment probably being the same as shown in the fillet, figure 127, a, b.

Several triangular arrowpoints of sheet brass were found with the skeleton. This account is taken principally from the communication sent by Dr. Thomas Webb, secretary of the Rhode Island Historical Society, to the secretary of the Société Royale des Antiquaires du Nord in 1838 and published in the Mémoires of that society for 1840–44. With the letter Dr. Webb sent a number of objects from the grave which he secured through Simeon Borden of Fall River. These were doubtless the greater part of the breast plate, a portion of the belt, and one of the arrowpoints described and figured in the above publication. In 1842 Jerome V. C. Smith sent to this society another arrowpoint from Fall River and a fragment of bulrush matting, probably from the same grave as the others.

Most of these objects are preserved in the Ethnographiske Museum at Copenhagen. Two of the brass tubes or beads were subsequently obtained in Copenhagen by Dr. Samuel Kneeland and presented to the Peabody Museum at Cambridge in 1886, one of which is shown in figure 127, g. The skeleton is said to have been destroyed by fire in Fall River about 1843.

Copies of the illustrations accompanying the article in the above Mémoires are shown in figures 126, d, e, h, and figure 132, c. The matting was of the ordinary bulrush type used principally for lining the interiors of wigwams and for other domestic purposes.

The fact that similar tubes arranged in like manner have been found in Denmark led to the erroneous belief that the Fall River specimens were of Norse origin. It was this belief, quite prevalent at the time, that led Longfellow to compose his "Skeleton in Armor."

Numerous other burials have been unearthed in New England accompanied by objects made from sheet copper and brass undoubtedly obtained from fishermen and traders during the century preceding the arrival of the Pilgrims. Most of these burials were accidentally discovered and no systematic effort was made to find other graves in the immediate vicinity. Some of the artifacts accompanying such burials have gradually found their way into the more important private collections or into our larger museums.

An interesting example probably dating about the first quarter of the seventeenth century is shown in figure 130. This is from the vicinity of Amoskeag Falls, Manchester, New Hampshire, a famous fishing station where many Indian artifacts have been found, a favorite camping ground of both the Algonquian and pre-Algonquian people. It represents the thunderbird which produced thunder by flapping its wings, and lightning by opening and closing its eyes. It is of copper, somewhat thicker than the ordinary sheet-copper, and was probably made from a piece of a copper kettle. It was undoubtedly worn as a gorget. It should be compared with the pictographs appearing in figure 94, and figure 50, a.

In figure 126, i, m, are shown a portion of a belt or headband and a small pendant, both of European sheet copper from a grave at Vassalboro, Maine. With this were also a number of tubular copper beads and several of shell (figure 140, m, n). A very similar sheet copper band, twelve and one half inches in length, also with serrated edges, was taken from the grave of a child by Dr. Moorehead, at Sandy point, about five miles below Bucksport, on the Penobscot River. This grave contained also twenty-seven tubular

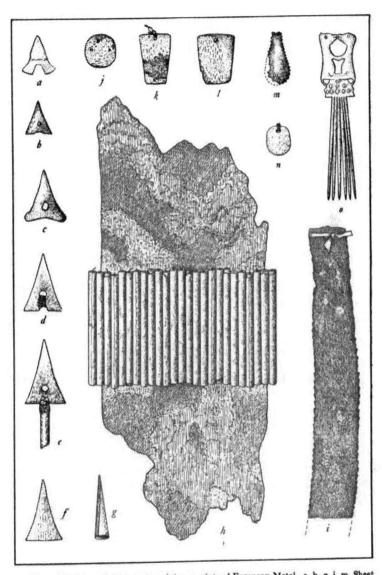

Figure 126. Personal Ornaments and Arrowpoints of European Metal. a, b, g, i, m, Sheet copper; c, d, e, f, h, j, k, l, n, sheet brass; o, cast brass. a, b, g, o, Graves in Rhode Island, after H. M. Chapin; d, e, h, Fall River, Mass. d, h, and probably e, also, are from the grave of the *Skeleton in Armor*, immortalized by Longfellow. This was, of course, the skeleton of an Indian accompanied by the usual objects of sheet metal. e, f, n, Grave at Revere, Mass.; j, k, l, grave at Winthrop, Mass.; i, m, grave at Vassalboro, Me. (1/3.)

beads of sheet copper and an iron axe. The beads were lying side by side on a piece of well dressed buckskin which had been colored red and which was perfectly preserved, owing to contact with the copper. There were also a few white and blue discoidal beads of shell strung alternately on thong or sinew.

In 1892 there was unearthed in Tiverton, Rhode Island, which adjoins Fall River, a skeleton with a number of long copper beads of the same form and size as those described above "fastened to a back of coarse woven bark-like material." This "back" was probably a portion of the mat in which the body was wrapped, and to which the beads became cemented by copper salts. There were also two brass arrowheads.

There is practically no difference in appearance externally between objects of sheet copper and of brass after they have laid many years in the ground, for their surfaces are nearly always covered with green carbonate, which is as noticeable in brass as in pure copper. In order, therefore, to identify the metal it is necessary to scrape away a small portion of the corrosion until a fresh surface is exposed.

In April, 1888, workmen, excavating for the narrow gauge railroad at Winthrop, just across the harbor from Boston, unearthed three or four skeletons near the site of the present Centre Station. The skull of one of these lay in contact with pieces of thin metal, evidently parts of a copper vessel which had been placed over the head. This had apparently been formed from a circular piece of sheet copper by laying it over a block with a depression on its surface, and beating it with a hammer of stone or other material having a convex face, after the manner of colonial sheet metal workers. It had no wire reinforcement at the rim. This is doubtless similar to the basins seen by Brereton at Buzzards Bay in 1602 and described as "large drinking cups made like skulls." As soon as the superintendent of the road heard of the discovery, he secured the bowl and also the skulls and such other bones as had not been destroyed, and presented them to the Peabody Museum at Cambridge. As circumstances permitted, further excavations were carried on by Professor Putnam in behalf of the Museum and eight additional graves were opened. Graves 6 and 7, of the plan, figure 128, were the ones destroyed by workmen, and the positions of the skeletons could not be accurately determined. Artifacts were found in all the graves opened by the Museum with the exception of Number 3.[97] All the burials were flexed except those of the two infants in Grave 4.

Grave 1. Thirty inches deep. Lying parallel to the spinal column of the skeleton was a much corroded bar of iron, twenty-three and one half inches long, seven eighths of an inch wide, and one quarter of an inch thick, one end of which tapered to a chisel-like edge. Over this were five bone points, and the incisor of a beaver such as

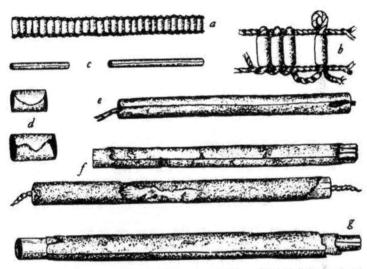

Figure 127. Beads of European Sheet Copper and Bass. a, Fillet of sheet copper and brass beads; b, a portion of a, enlarged to show technique; c, two of twenty-nine beads of sheet copper. All from a grave at Dorchester, Mass. f, Beads of elder wood covered with sheet copper, from grave at Winthrop, Mass.; g, bead of elder wood covered with sheet brass, grave of the *Skeleton in Armor*, Fall River, Mass.; e, bead of sheet copper, grave at Harpswell, Me.; d, beads of sheet brass from grave in the Whaleback Shellheap at Damariscotta, Me. All in the Peabody Museum, Cambridge. (1/1.)

those commonly hafted and used as chisels. On the opposite side of the body was another group of five bone points and a second beaver tooth. It seems probable that the two groups of bone points are all that remain of two lots of bone pointed arrows. A triangular brass arrowpoint was found embedded in one of the lumbar vertebræ. The Indian had been shot through the abdomen. Higgeson, writing in 1629 of the arrows in this region, says that

[97] C. C. Willoughby, *Indian Burial Place at Winthrop, Massachusetts.* Papers of the Peabody Museum of Arch. and Eth. Cambridge, vol. XI, no. 1.

some were headed with bone and some with brass. Both kinds occurred in this grave.

Grave 2. This had been dug to a depth of thirty inches, and contained the flexed skeleton of a woman. The body had been wrapped in matting. At its left side lay an unworked shell of *Fulgur canaliculata*, a species not uncommon on the Massachusetts coast. This probably served as a drinking cup. About a foot from the skull were three pottery vessels, two of which are illustrated in figure 113, c, e. Near the left shoulder were about twenty beads, approximately four inches long, one fourth inch in diameter, each apparently made of a section of elder with pith removed and covered with thin sheet copper, the salts of which had preserved

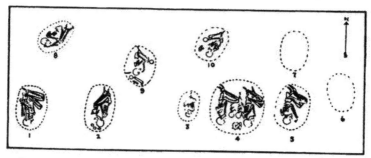

Figure 128. Burial Place at Winthrop, Mass. Sketch-plan showing position of objects in graves.

the two-ply twisted cord with which the beads had been strung. Two of these appear in figure 127, f.

Grave 3. Skeleton of a child about one year old. No artifacts found.

Grave 4. A shallow grave containing the skeletons of a man, a woman, and two children in the positions shown in the plan. Fragments of the pottery vessel, restored in figure 113, d, lay near the head of the woman. Beneath her head were eighty tubular glass beads, some white and others blue. There were also found one hundred and forty-eight white beads made from the columellae of large univalves.

Grave 5. A much decayed skeleton of a man lay two feet below the surface. The only artifacts found were a few tubular shell beads and five tubular glass beads which lay beneath the jaw.

Graves 6 and 7. Unearthed by workmen. Exact locality unrecorded. No artifacts found with skeletons.

Grave 8. Skeleton of a man two feet below surface. A bone awl lay about four inches from the vertebral column.

Grave 9. This contained the skeleton of a child, probably a girl, two to three years old. Near the head were fragments of a medium size pottery vessel and an antler spoon. Nearby was a stone pestle with its upper portion carved to represent the head of an animal (figure 81, g,), also a small water-worn stone, one end of which somewhat resembled an animal head. Near the knees was a toy pottery vessel two and one half inches in height. The pestle with the animal head, although a domestic implement, had evidently served as a plaything for the child.

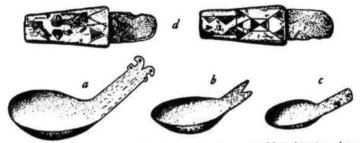

Figure 129. Knife and Sheet Metal Spoons from Indian graves, Massachusetts: a, brass, from near Plymouth; b, brass, c, copper, d, brass blade, antler handle. From graves at Winthrop. a, Peabody Museum, Salem; b, c, d, Peabody Museum, Cambridge. (1/3.)

Grave 10. Skeleton of a child about three years of age, probably a boy. Near the knees were fragments of a pottery vessel. Near the extremity of the forearm lay a deposit consisting of two spoons, the larger made of sheet brass and the smaller of sheet copper, figure 129, b, c; five pendants and a disc having two perforations, all of sheet brass, three of which are shown in figure 126, j, k, l; a terra-cotta pipe (figure 104, i); the remnants of a bag of coiled netting (figure 132, d), which had evidently contained the pipe; and what may have been the remains of a second bag, probably of dressed skin. These fragments had been preserved by contact with the metal.

With these objects were several seeds resembling those of the *Cornus,* having the ends ground down to the cavity, thereby forming a perforation for stringing for use as beads, probably as ornaments to one of the bags. With the skeleton were also several glass beads both blue and white, and a small iron adze blade.

At the time of the discovery of these burials, the place was known as the Pound. There was a house or shed and palisaded yard built here by the settlers of Boston for the protection of their cattle. On the 23rd of February, 1634, the authorities voted "that there shall be a little house built and a sufficiently payled yard to lodge cattle in of nights at Pullen Poynt Neck before the 14th day of ye next second month." William Cheeseborough, Constable of Boston, was appointed cattle guard for this place.[98] This definitely places the burials at a period previous to 1634. They probably belong to the first or second decade of the seventeenth century, possibly earlier.

From time to time other burials have been unearthed in various parts of Winthrop but they have usually been unaccompanied by artifacts, or if artifacts were present they were overlooked. The interesting knife illustrated in figure 129, d, was found with a skeleton on Hermon Street, in 1886. Its blade was apparently made from a piece of heavy sheet brass or a part of an old kettle. The handle is of antler and is ornamented with designs in incised lines. It is an old form such as was used for hafting chipped flint blades. On one side is a perforation made by drilling two holes diagonally until they meet, through which a suspending cord was passed.

In 1878 Rev. K. L. Washburn unearthed at Revere a grave containing numerous objects belonging to this proto-historic period. The artifacts consisted of a stone pipe with brass-bound bowl, figure 104, a; two arrowpoints, a knife blade, two pendants, and twenty-one small beads, all made of sheet brass. The two arrowpoints and one pendant are shown in figure 126, c, f, n.

Some years ago one of these old graves was found at Harpswell, Maine, containing numerous tubular beads of sheet copper, and many small brass or copper beads strung like those in figure 127, a, b. I do not know what became of most of this material. One of the larger tubular beads and a portion of one or two others, also numerous fragments of matting, dressed buckskin, cordage, etc., were given to the Peabody Museum, Cambridge, in 1877. The larger bead, figure 127, e, was a little less than three inches in length. On some of the pieces of buckskin were distinct impressions of a belt made of these long beads placed side by side as in the belt found with the "Skeleton in Armor." There were also the

---

[98] C. W. Hall, *History of Winthrop, Mass.*, 1902, p. 19.

impressions of a fillet of small beads similar to figure 127, a, although the beads were slightly larger than the ones shown in the drawing. The salts of copper from each of these had left its form clearly marked on the skin. There were also several pieces of thong. Among the fragments of matting used for wrapping the body were those of the common bulrush type, and also an entirely new form (figure 132, g) which will be described under the heading of textiles.

During excavations at Savin Hill Park, Dorchester, an Indian grave was discovered in which were found the following artifacts: several beads about an inch in length, of sheet copper, figure 127, c; a fillet, probably for binding the hair made of one hundred and nineteen small beads of sheet copper and brass; fragments of a copper belt or other ornament; a bone implement; several white, oval porcelain beads of the usual form; an iron head for a fish spear, an iron fish hook, and an axe of the same metal.

A portion of the fillet is illustrated in figure 127, a, and the method of joining the beads in b, of the same figure. The same technique was followed in making the belts and bandoleers of long cylindrical beads elsewhere described. A few iron axes were obtained at an early date. When Champlain visited the coast of Massachusetts in 1605 he found the Indians using stone axes and says "they have no others except some few which they receive from the savages on the coasts of LaCadie who obtain them in exchange for furs."[99]

In 1864 a pit was opened in a sandy gravel knoll in Manchester, Massachusetts.

Four entire skeletons were found buried there, three of adults and one of a youth; one of the adults was of very large size. They were found lying nearly side by side, with their heads toward the west, and were raised so as to face the east. They were found about fourteen inches below the surface which had been much cultivated. One of the skeletons had its head resting upon a round piece of copper about sixteen inches in diameter, and where the head touched the copper the skin and hair adhered firmly to the skull. The hair was black and bright and about two and a half feet long. With them were found an iron tomahawk, and an iron knife blade, much decayed by rust, some coarse cloth made of flags or rushes, a short stemmed smoking pipe, and a large number of bone arrowheads, preserved by the copper in sound condition. These arrowheads were formed something like a writing pen, sharp at the point; some were formed of stone, larger and in the form of a heart; some lobster's claws, a fishing line in good form but very rotten, a portion of

[99] Champlain's *Voyages*, Prince Soc. reprint, vol. II, pp. 73–74.

another line of larger size, both made from fibrous plant, a wooden ladle or bowl, and wooden spoons.[100]

The above account was written by John Lee, in whose possession the objects remained for many years. Upon his death most of them were presented to the Peabody Museum at Cambridge by his heirs.

The disc or platter is of sheet brass, not copper, and is less than one sixteenth of an inch thick. It was broken into many pieces while being taken from the earth. Its outer edge is irregular and has the appearance of having been cut with crude tools such as Indians might have used. Preserved by contact with the disc were fragments of what are probably four bags, two of which seem to have been of the ordinary Algonquian rectangular type. Drawings showing details of the different weaves are reproduced in figure

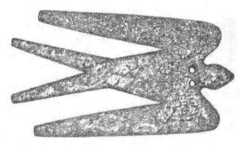

Figure 130. Gorget representing the Thunderbird. Probably made from a piece of a copper kettle. Amoskeag Falls, Manchester, N. H. Peabody Museum, Cambridge. Lowell collection. (1/4.)

133, a, b, c. The bowl of the tobacco pipe was broken and some of the pieces were not recovered. It was of the same general form as the slate pipe illustrated in figure 104, a, except that the bowl was not bound with sheet brass. The stem had likewise been broken and the end worked down in the same manner for receiving an extension of sheet metal which was not recovered. One of the bone arrowpoints is shown in figure 122, b. The fragments of cordage, an example of which appears in figure 133, e, do not seem to have been parts of fishing lines. They are three to four inches in length, some of them being larger at one end than at the other. The large braided example, f, is probably a portion of a bag handle or the running cord for closing the mouth of a bag. The wooden bowl and the iron axe and knife were not received by the Museum.

[100] D. F. Lamson, *History of Manchester, Massachusetts.*

After and during the first two or three decades of the seventeenth century the Indians received from European traders, especially from the French and Dutch, cloth, kettles, hatchets, and many other objects, and the graves of that period have yielded numerous articles of this nature. The native industries of the people rapidly declined. It was principally among the women that the finer arts survived for a time, such as the better class of bag and basket making, porcupine and moosehair embroidery, etc., although the men continued for a period the production of their excellent wooden bowls and drinking cups.

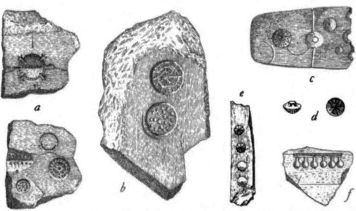

Figure 131. Stone Moulds for casting buttons and other objects of pewter and lead. All from Massachusetts: a, Natick, obverse and reverse sides; b, Yarmouth; c, d, Kingston (the pewter buttons shown in d, were found in the grave with the mould); e, Essex Co.; f, one half of a bullet mould from an island in Manchaug Pond, Sutton. a, b, c, d, Peabody Museum, Cambridge; e, Peabody Museum, Salem; f, C. C. Ferguson coll. (1/3.)

We have before referred to the statement of Roger Williams that the Indians had "excellent art to cast our pewter and brass into very neat and artificial pipes." They also cast buttons and other small ornaments in one-piece moulds which they made of slate or other suitable stone. A number of the latter are illustrated in figure 131. They simply melted the metal and poured a small amount of it on to the mould. When cool the cast was finished by trimming and grinding. One frequently comes across a mould of this type in local Indian collections. The one shown in c, is made of a piece of slate tablet and is from an Indian grave at Kingston, Massachusetts. The two lead or pewter buttons, d, were with it and were cast in this mould. The eye of the button was made by trimming the metal with a knife. There is a well made brass comb of Indian design in the Rhode Island Historical Society's collection at Providence from a grave at Charlestown, Rhode Island, a drawing of which appears in figure 126, o, which was probably cast by an Indian from an antler comb used as a model.

Textile Fabrics. The proto-historic tribes of this region, especially those of the southern half of New England, were expert makers of various kinds of textile fabrics which made up a large portion of the furnishings, utensils, and personal belongings of the people. This art was doubtless inherited principally from the old Algonquian group which entered New England from the Southwest. We know nothing of the textile productions of the pre-Algonquian inhabitants.

So far as we can judge by the few existing examples, our Indians were very proficient in this art and seem to have produced a great variety of woven objects showing approximately as high technical and artistic merits as those found among the most advanced tribes east of the Mississippi. Some of the soft bags, of which only two are known to the writer, are apparently equalled only by certain examples from the Pacific coast.

These textiles consisted of various types of matting, baskets of many varieties, certain forms of clothing such as capes or mantles, also bags, quivers, and burden straps.

Mats for covering wigwams were usually made of flag leaves firmly sewed together with twisted cords of bast, the needle used for sewing being often made from one half of the split rib of a deer (figure 124, f – h). Morton says of these exterior mats, some were

made of reeds and some of longe flagges or sedge firmly sewed together with needles made of the splinter bones of a cranes legge with threads made of their Indian hemp which there groweth naturally.[101]

Similar flagleaf covering mats from Algonquian tribes of the Great Lakes region, may be seen in our larger museums. They are made of leaves of the cat-o'-nine-tail strung together on cords in such a manner that each alternate leaf lies upon opposite sides and covers the junction of two other leaves. These mats are usually four to five feet in width and eight to ten feet long. The ends are furnished with a strip of wood to which tying cords are attached.

[101] Thomas Morton, *New English Canaan*, Prince Soc. reprint, pp. 134–136.

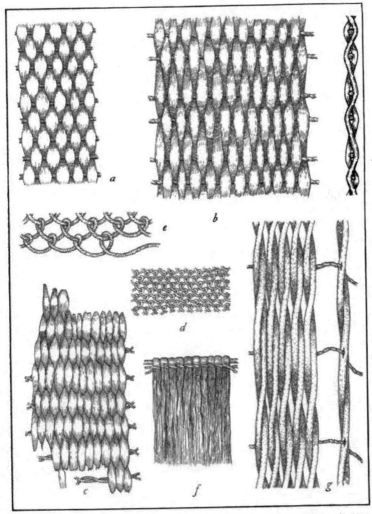

Figure 132. Textiles from Graves. a, b, c, Woven bulrush matting: a, Harpswell, Me.; b, Winthrop, Mass.; c, Fall River, Mass. d, Fragment of coiled netting bag, Winthrop; e, same as d, enlarged; f, fringe of bast or other fiber, Winthrop; g, sewed bulrush matting, Harpswell, Me. All Peabody Museum, Cambridge except c. (1/1, except e.)

I know of no existing example of this type from New England but there is no doubt of their extensive use in this locality.

Morton implies in the above quotation that some of these sewed mats were made of reeds. He probably refers to bulrushes. Woven bulrush mats were extensively used for interior furnishings, but sewn bulrush mats were, so far as I know, unknown to ethnologists up to the present time.

Recently in looking over a few odds and ends from a proto-historic grave in Harpswell, Maine, I found fragments of a sewed bulrush mat which had evidently been used for wrapping the body. This is illustrated in figure 132, g. The rushes were twisted together in pairs and sewed as in the drawing, the cords being placed at intervals of about an inch. I had never before seen this type of mat, nor do I recall a description of one.

Woven bulrush mats were used extensively for lining the interior of wigwams, for covering couches, to sit upon, for drying shelled corn, berries, etc., and for many other purposes.

According to Roger Williams these mats were embroidered. Josselyn says they were painted. Like the mats of the Algonquians of the Great Lakes they were doubtless woven of rushes in their natural tint combined with others dyed in various colors, which formed bands or simple patterns extending across the mat, the effect being similar to the coarser varieties of Chinese matting familiar to most New England housewives.

The few examples of this matting from New England that have come down to us have been taken from graves where small fragments were preserved by contact with copper or brass. They were used for wrapping the body or were placed in the grave as a protection to the body and to the various personal belongings buried with it. The Pilgrims opened a grave at Cape Cod in which they found several of these mats with various objects placed between them.

Three fragments from proto-historic graves are illustrated in figure 132, a, b, c. In each instance the warp consists of twisted cords of bast or Indian hemp, and the woof of bulrushes. In b, the warp is arranged in pairs, while in a, the cords are nearer together and equally spaced. The weaving is the ordinary in-and-out type. The example shown in a, is from the grave at Harpswell from which g, was obtained; b, is from a burial at Winthrop, across the harbor from Boston; and c is from the grave at Fall River, from which the "Skeleton in Armor" was taken. It is copied from the illustration in the first volume of Mémoires de la Société Royale des Antiquaires du Nord.

Of the woven garments of our Indians we know but little. They were probably confined principally to shoulder capes and mantles. Champlain, who explored our coast as far as the southeastern portion of Cape Cod in July, 1605, says that south of the Island Cape (Cape Ann) the Indians "wear neither robes nor furs, except very rarely: moreover their robes are made of grasses and hemp, scarcely covering the body, and coming down only to their thighs."[102] This of course was only a summer garment, worn probably as much as a protection from mosquitos as for warmth.

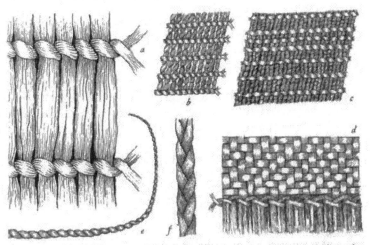

Figure 133. Textiles from grave at Manchester, Mass. a, Fragment of a typical Algonquian flat bag of bast, twined woven; b, a piece of what was probably a small bag; c, closely woven fabric with double warp cords; d, fragment of a twilled woven mantle (?) of bast, fringed; e, f, pieces of tying cords probably belonging to bags or mantles. All Peabody Museum, Cambridge. (1/1.)

In figure 133, d, is shown a fragment of what was probably a bast mantle in twilled weaving, the lower edge of which is fringed. This fringe is formed of the ends of the warp reinforced with loops of the same material to give additional thickness, all being nicely bound together by a single double woof cord of twined weaving. This is from the grave at Manchester, Massachusetts, preserved by contact with a brass plate. It is the only example of what was doubtless a woven New England mantle which I have seen, with the possible exception of c, in the same figure.

[102] Champlain's *Voyages*, Prince Soc. reprint, vol. II, pp. 84–85.

Another type of shoulder cape or mantle, of which no example has come down to us, was covered with the iridescent feathers of the wild turkey. These seem to have been fairly common. Morton says they were woven of twine of their own making, and Williams informs us they were usually the work of the old men. According to Josselyn they were sometimes made by women for their children. Other feathers may have been sometimes substituted for those of the turkey, for President Wheelock of Dartmouth College had a headpiece presented to him by an Indian, which had been worn by a Sagamore. This "would have graced the head of Wellington. It was covered with scarlet feathers, probably of the scarlet tanager, and in form not unlike a German cap, making an unique appearance." [103]

The fragments of cordage and other woven fabrics illustrated in figure 133 are also from a grave at Manchester. A piece of what was presumably a square flat bag of coarse bast is shown in a, such as was common among various woodland tribes of the Great Lakes region; b, and c, are of much finer material, probably Indian hemp (Apocynum cannabinum) or bast of the linden, slippery elm, or some other tree having fine inner bark. This twined weaving is widely distributed over both Americas, and is used in the production of nearly every kind of woven object from fish weirs to the finest cloth. It is a form of weaving which has never been duplicated by machinery, and the finer examples of cloth produced required an infinite amount of patience and skill in their making, the work being all done with the fingers.

There are several varieties of this twined weaving. The simplest form is shown in b. This may also have been a fragment of a small bag. In this example each warp cord is held in place by a single twist of the double woof strands. In c, there are two warp cords to each twist of the double woof strands which makes a much closer and warmer fabric. For this reason it seems probable that it may be a piece of a shoulder cape. Several fragments of tying cords were with the above specimens, f, having probably formed a part of the large bag, a.

A great variety of baskets and bags were made in ancient times, especially in southern New England, but very few examples of this early work have been preserved. The modern splint basketry commonly made by the Penobscot, Passamaquoddy, and some

[103] C. E. Potter, *History of Manchester, New Hampshire*, 1856, p. 47.

other tribes, and sold at summer resorts is a survival of the splint basketry of ancient times which was used largely in preparing corn foods. To meet the demands of White settlers these ancient forms were modified by the Indians many years ago, and in our great-grandmothers' days there were few families who did not possess covered storage baskets, and work and general utility baskets of many sizes and forms neatly made of splints and often ornamented with patterns painted or stamped in various colors. These stamps are said to have been cut from the potato after the

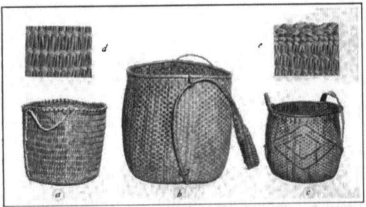

Figure 134. Carrying Baskets. a, Twined woven basket of bent grass, Gay Head Indians, Martha's Vineyard; d, e, enlargements showing weave of above basket; b, c, white oak splint baskets. The smaller one has a pleasing pattern in twilled weaving. Mashpee Indians, Cape Cod. Each of these baskets is furnished with a carrying-strap for the head or chest. Peabody Museum, Cambridge. (a, b, c, 1/13; d, e, 1/3.)

introduction of this tuber by the colonists, and were of many patterns. The making of commercial splint basketry has been an important industry among our surviving Indians for many years.

The process of preparing splints in the earlier days was as follows: small ash, white oak, or other suitable trees, were cut in the spring. The logs were sometimes soaked in water, although this was not always necessary. They were then peeled and beaten with wooden mauls until the annual growth layers were separated one from another. These were split into various widths and assorted, strips of uniform size being bound together in bunches or coils. Of the ancient forms of splint basketry we know but little. Gookin refers to basket sieves for sifting corn meal. These were in common use among agricultural tribes in general and were nearly square, about a foot in diameter, four or five inches deep, with flaring sides. The mesh which formed the bottom of the basket was woven in various degrees of coarseness for producing fine meal or the coarser hominy, etc. Hulling baskets were probably also in common use.

A knowledge of the great variety and excellence of the indigenous basketry of New England is gained principally from the accounts of early explorers and colonists. When the Pilgrims landed at Cape Cod one of their first acts was to open and rob an Indian cache of its winter supply of corn. They found therein a storage basket holding three or four bushels of shelled corn. It was round, with a narrow opening at the top, and was "handsomely and cunningly made." In one of the mat-covered wigwams they saw "baskets of sundry sorts, bigger and some lesser, finer and some coarser; some were cunningly wrought with black and white in pretty works." [104] When Captain Underhill returned from his memorable expedition against the Pequot Indians, he brought back many well woven mats and several "delightful" baskets. Winthrop lists among other articles stolen from a Nipmuc village during a raid by the Mohegans in 1646, "ten great hempen baskets." According to Gookin,[105] several sorts of baskets were made, both great and small. Some will hold four bushels or more, and so downward to a pint, some are made of rushes, some of bents (coarse grass), others of maize husks, others of a kind of silkgrass, others of a kind of wild hemp, and some of the barks of trees, many of them very neat and artificial with portraitures of birds, beasts, fishes, and flowers upon them in colors. Josselyn speaks of baskets, bags, and mats woven with sparke (spart? a plant of the broom kind, also a rush), bark of the lime tree, and rushes of several kinds, dyed as before, some black, blue, red, yellow, bags of porcupine quills woven and dyed also.[106] Wood writes, "In summer they gather . . . Hemp and Rushes, with dying stuffe of which they make curious baskets with intermixed colours and protractures of antique Imagerie; these baskets be of all sizes from a quart to a quarter." [107]

[104] *Journal of the Pilgrims at Plymouth*, Cheerer's reprint, pp. 34–39.
[105] Daniel Gookin, *Historical Collections*, Mass. Hist. Coll., 1st series (reprint 1859), vol. I, p. 151.
[106] John Josselyn, *Two Voyages to New England*, Veazie reprint, p. 111.
[107] William Wood, *New England's Prospect*, Boynton edition, p. 101.

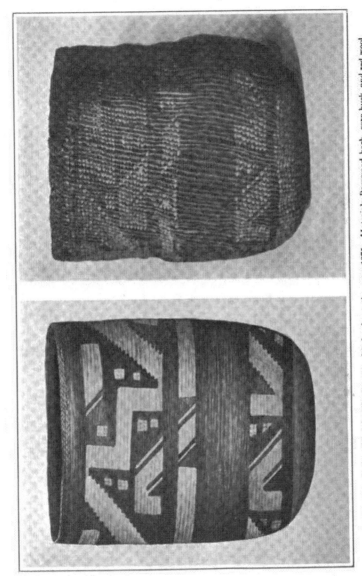

Figure 135. Narragansett Indian Basket. Made about the year 1675. Material: Basswood bark, corn husk, and red wool yarn, the latter destroyed by insects. The design, which is in corn husk, is shown in the drawing at the left. Rhode Island Historical Society, Providence. (About 3/4.)

251

It will be seen by the above quotations that these early writers were greatly impressed with the variety and excellence of the basketry of our more southern New England tribes; an excellence seemingly unequalled in any portion of eastern America.

The later splint basketry made by the Indians to supply the wants of their White neighbors, as we have already noted, had little in keeping with the earlier work, very few examples of which have come down to us. The two carrying baskets illustrated in figure 134, b, c, are of an ancient type and technique unmodified by White contact. They were used largely for gathering and transporting corn. The smaller basket was for collecting the ears in the field. It hung at the back, supported by the strap which passed across the chest. As the ears were gathered they were tossed over the shoulder into this receptacle. When filled it was emptied into the larger basket standing at the edge of the field for transportation to the wigwam. Of course this was but one of the many uses for which these baskets were fitted.

These two examples were made by the last surviving basket makers of the Mashpee Indian reservation of Barnstable County, Massachusetts, for their own use.

In figure 134, a, will be seen another carrying basket which is made of "bents," or coarse grass, in an ancient variety of twined weaving. It is the only example of this weave that I have seen from New England, although in ancient times it was not uncommon in the West.

This basket was obtained by the Peabody Museum at Cambridge from a Gay Head, Martha's Vineyard, Indian woman, and is said to have been made by Bashie Accouch in the early part of the nineteenth century.

Figure 135, shows a small basket with an interesting history. It was made, according to the old label which accompanies it, for a gift to Dinah Fenner, wife of Major Thomas Fenner, then (about 1675) living in a garrison in Providence, now Cranston, Rhode Island.

The squaw went into the garrison, Mrs. Fenner gave her some milk to drink, she went out by the side of a river, pulled the inner bark from the Wikup [Basswood] tree, sat down under the tree, drew the shreds out of her blanket, mingled them with the bark, wrought this little basket, took it to the garrison and presented it to Mrs. Fenner. Mrs. Fenner gave it to her daughter, Freelove, wife of Samuel Westcoat, Mrs. Westcoat gave it to her granddaughter, Wait Field, wife of William Field at Field's Point, Mrs. Field

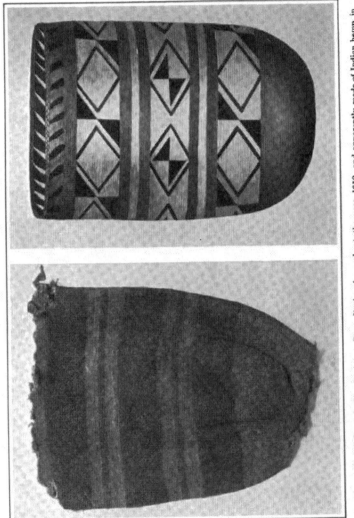

Figure 136. Mohegan Indian Basket or Bag. Dating from about the year 1650, and apparently made of Indian hemp, in twined weaving. The ornamental zones are in false embroidery, the material being porcupine quills in their natural light color or dyed a purplish black. The quills are much worn, but enough remain to show the complete design which is reproduced in the drawing at the right. Connecticut Historical Society, Hartford. (About 1/4.)

gave it to her daughter, Sarah. Sarah left it to her sister, Eleanor, who now presents it to the Historical Society of Rhode Island. Field's Point, September, 1842.

The basket has the appearance of having been made of such material as could be easily procured, and not of carefully selected substances such as would be brought together by the older basket makers. The vertical elements are of crudely prepared bast probably from the inner bark of the basswood tree, as stated in the label. The light colored design made by the horizontal woof is in corn husk, and the background was evidently made of red ravelings from a blanket, as also stated in the label, or of red woollen yarn which has been almost wholly destroyed by insects; only a few small shreds remain. The pattern which I have carefully worked out from the basket itself is shown at the left in the illustration.

The basket is twined woven and the designs in each of the decorated zones are produced not by false embroidery, as in figure 137, but by twined weaving alone. The light figures of a zone are formed by twining in the usual manner the two corn husk strands making up the woof cord. When a unit of the design is complete these husk strands are carried forward on the inner side of the basket to form the next light colored unit, as will be seen by a close inspection of the photograph. The wool strands making up the dark units of the design were doubtless manipulated in like manner, but as they have been destroyed by insects we cannot be sure.

The soft basket or bag represented in figure 136, is of great interest, illustrating as it does the finest type of native New England textile art. This was presented to the Connecticut Historical Society by William C. Gilman, who lived in Norwich and took great interest in the neighboring Mohegan people. The following is a copy of the record which accompanies it:

Yohicake Basket, a bag or basket as termed by the Mohegans. Received from Cynthia, now 60 or 70, and daughter of Lucy Tocamwap, the first member of the Mohegan church. By tradition of her own family Cynthia believes the basket to be near 200 years old. It has at any rate seen service. July 4, 1842. Presented by William C. Gilman.

It is apparently made of Indian hemp (Apocynum cannabinum) and is twined woven. There are sixteen or seventeen warp cords, and eighteen or nineteen double woof cords to the inch. There are three wide and two narrow zones in false embroidery wrought with porcupine quills in their natural white color or dyed a purplish black. This quill embroidery is very much worn but enough remains to clearly show the designs which are more apparent in the bag itself than in the photograph.

It will be noticed in the drawing at the right that the three wide zones thickly covered with quill embroidery showing black geometric figures on a white ground, also the two one-fourth-inch white zones between them appear much darker in the photograph. This is owing to the preservation of the original dark color of the fiber beneath the solid quill embroidery, which, being somewhat brittle, has largely disappeared through wear. Those portions of the bag not originally covered with embroidery have faded to a dull gray.

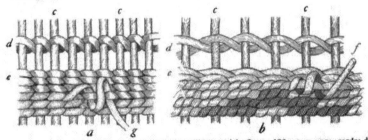

Figure 137. a, Method of weaving the bag illustrated in figure 136: c, c, warp cords; d, double woof cord; e, woof cords pressed close together; g, method of applying the porcupine quills. b, Technique of the weave of wallet shown in figure 138: c, c, warp cords; d, double woof cord; e, woof cords pressed close together; f, way of applying the moose hair which is wrapped three times around each twist of the woof strand instead of once as in the quill. g. (Enlarged.)

The upper edge of the bag originally terminated in about twenty-four projections somewhat less than an inch in length, one of which remains intact. From each of these, two or more warp-cords seem to have projected, all of which being braided together formed the upper rim of the receptacle. The openings thus produced were for the passage of a draw string. Similar openings are often present in bags from various sections of the country.

The method of weaving this bag is illustrated in figure 137, a; c, c, represent the warp cords; d, the manner of twisting the double woof cords, enclosing with each twist a single warp element; e, the woof cords pressed close together; g, the method of applying the porcupine embroidery. This was done while the woof strands were being added, and before they were tightly drawn, not after the body of the bag was finished.

In figure 138, we have an illustration of the highest development of the native textile industry which has been found among any of our eastern tribes. It is a two-fold pocket-book, of colonial form, unfolded, and the back or outer side only is shown. The side not illustrated is furnished with two pockets of green flannel. It is supplied with a silver hasp with the date, 1778 engraved upon it. The form of the pocket-book, the hasp, and the green flannel, are of course European. The heavy cloth forming the body of the book, the material of which it is made, the style of weaving and embroidery, and the colored designs are all purely native. The entire surface of the side shown is covered with an artistic native design embroidered with the long white hairs of the moose in their natural color, or dyed red, green, blue, or yellow.

This wallet was made by Mollocket, an old Indian woman of considerable local fame living in Oxford County, western Maine. She was one of the last of the Arosaguntacooks, a tribe claiming dominion over the Androscoggin Valley. It was given by her to Eli Twitchel of Bethel, Oxford County, about the year 1785. It is now in the collection of the Maine Historical Society, having been presented to that institution by Mrs. Lucia Kimball in 1863.

The technique of the weaving is shown in figure 137, b. The fiber of the cordage is apparently a very fine bast. The weaving is practically the same as in the bag last described. The warp cords are slightly farther apart, however, and moose hair used in the false embroidery is wrapped three times around each twist of the woof strand instead of once, as in the case of the coarser porcupine quill.

Martin Pring, who visited our coast in 1603, describes a quiver for holding arrows seen near Plymouth harbor in the following words:

Their Quivers are full a yard long made of long dried Rushes wrought about two handfuls broad above, and one handful beneath, with pretty workes and compartments, Diamant wise of read and other colours.[106]

Compartments as above used refers to the divisions of the colored decoration and not to divisions of the quiver itself. Diamant is the middle English form of diamond, and read is an obsolete form of red. In modern English the reading would be something like this: wrought . . . with pretty works in divided designs, diamond-wise, in red and other colors.

[106] G. P. Winship, editor, *Sailors' Narratives and Voyages along the New England Coast*, pp. 56, 57.

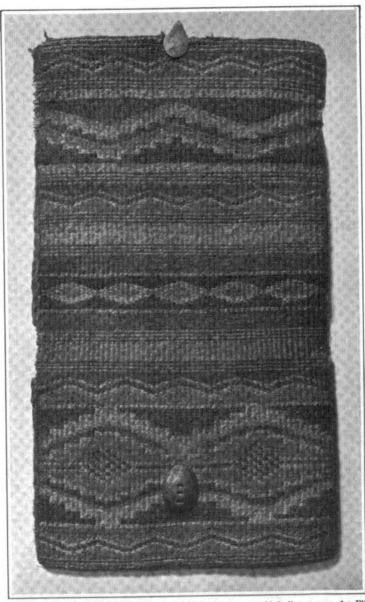

Figure 138. Twofold Pocket-book. Made by Mollocket, an old Indian woman, for Eli Twichel of Bethel, Oxford Co., Me., about the year 1785. Its form is European, but the methods of weaving, embroidering, and the colored decorative designs are strictly of Indian origin. Maine Historical Society, Portland. (3/5.)

If we omit the word red, this description would apply perfectly to the embroidered design on the bag illustrated in figure 136. We may be quite sure, therefore, that woven quivers of the form described by Pring were sometimes made and ornamented with artistic designs wrought with porcupine quills or possibly moose hair dyed in various colors, such as were used for decorating the beautiful bags or soft baskets made by our more southern New England tribes.

Figure 132, d, illustrates the technique of a fragment of a small bag in coiled netting. The mesh is shown enlarged in e. It was found with various other objects in Grave 10, at Winthrop, previously described. This is the only example that I have seen from New England. Two somewhat similar specimens were recovered from the Hopewell Mounds, Ohio. This form of netting is not uncommon in the Southwest, and recent examples occur among the northern Athapascans. It is a type widely distributed among primitive peoples in many parts of the world.

Bags of many sizes and of different weaves were doubtless in common use. Large bags or sacks were employed in storing corn in caches, as witnessed by Champlain. So far as I am aware no examples of New England nets for taking fish have come down to us.

Wooden Dishes. The proficiency attained in the making of certain wooden household utensils by the New England Indians is shown by the few ancient bowls, plates, and spoons that are occasionally found in old collections or which have been preserved as heirlooms in Indian families.

These old utensils are strictly of Indian origin and are not, as one might suppose, the result of copying similar objects in use among the colonists. The early settlers, however, were familiar with the serviceable wooden dishes of the Indians and adopted the same materials, including birdseye maple, and the burly portions of certain other woods, for bowls of their own make. Good examples of these may be seen in colonial museums.

In 1635, during the epidemic of smallpox among the Indians living near the Dutch trading station on the Connecticut River, being too ill to gather firewood, they kept themselves from freezing by burning "ye woden trays & dishes they ate their meals in."[109] Morton, writing of the Indians of eastern Massachusetts,

[109] Bradford. *History of Plymouth, Plantation.* Boston, 1879. p. 389.

says "They have dainty wooden bowls amongst them; and these are disposed by bartering one with the other and are but in certain parts of the country made, where the several trades are appro-

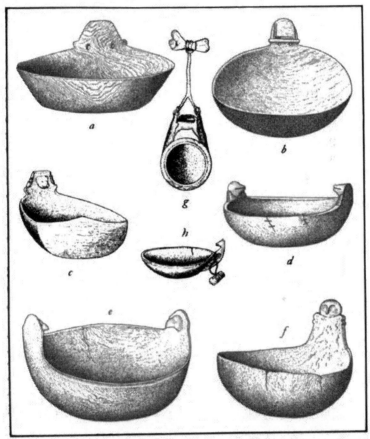

Figure 159. Wooden Bowls and Drinking Cups of the New England Indians. a, Wampanoag; b, c, d, Mohegan; e, probably Mohegan; f, Niantic; g, Abnaki, probably Penobscot; h, probably Nipmuc. (About 1/7.)

priated to the inhabitants of those parts only."[110] Josselyn refers to Indian "dishes, spoons and trayes wrought very smooth and neatly out of the knots of wood."[111] Gookin also writes of dishes,

[110] Thomas Morton, *New English Canaan,* Prince Soc. reprint, p. 159.
[111] John Josselyn, *Two Voyages to New England,* Veazie reprint, p. 111.

spoons, and ladles made "very smooth and artificial and of a sort of wood not subject to split."[112]

It should be remembered that before the arrival of Europeans these utensils were made with flint knives, scrapers, and stone adze blades supplemented by the use of fire, the artisan choosing the knotty or burly portions of maple, elm, pepperage, or other woods because such parts were not likely to split either in the making or during the use of the finished bowl. With the aid of charring and the above mentioned tools the shaping could be completed with less difficulty than one would suppose. Similar utensils were made by the Iroquois, some of the Siouan tribes, and several of the Algonquian groups beyond the borders of New England. Only a few old dishes of the New England tribes have come down to us and most of them are, fortunately, now in our larger museums where their preservation is likely to be permanent.

The utensils consisted of spoons, ladles, plates, and bowls, all of excellent workmanship. The ladle was of the same general form as used by the Iroquois and some of the more western Algonquians. Its bowl was relatively deep and the handle rose quite abruptly from its rim. I have seen but a few fragments from New England graves, but enough to indicate the original form.

The handles of spoons were sometimes quite elaborately carved with openwork or other ornamental figures, but those that I have examined have been broken and some of the parts were missing, and the complete designs could not be accurately restored.

But few plates are in existence. A good example, eleven inches in diameter, is in the Peabody Museum at Cambridge. This was obtained from the Passamaquoddy Indians, and is made of the burly portion of what appears to be elm wood. It is slightly more concave than the majority of the plates which are still to be found among the Micmac of Nova Scotia where they were until recently not uncommon, having been preserved, like the Passamaquoddy example, by use as an accessory in the well known Indian dice game. In 1585–8, John White pictured a plate of similar form nearly two feet in diameter used in serving food by the Virginia Indians.

In figure 139 are illustrated several of the finest examples extant of the ancient bowls and drinking cups of our New England

[112] Daniel Gookin, *Historical Collections*, Mass. Hist. Coll. 1st series, reprint of 1859, vol. 1, p. 151.

tribes. A very old bowl of Wampanoag origin is shown in a. It was for many years in possession of a family near Plymouth. It measures fourteen and one fourth inches across the rim and is made of elm wood. The handle, or projection rising from the rim, seems to be a conventionalized representation of the head of an animal. The two perforations for the eyes probably served for the passage of a suspending cord. This specimen has long been known as "King Philip's samp bowl." Presented to the Massachusetts Historical Society late in 1803, it was used for many years in balloting with corn and beans for members. At the quarterly meeting of January, 1804, it was voted "That the Committee of Publication . . . be requested to cause an inscription to be put on King Philip's Bowl, and to procure an affidavit ascertaining its authenticity." [113] The following is a copy of the inscription appearing upon its inner side:

> A Trophy from the Wigwam of King Philip when he was slain in 1676 by Richard. Presented by Elez' Richard his Grandson.

The following memorandum seems to be the only document relating to its authenticity that the Committee was able to secure.

> Plymouth Sept. 14, 1803. Received of Isaac Lothrop, eight dollars in full for a wooden bowl formerly belonging to that illustrious soldier known by the name of King Philip, son of the celebrated Indian Sachem, Massasoit, and was a portion of the trophy assigned to Eleazer Richard, great grandfather of the subscriber, who made one of the party that terminated the existence of the once princely proprietor
>
> his
Eleazer x Richard
mark

Isaac Lothrop was Register of Probate for the county of Plymouth and a member of the Massachusetts Historical Society. The bowl was evidently presented to the Society by him in the name of Eleazer Richard, from whom he purchased it. In the list of donations prepared for the quarterly meeting of Oct. 3, 1804, appears the entry: "The bowl of Sachem Philip from a friend."

In the Dexter Edition of Church's History of King Philip's War [114] is the following note relating to this bowl:

[113] Mass. Hist. Soc. Proceedings. Vol. 1, p. 163.
[114] Part 1, p. 153.

Church's narrative furnishes no evidence, either way, in regard to the genuineness of this relic. I find, however, no trace, either in Savage's fertile pages, or the Colony Records of Plymouth, Massachusetts, or Rhode Island of any Eleazer Richard (or Richards or Richardson) as then living in New England, nor any evidence that any person of that surname served under Church in that campaign.

Philip was slain by the deserting Wampanoag Indian who guided Church's party at night to the temporary camp of Philip. The bowl is doubtless of Wampanoag origin and it may have been brought with other booty from Philip's village on a previous expedition, for it was the custom of the English to pillage on such occasions. It is doubtful, however, if it was ever the personal property of that chief. In 1927 this bowl was transferred to the Peabody Museum at Cambridge.

A somewhat similar bowl shown in b, of the above figure was, in 1908, the property of Mrs. Emma Baker, a woman of Mohegan blood, and it descended to her from Lucy Tantaquidgeon, a sister of the noted Mohegan minister and missionary Samson Occom (1723–1792). The writer is indebted to William C. Gilman, Esq. for its history, and the photograph from which the drawing was made. The bowl is nearly circular, about eleven inches in diameter and four inches deep. The worn condition of the handle indicates long use. This handle seems to have been originally somewhat wider and decorated with lines and notches as in that of c. At a period apparently later than the date of its making its inner face was inlaid with two rows of white wampum joined at right angles. Six of the beads are missing. This is the letter L, the initial of Lucy, the sister of Occom and an early owner of the bowl.

There is a Pequot or Mohegan bowl in New London which has a zone of wampum inlay below the rim upon the outer side.

In the Memorial Museum at Deerfield is a fine old bowl of Indian make similar to the two above described, which came into the possession of the family of one of the early settlers many years ago. Like most bowls of Indian origin the walls are quite thin, but the bowl itself is somewhat less symmetrical than is usual. The single side handle is a characteristic of certain forms of these old utensils.

About the year 1850 John W. De Forest saw in the possession of a woman living near the Mohegan cemetery at Norwich, Connecticut, two bowls carved from pepperage knots, each holding about three pints, and said to have once been the property of the great Uncas. One of these was circular and had a handle like the head of an owl; the other was oblong and had two handles like the heads of dogs, facing each other.[115] Through correspondence I was able to locate two bowls answering the description of the second specimen described by De Forest, both being known as Uncas bowls.

The first is illustrated in d, and is the property of Miss Emily S. Gilman, to whom it descended as a family heirloom. Her Coit ancestors from whom she received it had lived in the Pequot-Mohegan region since 1650. Nothing further is known of its history. It is skilfully made from a knotty piece of hard wood, is ten and seven eighths inches long, and eight and one fourth inches wide, and has the appearance of great age. The somewhat conventionalized head rising from either end is well executed; the mouth is shown but the eyes are not indicated.

The second specimen, much like the first, is in the Slater Memorial Museum at Norwich. The heads forming the handles are much like the ones shown in d.

The bowl appearing in c, is also in the Slater Museum. It is said to have been taken from a grave near Norwich many years ago. It has a somewhat weathered appearance probably caused by exposure to the weather for a few months. It is made of a burly piece of hard wood and is accompanied by a metal spoon of a type common in the colonies during the seventeenth century.

An unusually fine Indian bowl is illustrated in e, which is in the King Philip Museum at Bristol, Rhode Island. It is recorded as having been obtained from the vicinity of Congammond Ponds, Southwick, Massachusetts. These lakes form the boundary between Massachusetts and Connecticut at a point some eighteen miles northerly from Hartford. I have been unable to learn more of the history of this excellent piece of Indian work. Effigy heads of a turtle or bird ornament the handles.

There is a fine old Niantic bowl, f, in the Peabody Museum at New Haven. Its record is as follows:

This succotash dish belonged to the queen of the Niantick Indians, Annie Walkheed. It is nearly 200 years old. Obtained in Niantick a few days ago. Cochester, May 3, 1868. Charles M. Taintor.

This may have been the circular bowl with handle like the head of an owl which is recorded by De Forest.

[115] De Forest, *History of the Indians of Connecticut*, p. 13.

I do not know to what extent the personal drinking cup furnished with a cord or thong and a toggle for suspension from the belt, was used by our New England tribes. Two excellent examples, however, have come down to us. These are illustrated in g, and h. The latter is in the cabinet of the Worcester Historical Society and I am indebted to its executive director, Mr. V. Waldo Cutler for the photograph from which the drawing was made and its history which I quote:

Drinking Cup made of cherry wood by the last of the Grafton Indians, and given by him to John Milton Earle of Worcester, Indian Commissioner for Massachusetts, about 1840. Commissioner Earle was grandfather to the donor, Miss Southwick.

The other cup, g, is skilfully carved from birdseye maple. On the handle are cut in relief four deer, two bucks and two does, the bucks appearing on the front and back, and the two does upon the sides. There are also two does and a bull moose in low relief on the bowl of the cup just below the rim. The back of the cup is covered with an intricate design in incised lines of which the typical double curve and trifoliate figures form parts. The cup was suspended from the belt by a thong, and the leg bone of a turtle used as a toggle. This cup was obtained by the writer from a private collection in New York. No data accompanied it, but it is probably the work of a Penobscot Indian. It is now in the Peabody Museum at Cambridge.

Shell Beads. With a few exceptions the shell beads from the graves of this section belong to the later Algonquian group. The seashore of New England, especially that portion south of Cape Cod, is well supplied with shells of various kinds which are suitable for the production of nearly all types of shell beads found in this region.

The oldest New England beads of this material of which we have knowledge were obtained from graves of the old Algonquian group and were usually accompanied by beads of native copper, and a few Marginella shells. Good examples are shown natural size in figures 61, and 140, j, k, l. They are probably made from the columellæ of *Fulgur carica*, the largest univalve of the north Atlantic. This is abundant south of Cape Cod but generally does not reach its maximum growth north of New Jersey, and some of the largest beads like figure 61, b, may have been made of shells from this more southern region. Other beads of this type were made of the columellæ of *Fulgur canaliculata* which is also common south of Cape Cod. This species, however, does not attain quite as large a size as the former. The medium and smaller tubular beads of this type may have been produced from either of the above species, or occasionally from some of the smaller "periwinkles," a term loosely applied to Fulgur shells and also to some other species of New England univalves. It should be noted that in all of the beads illustrated which show a portion of the spiral canal, the whorl is dextral like that of the two species above mentioned. *Fulgur perversa*, a Floridian shell, with a sinistral whorl, is not found in the North.

The above forms of tubular shell beads of various sizes were used down to historic times but appear not to have been very common in prehistoric days. A considerable number, however, have been taken from graves of the early historic period which have been accompanied by tubular beads of European copper or brass, or other objects obtained from Whites. Figure 140, m, n, are from a grave of the historic period at Vassalboro, Maine. With them were several beads of European sheet copper.

One hundred forty-six of this type, averaging one half inch in length which were taken from one of the graves at Winthrop, across the harbor from Boston, may be seen in the Peabody Museum at Cambridge. They were accompanied by sixty-six glass beads, white, blue, and black in color, of about the same size as those of shell.

The columella type of beads varied in length from about three sixteenths of an inch to about two inches. The older examples were usually large. In later days the smaller sizes were more common and the earlier white trade wampum was sometimes made from small columellæ. A good example taken from a string of about sixty from a grave at Saugus, Massachusetts, is shown in g.

After the introduction of commercial wampum at Plymouth by the Dutch and the development of the industry of its making by the tribes of southern New England, especially the Narragansets and Pequots, the white as well as the purple variety seems to have been made almost wholly from shells of the quahog or hardshell clam, *Venus mercenaria*. The principal part of the shell of this bivalve is white, but a portion of it, ranging from light purple through various shades to nearly black, was used for making the colored beads, which had a commercial value double that of the white. Certain shellheaps which I have examined on the southern shore of Cape Cod consist almost wholly of discarded fragments of this shell thrown aside while procuring suitable pieces for making these beads. This indicates that the Wampanoag or the Nauset also made wampum. While the term wampum, or wampumpeage was usually applied by the New England tribes to the white beads, and suckauhock, mowhackees or mohacheis to the purple variety, both types were generally known to the English as wampum.

In h, i, are shown examples of standard commercial wampum of Indian make. These were ground into shape on stones, and perforated with sharpened nails or steel awls obtained from traders. The beads vary slightly in size and are usually somewhat unsymmetrical as one would expect when worked out by hand.

A section of a Penobscot Indian arm band cut from an old wampum belt is illustrated in q, showing white figures on a purple ground. The diagrammatic drawing, r, explains the method of weaving. This is the usual technique of belts, collars, garters, and other objects made of wampum.

The cordage in this instance is of native fiber, probably Indian hemp (*Apocynum cannabinum*), although sinew is sometimes employed. Narrow strips of buckskin are frequently used for separating the rows of beads instead of twisted cord, as in the example illustrated.

Long Island seems to have been the original home of purple wampum, and it was probably here that the Dutch obtained their first supply. We do not know how early this was. Their first trading expedition to the Hudson River occurred in 1610. By 1628 they had a lucrative trade established at Aurania, now Albany, where they received furs in exchange for these beads.

Wampum was not known to the English until introduced by the Dutch in 1628. During this year Secretary Rasier and his party visited Plymouth and induced the English to purchase 50" worth of these beads, telling them of their trade value among the tribes of the Hudson River and suggesting that they would find them of equal value in trading with the Indians of the Kennebec, where the Plymouth colony had received a grant of land and established a trading house. It was two years before this small amount was disposed of. The demands for it, however, steadily increased and the English could with difficulty get enough to supply their needs. The following account of this transaction and its important bearing upon the future trade relations with the New England tribes is quoted from Governor Bradford's report for the year 1628.

This year the Dutch sent againe unto them [the English] from their plantation both kind leterss, and also diverse comodites, as sugar, linen cloth, Holland finer & courser stufes, &c. . . . But that which turned most to their profite, in time, was an entrance into the trade of Wampampeake; for they

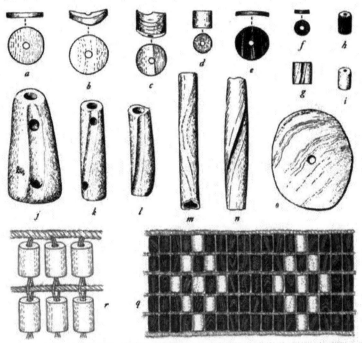

Figure 140. Shell Beads. All from graves excepting h, i, q, r. a, b, Waterville, Me.; c; Bridgewater, Mass.; d, Atlantic, Mass.; e, f, Revere, Mass.; g, Saugus, Mass.; h, i, typical wampum beads, white and purple; j, k, l, Highgate, Vt., old Algonquian; m, n, Vassalboro, Me., o, Deerfield, Mass.; q, section of Penobscot Indian wampum belt; r, diagrammatic sketch showing construction of wampum belt. (1/1, except r.)

now bought aboute 50ˢ worth of it of them; and they tould them how vendable it was at their forte Orania [Albany]; and did perswade them they would find it so at Kenebeck; and so it came to pass in time, though at first it stuck, & it was 2. years before they could put of this small quantity, till ye inland people knew of it; and afterwards they could scarce ever gett enough for them, for many years together. . . . And strange it was to see the great allteration it made in a few years amonge ye Indeans them selves; for all the Indeans of these parts, [the Wampanoag] & ye Massachusets, had none or very litle of it, but ye sachems & some spetiall persons that wore a litle of it for ornamente. Only it was made & kepte amonge ye Nariganssets, & Pequents, which grew rich & potent by it, and these people [the Wampanoag and Massachusetts] were poore and begerly, and had no use for it. Neither did the English of this plantation or any other in the land, till now that they had knowledg of it from ye Dutch so much as know what it was, much less yt it was a comoditie of that worth & valew. But after it grue thus to be a comoditie in these parts, these Indeans fell into it allso and to learne how to make it; for ye Narigansets doe gather ye shells of which y^{ey} make it from their shors. And it hath now continued a current comoditie about this 20. years. . . . In ye mean time it makes ye Indeans of these parts rich and powerful and also prowd thereby.

The above was written about the year 1647. In Governor Winthrop's Journal under the date of October 2, 1633, are the following entries:

The bark *Blessing* which was sent to the southward returned. She had been at an island over against Connecticut called Long Island . . . there they had a store of the best wampampeage both white and blue. The Indians there are very treacherous people. They have many canoes so great that one will carry eighty men.

There seems to have been direct communication between the Indians of Long Island and their kindred in Rhode Island and Connecticut. On July 9, 1634, it is noted that when the Plymouth magistrates came to Boston to consult about the Kennebec country, they had "drawn down thither the greatest part of the trade by carrying wampampeage thither which none of the English had known the use of before."

On August 12 Winthrop again writes: "Our neighbors at Plymouth had great trade this year at Kennebec so as Mr. Winslow carried with him to England, this year, about 20 hogsheads of beaver, the greatest part whereof was traded for wampampeage."

The readiness with which wampum could be woven into striking personal ornaments with white figures on a purple ground or vice versa, was largely responsible for its great popularity among the natives. It is of interest to note that some of the finest examples of woven wampum from New England in our collections have been obtained in recent years from the Penobscot and other Maine Indians, by whom it has been preserved through several generations.

Writing of wampum as late as 1723 from his mission at Norridgewock on the Kennebec, Father Rasle says:

It is with these beads that our Indians bind up and plait their hair on their ears and behind. They make of them pendants for their ears, collars, garters, large sashes five or six inches in breadth, and on this kind of ornament they pride themselves much more than a European would on all his gold and silver.

Rasle also says that the black and white beads were strung together in such a way as to represent different showy figures with great exactness. Most of the wampum used in this section seems to have been made by the Narragansets, Pequots, and some other tribes of southern New England, although some was brought from Long Island. As good quahog shells became scarce in Rhode Island the Narragansets imported them from Long Island.

An idea of the great amount of these beads made by these Indians and their neighbors may be gathered from the following: In a treaty made with the Narragansets in 1645 they agreed to pay the English 2000 fathoms of good white wampum as a remuneration for the trouble they had caused them and their Mohegan allies. In 1647 the commissioners received 200 fathoms, by 1649, 1100 fathoms had been paid. In all 1529½ fathoms were finally credited, although a portion of this was in other goods. Assuming that 1000 fathoms were actually received, which seems a moderate estimate, and reckoning eight white beads to a penny or four hundred eighty to the fathom, its current value at that time, we have a total of 480,000 beads, a large number when we consider that each one had to be shaped, polished, and drilled by hand. Tribute was collected by the English from certain tribes over a period of many years on account of their murders, wars, and so forth. It had been due from the Pequots since 1638. In 1651 they paid 312 fathoms. They were then told that henceforth the children born to them should be exempt, and that all tribute should end in ten years.

Spurious wampum, such as was made of quahog shells by the Dutch and Swedes for Indian trade does not seem to have been made in New England, at least to any great extent, but more or less of it was imported and the Connecticut colonies were obliged to pass laws prohibiting its use as currency. Examples of these spurious beads may be seen in most large collections; they may be readily recognized, however, by their symmetry and uniformity, whereas those of Indian make are usually more irregular and are obviously worked out by hand.

Roger Williams came to Massachusetts in 1631. In 1636 he went to Providence. In 1643 he sailed for England as agent for that colony. During this voyage he composed his *Key into the Language of America*, which was printed soon after his arrival in England. The following excellent account of wampum and its use is taken from Chapter XXIV of this work.

The Indians are ignorant of Europes Coyne. . . . Their owne is of two sorts; one white, which they make of the stem or stocke of the Periwincle, . . . and of this sort six of their small Beads (which they make with holes to string the bracelets) are currant with the English for a Peny. The second is black, inclining to blew, which is made of the shell of a fish, which some English call Hens, Poquaûhock [quahog], and of this sort three make an English peny. They that live upon the Sea side generally make of it, and as many make as will. The Indians bring downe all their sorts of Furs, which they take in the countrey, both to the Indians and to the English for this Indian Money: this Money the English, French and Dutch, trade to the Indians, six hundred miles in severall parts (North and South from New-England) for their Furres and whatsoever they stand in need of from them. . . . Puickquat, 10 six pences. This Piûckquat being sixtie pence, they call Nquittómpeg, or Nquitnishcaûsu, that is, one fathom, 5 shillings. This one fathom of this their stringed money, now worth of the English but five shillings (sometimes more) some few yeeres since was worth nine, and sometimes ten shillings per Fathome: the fall is occasioned by the fall of Beaver in England. . . . Their white they call Wompam (which signifies white): their black Suck-auhock (Sácki signifying blacke). Both amongst themselves, as also the English and Dutch, the blacke peny is two pence white; the blacke fathom double, or, two fathom of white. . . . They hang these strings of money about their necks and wrists; as also upon the necks and wrists of their wives and children. Máchequoce, a Girdle; which they make curiously of one, two, three, foure and five inches thicknesse and more, of this money which (sometimes to the value of ten pounds or more) they weare about their middle and as a scarfe about their shoulders and breasts. Yea, the Princes make rich Caps and Aprons (or small breeches) of these Beads thus curiously strung into many forms and figures: their blacke and white finely mixt together.

Purple or "black" beads had an established value double that of the white. At the time the above was written the current value of white beads was six for a penny and purple beads three for a penny. By 1648 the value had diminished and during this year Massachusetts ordered that wampum should be legal tender to the amount of 40 shillings. White was to be eight for a penny and purple four. The measure of wampum was usually by the fathom. When strung, the average wampum beads number about five to the inch, sixty to the foot, and three hundred and sixty, to six feet or a fathom.

In Williams's time a fathom of wampum was reckoned by *count*, not by measure. He says six white beads were equal in value to a penny, thirty-six beads would therefore be worth a sixpence, and three hundred sixty white beads, or a fathom, would equal in value ten sixpences, or five shillings. These three hundred sixty beads if strung might exceed or fall short of a measured fathom.

As purple wampum had twice the value of white, a fathom of this would seem to have consisted of one hundred eighty beads, which if strung would be but half of a measured fathom but its value would also be five shillings. According to this system, after 1648, a fathom would consist of four hundred eighty white beads or two hundred forty purple beads. The money value of the fathom remained the same (five shillings) but the number of beads and its measured length were much increased.

The gradual decadence of the use of wampum as currency in New England took place not long preceding the period of King Philip's War. In New England, besides its use as currency, wampum was woven into caps, aprons, garters, belts, collars, neck ornaments, and so forth. It was also occasionally used for inlay in bowls and other objects of wood. Mrs. Rawlinson describing a dance in which Weetamoo the distinguished Squaw Sachem took part, says she wore a "kersey coat covered with girdles of wampum from the loins upward, her arms from her elbows to her hands were covered with bracelets; there were handfuls of necklaces about her neck."

One of King Philip's belts, curiously wrought with "black and white wampum in various figures and flowers and pictures of many birds and beasts" was nine inches broad and when hung about Captain Church's shoulders reached to his ankles. Philip had two other belts, one with two flags upon the back which hung from his head, the other with a star upon the end which hung from his breast. When Philip visited Boston he wore a coat and leggings, set with wampum "in pleasant wild works" and a broad belt of the same.

The symbolic use of wampum seems to have been far less prevalent in New England than among the Iroquoian tribes, among whom it continued in vogue many years after its practical disappearance in this region.

Discoidal beads both white and purple similar to those illustrated in a-f, of figure 140, are not uncommon in the later Algonquian graves of New England, and occasionally they occur in considerable numbers. Both kinds vary in diameter from about three sixteenths to about seven sixteenths of an inch. It is difficult to determine the species of shell from which these white beads were made but it is probable that the quahog and the larger "periwinkles" were used.

The purple discoidal beads, e, f, were made from the common mussel shell, and while the white beads are generally much more numerous in a given burial, a few purple beads often accompany them.

Discoidal beads are often found associated with objects of European origin and this type may be considered as belonging principally to the early historic period. Champlain saw shell beads used in embroidery and also as ornaments for the hair. On the arms of the skeleton of a child in a grave opened by the pilgrims at Cape Cod were bracelets of small shell beads. We are not told whether these were of the tubular or discoidal variety.

In the Peabody Museum at Cambridge is an unusually fine necklace of about nine hundred white and purple beads, each about three sixteenths of an inch in diameter. The purple beads are of mussel shell. This was found with a skeleton at Atlantic, near Boston. The white beads are thicker than the purple, and in a few instances their thickness equals their diameter. Figure 140, d, is an example. The two varieties were strung alternately. A noticeable peculiarity is the uniformity of their diameters. It was a custom among the Dutch and Swedes to make wampum for Indian trade. Much was produced in private families and workshops were established in a few communities. The shells were broken into suitable pieces, drilled, and strung on wires, which were hung from a framework above a grindstone having several grooves cut in its face or periphery. These strings of roughly shaped beads were then held against the grooves of the revolving stone till the edges of the shell were ground smooth and the beads became symmetrical and uniform in size.

It is very apparent that the beads of this necklace were the product of a similar manipulation. A wooden pendant in the form of a bird's head was found with the necklace. Two beads were inlaid for eyes and its surface was ornamented with checker work, each alternate square being produced by laying parallel to each other and a short distance apart, several pieces of brass wire about half an inch in length with their ends bent at right angles and pressed into the wood, the presence of copper in the brass acting as a preservative for the wood.

Figure 140, a, b, shows two typical beads selected from a group of about five hundred from a grave on the west side of the Kennebec River at Waterville. While the diameter of the beads varies considerably, their peripheries, like most of our discoidal beads, are very regular. They are probably a mixture from several original lots. Only three beads of mussel shell were found with them.

In c, we have a more massive and less common form, from a grave at Bridgewater, Massachusetts, apparently made from the columella of a large periwinkle. This type also is usually accompanied by a few purple beads of mussel shell.

In the archæological museum at Andover are upwards of five thousand white discoidal beads approximately one fourth of an inch in diameter, and a very few massive tubular beads, all of which came from a grave in the small cemetery at Sandy Point, five miles below Bucksport on the Penobscot River. Similar small beads were found here with three other skeletons. Various graves in this burial place contained objects of European origin. A large iron kettle had been placed over the head in two burials. An iron axe, a sheet copper head-band, tubular beads of sheet copper, and also a few white discoidal shell beads strung alternately with purple beads of mussel shell were found in the grave of a child.

A grave was opened on the home lot of Mr. George Sheldon at Old Deerfield some years ago which contained a few discoidal shell beads, one of which is illustrated in o, of the above figure. These are unusually large, and are undoubtedly of Indian make, although probably not very old. In this grave were also found several typical white wampum beads, six fairly large polychrome glass beads, red, blue, and white in color, a few small globular glass beads and the pottery vessel illustrated in figure 116, b.

From the foregoing study of New England shell beads the following deductions seem permissible: 1st, there seems to be no evidence of their occurrence in this region in pre-Algonquian days; 2nd, the tubular variety made from the columellæ of large univalve shells was used sparingly by the old Algonquians, presumably by shamans or other persons of note; 3rd, They occurred more commonly among the later Algonquians, especially the smaller sizes, which were probably the forerunners of the form known as wampum; 4th, The purple (quahog shell) and white wampum industry among the tribes of southern New England during the second quarter of the seventeenth century was doubtless adopted from the natives of Lond Island, where the traffic had been stimulated through Dutch contact; 5th, The production of purple (mussel shell) and white discoidal beads was greatly stimulated by English traders. In colonial days these seem to have been made at least partially by appliances of European origin, and probably large numbers were produced by the Whites for trade purposes. It is not improbable that a few discoidal shell beads, both purple and white, were made by our New England tribes in prehistoric days, but I have seen no examples which may be definitely assigned to that period.

But few of the large, thin, discoidal beads called runtees have been found in New England, although quite common in New York State. They are usually about one and one half inches in diameter and have two parallel perforations about one fourth of an inch apart running from edge to edge, which serve to keep the beads on the same plane when strung. One side of the bead is usually ornamented with a cross, star, or concentric circles often made up of small circles with a central dot. They were probably made by Europeans for Indian trade. According to Beauchamp (Bulletin of the New York State Museum No. 41) they were first used late in the seventeenth century and were mostly dispersed when silver ornaments came into fashion.

European glass beads were obtained by our Indians at an early date. Verarzanus, who visited New England in 1524, says the objects which the natives esteemed most highly "of all those which we gave them were bells, crystals of azure color and other toys to hang in their ears and about their necks." There can be no doubt that the fishermen and traders of the latter half of the sixteenth, and the first quarter of the seventeenth centuries furnished the natives with many glass beads of various shapes and colors in exchange for furs. Governor Bradford speaks of the store of English beads brought to Plymouth in 1622 by Captain Jons "which were then good trade."

The importance of glass beads as a medium of exchange with the Virginia tribes is shown by the following:

In 1620 a subscription list was started in Jamestown to erect a factory for the manufacture of beads for trade with the Indians, and in 1621 the London company sent Italian workmen to make them. This plant, which was situated some distance from Jamestown, escaped the massacre of 1622, and is heard of as late as 1623.[116]

A few years ago a cache of glass beads was unearthed near Leedstown, about sixty miles north of Jamestown. I was fortunate in securing about a hundred for the museum at Cambridge. These consisted mostly of the polychrome variety about one-fourth inch in diameter, with blue and white stripes in groups of three on a red ground. There were also monochrome tubular beads, red, white, and gray, about one half inch long, and several more or less oval semi-translucent whitish beads a half inch or more in diameter, and quite crudely fashioned. It is very probable that the beads in this cache were made at the Jamestown factory. There is in the Peabody Museum at Cambridge one of the crude semi translucent beads like those above mentioned from a grave at Gardiner, Maine, which may well have been procured through Plymouth traders whose Kennebec grant included the present site of that town. It was the custom of the English trading vessels to call at New England on their way to and from Virginia.

Many glass beads have been found in New England graves. Among the oldest of these may be mentioned an oval or lenticular form about three eighths of an inch or less in length, having the appearance of white porcelain. These are usually accompanied by a much lesser number of the same shape in dark blue or black. They are found throughout most of the coastal region and were probably obtained from fishing and trading vessels. Sometimes occurring with them are blue or white globular beads of relatively the same diameter (about one eighth of an inch) and occasionally also a few small tubular beads.

Tubular monochrome beads of glass about one half inch in length and varying from one sixteenth to three sixteenths of an inch in diameter, in white, blue, and black, are not uncommon. Other varieties are found with burials, including blue and white oval and globular forms about one eighth to one fourth inch in diameter, also the simpler types of polychrome beads, but these are not common. The well known embroidery beads used in such numbers by the tribes of the West during the century just passed seem to have been practically unknown in this region in early historic times. Only a very few of the larger sizes have been found.

[116] N. Hudson Moore. *Old Glass*, pp. 209, 210.

General Culture of the Historic New England Tribes. The historic Indians of New England may be divided into two cultural groups by a line running from a point just south of Cape Ann. The general culture of the northern and eastern group, comprising the Abnaki and Pennacook confederacies, (see Figure 141), was similar in many respects to that of their kindred of the eastern British provinces, while the culture of the southern group had more in common with that of the coast Algonquians of the more southern states. There were many cultural resemblances, however, between these two groups, and both belonged to the great Algonquian family. The dialects of New England are grouped as follows by Swanton and Michelson: The Abnaki and Pennacook are classed with the Cree, Montagnais, and Micmac of Canada. The Massachuset, Wampanoag, Narraganset, and Nipmuc, together with the Montauk of Long Island, form a group by themselves. The Pequot, Wappinger and Mahican, are classed with the tribes of southeastern New York, New Jersey, Delaware, and eastern Pennsylvania.

The Abnaki division, which occupied the greater part of Maine, was composed of a loose confederacy of tribes united for offensive and defensive purposes. They formed an early attachment for the French, and largely through the influence of the French priests carried on an almost constant war with the English colonists. The records are insufficient to define accurately the political and social organization of all the New England divisions, but it is known of various Abnaki tribes that each had its war chief, and also its civil chief, whose duty was to preserve order and give advice. The grand council consisted of the chiefs and two men from each family, who determined for the tribe matters of importance, and pronounced sentence of death on those deserving capital punishment. The general council, consisting of both men and women of the tribe, decided questions relating to war. Descent seems to have been reckoned through the male line.

The southern cultural group comprised several tribes and confederacies. The more important were the Massachuset, Wampanoag, Narraganset, Nipmuc, Pequot, Niantic, Wappinger, and the Mahican, including the Mohegan. Their distribution is shown on the map. But little is known of the Connecticut River tribes of Massachusetts and Northern Connecticut. They were considerably reduced in number through an epidemic of smallpox in 1635.

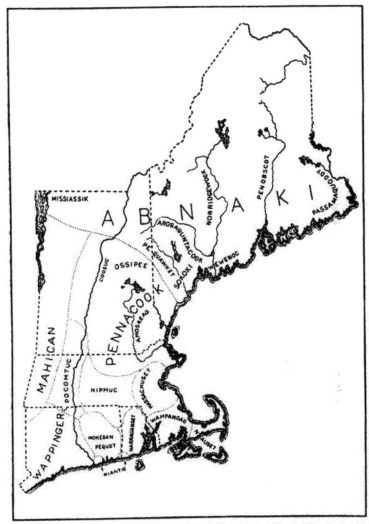

Figure 141. Map showing distribution of the principal Indian Tribes in New England in the Seventeenth Century.

With few exceptions the divisions of the southern group are generally considered independent tribes. The Nipmuc had lost their tribal independence and certain of their villages were tributary to the Narraganset, Massachuset, or Pennacook. The Nauset was probably a subtribe of the Wampanoag. The Mattabesec of western Connecticut belonged to the Wappinger confederacy.

The government of probably most of the divisions of the southern group was vested in a head chief called Sachem, and in one or more bodies of councillors or advisers. The office of sachem was in general hereditary, and if male heirs were wanting, it descended upon a female. The subchiefs were commonly known among the colonists as sagamores. In most of the southern tribes descent was probably reckoned through the female line instead of through the male line, as among the Abnaki.

The unit of tribal organization was the family. In New England, one wife seems to have been the rule, although two or more were allowed chiefs and men of wealth and distinction.

A clan or gens was a consanguineous division of a tribe, and consisted of a number of families joined by ties of blood and adoption, its head being a subchief whose duty was principally to counsel and advise his followers. If descent was reckoned through the female line, such a division was called a clan; if through the male line, a gens.

A band was a group of families of a given tribe brought together by conditions more or less temporary. Such a band often formed a village which may or may not have been composed of a specified clan group.

A tribe formed a political and territorial group, and was commonly composed of several clans or gentes, organized politically for the commonweal of its members, who occupied a given territory, and were ruled by a sachem or head chief. Although the tribe frequently constituted an independent state, it sometimes formed an alliance with a neighboring tribe or tribes against a common enemy. Such an alliance, of greater or less permanency, formed a confederacy.

The present writer has made a somewhat extended investigation of the probable number of Indians occupying New England at about the beginning of the seventeenth century. These data would be out of place here. It is sufficient to say that there seem to have been about twenty-four thousand in all. The most densely populated sections were eastern Massachusetts, Rhode Island, and Connecticut. There seem to have been but few Indians in Vermont at that time. Western Massachusetts, northern New Hampshire, and the greater part of Maine were sparsely inhabited compared with the more southern sections. The pestilence which spread through the tribes of eastern Massachusetts in 1616–17 materially reduced the numbers of the Pennacook, Massachuset, and Wampanoag, and enabled the English to secure a foothold.

John Verarzanus, the Florentine explorer, arrived on the New England coast in 1524. He spent fifteen days either in Buzzard's Bay, Narragansett Bay, or Boston Harbor, and was much interested in the natives with whom he came in contact. He writes:

There were amongst these people 2 kings, of so goodly stature and shape as is possible to declare, the eldest is about 40 yeares of ag, the second was a yong man of 20 yeares old. Their apparell was on this manner: the elder had upon his naked body a harts skin, wrought artificialie with divers braunches like Damaske, his head was bare, with the hair tied up behind with divers knottes: About his neck he had a large chaine garnished with divers stones of sundrie colours, the yong man was almost apparelid after the same manner.

This is the goodliest people, and of the fairest conditions, that wee have found in this our voyage. . . . The women are of like conformitie and beawtie, verie handsome and well favored, they are as well mannered and continente as anye women of good education. There are also of them whiche weare on their armes verie riche skinnes of leopards [bay lynx]. They adorn their heades with divers ornaments made of their own haire, whiche hange downe before on both sides of their breasts, others use other kinds of dressing them selves.[117]

It is interesting to compare this first description of the natives of southern New England with later accounts. The harts skin mantle above mentioned was undoubtedly the same type as described a hundred years later by Morton as follows:

they have likewise another sort of mantels, made of Mose skinnes . . . these skinnes they commonly dresse bare, and make them wondrous white, and stripe them with size round about the borders, in forme like lace set on by a Taylor, and some they stripe with size in workes of severall fasions very curious, according to the severall fantasies of the workemen, wherein they strive to excell one another.[118]

It is a pity that none of these beautiful mantles have come down to us. The nearest approach to the intricate designs with which they were decorated appears painted in red, blue, and yellow pigment on the buckskin mantles and coats of the Nascapee and Montagnais of the Labrador Peninsula and in bead work on the cloth coats of the Malecite, an Abnaki tribe of the St. John River. The paint was prepared by mixing finely ground color with fish roe, and applying with paint sticks of wood or antler.

[117] John Verarzanus, in The Relation of Hakluyt's Divers Voyages (1582), Hakluyt Soc' reprint, p. 65.

[118] Thomas Morton, New English Canaan, Prince Soc. reprint, p. 142.

The "verie riche skins of leopards" seen on the arms by Verarzanus, were the spotted skins of the bay lynx, or bob cat. When
the Indians first visited the Pilgrims at Plymouth under the guid-
ance of Samoset, it was noticed that one of the company wore a
"wild cat's skin or such like on one arm."

The common way of wearing a deer-skin mantle was to pass it
under the right arm and fasten it over the left shoulder. This left
one arm exposed, which in cold weather was covered with the
whole skin of some animal of the proper size. Wood says it was
covered with a "deepe furr'd cat skin like a long large muffe which
hee shifts to that arm which lyeth most exposed to the winde."
It seems that the skin of the bob cat was preferred for this purpose, but the skins of the otter and beaver are also mentioned.
Pendants and necklaces of flat, oval stones have already been
illustrated (figure 103). Probably these were similar to the ones
mentioned by Verarzanus.

The indispensable garment worn by both sexes was the breech
clout which was carried between the legs of the wearer and was
supported by the girdle over which its ends hung," a flap before
and a tail behind." This was worn by both sexes, and was frequently the only garment used indoors in warm weather. The
women also usually wore an additional short garment of skins or
European cloth wrapped like a blanket around their loins. Robes
or mantles for cold weather were made of the skins of the bear,
moose, deer, wolf, beaver, otter, fox, raccoon, and squirrel. A robe
of raccoon skins was "of more esteeme than a coat of beaver, because of the tayles that (hanging around in order) doe adorne the
garment."

Deer skin mantles were dressed with or without the hair, the
latter were preferred for summer wear. In winter the hair side
was worn innermost. While one deer or bear skin usually served
as a mantle for men, two were sewed together at full length in
making a woman's dress.

Leggings were worn by both sexes, those for women being shorter
than for men. They were worn for warmth in cold weather, on
dress occasions, and by the men as a protection against brush and
briers while hunting. They were often ornamented with designs
in red, blue, and yellow. Their lower ends were fastened within
the moccasins, which were usually made of mooseskin. Weymouth speaks of two little Abnaki boys, all naked except their

legs, which were covered with leather buskins, fastened with straps to a girdle about their waists which they gird very straight and which was decked round about with little round pieces of red copper. The woven garments made by our New England tribes are described in the chapter on textile fabrics.

Wood has this to say regarding the method of wearing the hair,

Their black haire is naturall, yet it is brought to a more jetty colour by oyling, dying, and daily dressing. Sometimes they weare it very long, hanging down in a loose dishevel'd womanish manner; otherwhile tied up hard and short like a horse taile, bound close with a fillet, which they say makes it grow the faster: they are not a little phantasticall or customsick in this particular; their boyes being not permitted to weare their haire long till sixteene yeares of age, and then they must come to it by degrees; some being cut with a long foretop, a long locke on the crowne, one at each side of his head, the rest of his haire being cut even with the scalpe: the young men and souldiers weare their haire long on the one side, the other side being cut short like a screw; other cuts they have as their fancie befools them, which would torture the wits of a curious Barber to imitate. But though they be thus wedded to the haire of their head, you cannot wooe them to weare it on their chinnes, where it no sooner growes, but it is stubbed up by the rootes.[119]

The hair of Philip's warriors was trimmed "comb fashion,"[120] the sides of the head being shaved, leaving a ridge of comparatively short upright hair crossing the crown from front to back.

We know but little as to the methods of dressing the hair of women. Champlain mentions a girl with her hair very neatly dressed with a skin colored red and bordered on the upper part with little shell beads. A portion of it hung down behind, the rest being braided in various ways.

Verarzanus as above mentioned speaks of the adornment of the heads of women.

Turkey and eagle feathers were worn in the hair by men. A headdress of upright feathers was sometimes worn fashioned "like a coronet," "broadwise like a fan," or "like a turkey-cock's train." The well known warriors' head ornaments of certain western tribes made of deer hair colored red were also worn in New England. Gookin describes them as "deer shuts made in the fashion of a cock's comb dyed red and crossing their heads like a half moon." Weymouth saw a headdress on the coast of Maine which he describes as a "kind of coronet . . . made very cunningly

[119] William Wood. *New England's Prospect*, Boynton edit., p. 67.
[120] Drake. *History of Philip's War*, p. 23.

of a substance like stiff hair colored red, broad and more than a handful in depth."

Face painting was common among both sexes. Tattooing was quite general. Wood writes that many of the better sort bear

upon their cheekes certaine pourtraitures of beasts, as Beares, Deeres, Mooses, Wolves, &c, some of fowls as of Eagles, Hawkes, &c. which be not a superficiall painting, but a certaine incision, or else a raising of their skin by a small sharpe instrument, under which they conveigh a certain kind of black unchangeable inke, which makes the desired forme apparent and permanent. Others have certaine round Impressions downe the outside of their armes and brests, in forme of mullets or spur-rowels, which they imprint by searing irons: whether these be foiles to illustrate their unparalleld beauty (as they deem it) or Armes to blazon their antique Gentilitie, I cannot easily determine: but a Sagamore with a Humberd in his eare for a pendant, a black hawke on his occiput for his plume, Mowhackees [purple beads] for his gold chaine, good store of Wampompeage [white beads] begirting his loynes, his bow in his hand, his quiver at his back, with six naked Indian spatterlashes at his heels for his guard, thinkes himself little inferiour to the great Cham; hee will not stick to say, hee is all one with King Charles.[121]

The animal figures tattooed upon the cheeks were undoubtedly totems or clan marks, and as Wood thought possible, were doubtless "arms to blazon the antique gentility of the wearer."

We are apt to picture the country when first seen by Europeans as thickly covered with primeval forests and as having few open spaces and fields. This was probably true of the more remote uninhabited sections, but does not apply to all tribal lands, especially those of the southern half of New England. These were burnt in the fall and spring for the purpose of killing the undergrowth and keeping the fields and woodlands open. It was principally in the swamps where the fire did not penetrate that nature took its course. Wood writes: [122]

And whereas it is generally concieved, that the woods grow so thicke, that there is no more cleare ground than is hewed out by labour of man; it is nothing so; in many places, divers Acres being cleare, so that one may ride a hunting in most places of the land, if he will venture himselfe for being lost: there is no underwood saving in swamps, and low grounds that are wet, in which the English get Osiers, and Hasles, and such small wood as is for their use. Of these swamps, some be ten, some twenty, some thirty miles long, being preserved by the wetnesse of the soile wherein they grow; for it being the custome of the Indians to burne the wood in November, when the grass is withered, and leaves dryed, it consumes all the underwood, and rubbish,

[121] Wood, op. cit., pp. 69, 70.
[122] Ibid, p. 16.

which otherwise would over grow the Country, making it unpassable, and spoile their much affected hunting: so that by this means in those places where the Indians inhabit, there is scarce a bush or bramble, or any cumbersome underwood to bee seene in the more champion ground. Small wood growing in these places where the fire could not come is preserved.

An account of this custom is also given by Morton: [123]

The Salvages are accustomed to set fire of the Country in all places where they come, and to burn it twice a yeare, viz: at the Spring, and the fall of the leafe. The reason that moves them to doe so, is because it would other wise be so overgrowne with underweeds that it would be all a coppice wood, and the people would not be able in any wise to passe through the Country out of a beaten path. . . . The burning of the grasse destroyes the underwoods, and so scorcheth the elder trees that it shrinkes them, and hinders their grouth very much: so that hee that will looke to finde large trees and good tymber, must not depend upon the help of a wooden prospect to find them on the upland ground; but must seeke for them (as I and others have done) in the lower grounds, where the grounds are wett, . . . for the Salvages, by this custome of theirs, have spoiled all the rest: for this custonme hath been continued from the beginninge. . . . And this custome of firing the Country is the meanes to make it passable; and by that meanes the trees growe here and there as in our parks: and makes the Country very beautiful land commodious.

During Champlain's exploration in July, 1605, and again the following year, he found along our shore much land cleared. He says the country was very agreeable and there was no lack of fine trees. On his maps of the various harbors which he surveyed are numerous small sketches of Indian habitations with their fields of corn. Some of these are reproduced in figure 142. In 1616 Captain John Smith refers to

the country of the Massachusetts which is the Paradise of all these parts. For heere are many isles all planted with corn; groves, mulberries, salvage gardens and good harbours. . . . The Sea Coast as you pass, shews you all along large corn fields and great troups of well proportioned people.

This was just before that fatal pestilence which nearly depopulated eastern Massachusetts.

Five years later when Governor Bradford sent an expedition to Boston Bay, he found that most of the islands had been inhabited and that some had been cleared from end to end; but the people were all dead or had removed.

During the journey of Edward Winslow and Stephen Hopkins to Pokanoket, near the present site of Bristol, Rhode Island, to visit Massasoit, they went through Namasket to the Taunton

---

[123] Morton, op. cit., pp. 172, 173.

River, along the banks of which they journeyed. They tell us that upon this river there

are and have been many towns. The ground is very good upon both sides, it being for the most part cleared. Thousands of men have lived here which died in the great plague not long since, and pity it was and is to see so many goodly fields so well seated without men to dress and manure the same.

In this partially open country were the villages of the natives, which varied in size and permanency. The larger settlements were the headquarters of a tribe or tribal division and when palisaded were the strongholds or forts which formed a refuge for the people when attacked by an enemy.

During summer excursions and the later hunting season such villages were often nearly deserted, the infirm and aged being the principal occupants. The more common type of village sheltered perhaps a hundred people or less. Many of these were not palisaded. During the planting and harvesting seasons or when camping at fishing stations, a few small houses sufficed. The coverings of these houses and also many of the more permanent ones were in the form of mats which were easily removed and transported, the framework being left standing for use another season. Roger Williams says the Indians were very expeditious at their removals. "They are quicke; in halfe a day, yea, sometimes at a few houres warning to be gone and the house up elsewhere, especially if they have stakes ready pitcht for their Mats." Josselyn writes: "I have seen half a hundred of their Wigwams together in a piece of ground, and they show prettily, within a day or two or a week they have been all dispersed."

Most communities had as their headquarters one or more fortified enclosures, where the people dwelt at certain seasons, or into which they moved in time of danger. The larger forts consisted of a score or more of cabins enclosed by a palisade. The smaller ones were forty or fifty feet in diameter and contained a single cabin. The construction of the fortifications was practically the same whether they contained one or fifty houses. The smaller forts had but one entrance, while the larger had two, one on each side, formed by overlapping the ends of the stockade, leaving a narrow passage between them. During the early colonial period there were numerous Indian forts in various sections of New England. The later ones were abandoned at or about the time of Philip's war. Roger Williams says that "with friendly joyning" the Indians built their forts; that is, the men of a community and their friends took part in the work, which was probably accompanied by feasts and dances. The historic stockades were usually circular or square and enclosed areas about 50 feet in diameter to about 4 acres in extent. The more important references to historic Indian fortifications in New England follow, and, while the descriptions fail to give many desirable details, they furnish a good general idea of these strongholds.

The first account is by Champlain and refers to a fort on the right bank of the Saco River near its mouth. He figures a square enclosure containing a single house. See figure 142, d.[124]

The savages dwell permanently in this place, and have a large cabin surrounded by palisades made of rather large trees placed by the side of each other, in which they take refuge when their enemies make war upon them.

The first fortifications seen by the Pilgrims were at Cape Cod. The remains of an old fort or palisade was found near the mouth of Pamet River, at Truro,[125] which they attributed to Christians, being without knowledge of Indian works of this nature. Farther south on the Cape, below Wellfleet Bay, what appears to have been a second fort was encountered. If a fort, it had evidently been abandoned at the time of the epidemic which prevailed in eastern Massachusetts a few years previous to the arrival of the Pilgrims. The dead were buried both within and without the enclosure. Within the enclosure were frames of houses, the coverings of which had been removed and carried away. The Pilgrims thought this to be a palisaded cemetery, and thus described it:

we found a great burying place, one part whereof was incompassed with a large Palazado, like a Church-yard, with yong spires foure or fiue yards long, set as close one by another as they could, two or three foot in the ground: within it was full of Graues, some bigger, and some lesse, some were also paled about, & others had like an *Indian*-house made over them, but not matted: those Graues were more sumptuous then those at *Corne-hill*, yet we digged none of them vp, but onely viewed them, and went our way; without the Palazado were graues also, but not so costly.

The following autumn the Pilgrims discovered two small forts, near the present site of Boston. These are described as follows:

Not farre from hence in a bottome, wee came to a Fort built by their deceased King, the manner thus; There were pools some thirtie or fortie foote long, stucke in the ground as thick as they could be set one by another, and

[124] Champlain's *Voyages*, Prince Soc. reprint, vol. II, p. 67.
[125] *Journal of the Pilgrims at Plymouth*, Cheever reprint, p. 34.

with these they inclosed a ring some forty or fifty foote ouer. A trench breast high was digged on each side; one way there was to goe into it with a bridge; in the midst of this Pallizado stood the frame of an house, wherein being dead he lay buryed. About a myle from hence, we came to such another, but seated on the top of an hill: here *Nanepashemet* was killed, none dwelling in it since the time of his death.

The height of the palisades as given above, 30 or 40 feet, is evidently too great. The trenches were "breast high," measuring probably from the bottom to the top of the embankment which supported the palisades.

Wood writes:

These Forts some be fortie or fiftie foote square, erected of young timber trees, ten or twelve foote high, rammed into the ground, with undermining within, the earth being cast up for their shelter against the dischargements of their enemies, having loopholes to send out their winged messengers.

Vincent's account is drawn largely from Wood's, but, as he was one of the party that attacked the Pequot fort near Mystic, Connecticut, to which he has reference, his account is of value as it supplements that of Wood:

They choose a piece of ground, dry and of the best advantage, forty or fifty foot square (but this was at least two acres of ground). Here they pitch, close together as they can young trees and half trees as thick as a man's thigh or the calf of his leg. Ten or twelve feet high they are above the ground and within [the ground] rammed three foot deep with undermining, the earth being cast up for their better shelter against the enemy's dischargements. Betwixt these palisadoes are divers loopholes, through which they let fly their winged messengers. The door is for the most part entered sideways which they stop with bows and bushes as need requireth. The space therein is full of wigwams, wherein their wives and children live with them.[126]

The palisades were set close together, but open spaces between logs not perfectly straight were unavoidable. These open spaces were probably used as loopholes. Underhill, describing the same structure, says:

This fort or palisado was well nigh an acre of ground which was surrounded with trees and half trees, set into the ground three feet deep, and fastened close to one another, as you may see more clearly described in the figure of it before the book.

The illustration referred to, which appears in Underhill's *News From America* (1638), was evidently made by a wood engraver from a rough ground plan. It is of little value except as showing the fort to have been circular, with two entrances, one upon either

[126] *Vincent's narrative* in Orr's History of the Pequot War, p. 105.

side, each formed by overlapping the ends of the stockade, leaving a passageway between them. This fort is said to have contained about 60 or 70 wigwams.

Gookin says that at Natick "there was a handsome large fort, of a round figure, palisaded with trees." The fort at Penobscot was 70 feet long and 50 feet broad and within it were 23 wigwams.[127] Philip's fort, the site of which is at South Kingston, Rhode Island, had "besides high palisades, an immense hedge of fallen trees of nearly a rod in thickness, surrounding it, encompassing an area of about five acres." It is said to have contained about 500 wigwams. Another estimate gives the size of the enclosure at 3 to 4 acres.

A few instances are recorded of the apparent use by Algonquians of a trench and embankment without palisades as a defensive work under circumstances which probably rendered the erection of a stockade impracticable. Two traditions current in past years are as follows: A party of Nipmuc entrenched themselves on the shore of Quinebaug River against the Narraganset, where they remained three days. Fifty years ago these earthworks were visible (De Forest, *Indians of Connecticut*, p. 268.) We are also told (Mass. Hist. Coll., 3d series, vol. VI, p. 197) that a company of Mohegan invaded Block Island and were driven to a bluff, where they "by some means dug a trench around them toward the land, to defend them against the arrows of their enemies." This earthwork was known locally as the Mohegan fort.

In all there are about twenty Indian forts mentioned by the early explorers and colonists of New England between the years 1605 and 1676.

Indications of these old palisaded villages have largely disappeared through cultivation of the land and other modern improvements. The trenches and embankments, however, are occasionally found where the surface has remained unchanged through intervening years. One of the best examples that I have seen is located near the head of Mill River in Mendon, Massachusetts, on land the greater part of which has remained uncultivated since its abandonment by the Indians. It is located upon a sandy hill which is about three hundred feet in diameter at its base. The trench, now shallow in places, can be traced for about half of its length. It apparently encircled the knoll, and its embankment

[127] Drake's *Indian Wars*. p. 325.

undoubtedly supported palisades with the trench upon the inner side. The enclosed space was about two hundred fifty feet in diameter. Portions of hearths of field stones may be seen within the enclosure and a few chipped implements have been found there. Mill River, navigable for canoes at this point, lies not far distant, and in the immediate neighborhood of the hill is an Indian corn field, the contours of the irregularly placed corn hills being perfectly preserved, as the land is wooded and probably has been for many generations.

De Forest mentions the remains of an old Indian fort in Thompson, northeastern Connecticut. These are on a hill about three fourths of a mile east of the town, and people still find here and there in the neighboring forest hills and rows of Indian corn fields, now thickly covered with sturdy trees.[128] A considerable number of these old sites, once palisaded, have been reported, and others will doubtless come to light as time progresses.

Caution, however, must be exercised not to confuse these old Indian remains with the many trenches and embankments which were the work of the early English colonists. These are quite common, especially in Massachusetts. They occur in Sudbury, Wayland, Concord, Andover, Millis and in various other places. The Peabody Museum of Cambridge has mapped many of those in the Sudbury River valley. The trench and embankment at Stony Brook, Weston, thought by the late Professor Horseford to mark the site of ancient Norumbega,[129] probably belong to this category. A careful examination of these earthworks indicates that they are old boundary lines or *fences*; a term according to the Century Dictionary, applicable to a trench or ditch when used as a boundary or barrier. One of the longest of these trenches measures upwards of thirteen hundred feet. They are, however, usually much shorter, and often have one or more branches extending from them. From the top of the embankment, which is upon one side only, to the bottom of these old colonial trenches, the vertical measurement is usually about two to four feet, and from the outer edge of the embankment to the opposite edge of the trench, seven to twelve feet or thereabout. As a rule they seem to have no relation to the present boundary of the fields and are often fragmentary, portions of them having apparently been

[128] De Forest, *History of the Indians of Connecticut*, p. 377.
[129] E. N. Horseford, *The Defences of Norumbega*, 1891.

levelled in recent cultivation of the land. They often occur on thickly wooded land. It is noticeable that some of them extend along the sides of highways, and in two instances, one at Millis and another at Sudbury, I have found the trench and embankment continued by a stone wall.

The well preserved embankments and trenches at Millis, Massachusetts,[130] enclosing the hill near South End Pond, an expansion of Boggestow Brook which flows into the Charles River, probably belong to this group of remains, although originally taken by the present writer to be of Indian origin, their resemblance to similar Indian earthworks being very marked.

The habitations of the New England Indians were of three general types — the round house, the long house, and the conical house. The first two forms occurred throughout this area. The conical house seems to have been more common in Maine than in other sections of New England, where if used at all it was probably employed as a temporary shelter only.

The outline of the round house (figure 142, g, h) closely approached that of a hemisphere. The ground plan was circular, with an approximate diameter of ten to sixteen feet. The probable height of these lodges over the central fireplace was six to eight feet. They were occupied by one or two families. According to Williams "two families will live comfortably and lovingly in a little round house of some fourteen or sixteen feet over."

The framework consisted of small poles set in the ground two to three feet apart, enclosing the circular floor space. Several arches were made, each formed by bending and lashing two opposite poles together. The remaining poles were bent over and joined to these arches, and horizontal poles were added, the whole being firmly bound together. Morton's description is as follows:

They gather Poles in the woodes and put the great end of them in the ground, placinge them in forme of a circle or circumference and, bendinge the topps of them in form of an Arch they bind them together with the Barke of Walnut trees which is wondrous tuffe so that they make the same round on the Topp.

The men usually prepared the poles and made the framework, over which the women fastened the mats and other coverings.

There were usually two entrances to wigwams of this type, one

[130] C. C. Willoughby, *Certain Earthworks of Eastern Massachusetts*, Am. Anthropologist, n. s., Vol. 13, pp. 566–576.

at the north, the other at the south. These were about three feet in height, "and according as the wind sets, they close up one door with bark and hang a deer's skin or the like before the other." An opening in the roof about eighteen inches square allowed the smoke to escape. In windy weather, if the smoke became troublesome, this aperture was screened with a small mat placed upon the top of the lodge and arranged with a cord so as to be turned to the windward side. That houses of this type were sometimes used by the Abnaki of central and eastern Maine seems evident from the remark of John Gyles, who was captured at Pemaquid in 1689, and lived with the Indians for seven or eight years in the region of the Penobscot and St. John Rivers. Describing the houses of the beaver, he says "they are round in the figure of an Indian wigwam."[131]

In the second group are included those lodges having an oblong, rectangular ground plan (figure 142, a, d, e, f) and an outline resembling that of a semicylinder. The medium and smaller sizes were generally used as communal dwellings. Those with two fires usually sheltered four families, those with three, four, or more fires contained six, eight, or more families. The larger houses were also built for ceremonial purposes and were "sometimes a hundred, sometimes two hundred feet long," and thirty feet broad.

The framework was made by setting poles in two parallel rows enclosing the floor space. Opposite poles were bent over and joined to each other in pairs, forming a series of arches of equal height, which were joined together by horizontal poles placed at intervals, forming an arbor-like framework. The poles for the ends of the framework were set either in a straight line and joined to the end arches in a perpendicular position, giving the form to the finished hut shown in the drawings above mentioned, or were arranged in a segment of a circle and bent over and joined to the main framework, thereby giving a more rounded appearance to the ends of the huts. These wigwams had, according to their size, two or more entrances, which were covered with a deer-skin or with a mat which could be rolled up. According to Wood: "Their houses are smaller in the Summer when their families are dispersed, by reason of heate and occasions. In Winter they make some fiftie or three score foote long, fortie or fiftie men being

<hr>

[131] John Gyle's Captivity, in S. G. Drake's Tragedies of the Wilderness, p. 94.

inmates under one roof." There is evidence, however, that long houses were sometimes occupied as summer dwellings, and while the winter wigwams were more commonly of the long type, especially in the southern half of New England, smaller cabins were also used for winter habitations.

Verarzanus, describing the New England habitations in 1524, writes:

We sawe their houses made in circular or rounde fourm 10 or 12 foote in compasse. . . . They moove the foresaide houses from one place to another according to the commoditie of the place and season, wherein they will make

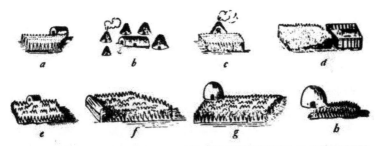

Figure 142. Habitations and Gardens: a–d, Saco River Valley, Me.; a, c, "Cabins in the open fields near which they cultivate the land and plant Indian corn"; b, "Another place where they have their dwellings all together after they have planted their corn"; d, "Place where they have their fortress"; e–h, houses and gardens, coast of Massachusetts: e, at Chatham; f, g, at Nauset Harbor; h, at Gloucester. After Champlain, 1605–06.

their aboade and only taking of the cover, they have other houses builded incontinent. The father and whole familie dwell together in one house in great number: in some of them we saw 25 or 30 persons.

The long house was used for council or ceremonial purposes throughout New England. It is recorded as occurring on both the Saco and Kennebec Rivers. The one on the Penobscot was twenty feet wide by forty feet long.[132]

The conical wigwam (figure 142, b, c) seems to have been most common among the Abnaki; it is the traditional lodge of the modern Penobscot Indians. The framework was made of straight poles with their lower ends set into the ground enclosing the circular floor space, their upper ends being brought together and fastened. This frame resembled that of the skin tipi of the Plains tribes, and was covered with bark mats or pieces of bark which were sometimes held in place by a second series of poles placed

[132] Maine Hist. Soc. Coll. 1876, vol. vii, p. 14.

over them. Father Rasles, in a letter written at the Indian village of Nanrantsouak (Norridgewock) on the Kennebec, in 1723, describes the type as follows:

Their cabins are easily built. They plant poles in the earth, which they join at the top, and then cover them with large pieces of bark. The fire they make in the middle of the cabin and all around it. . . . they sit during the day and sleep at night.[133]

Little hunting houses of bark and rushes, "not comparable to their dwelling houses," were built by hunters for temporary occupancy while on their fall hunts.

In common with most American tribes the New England Indians erected little wigwams, in which the women lived alone during catamenia, "which custome in all parts of the country they strictly observe."

Williams describes the men's sweat-lodge as a

little Cell or Cave, six or eight foot over, round, made on the side of a hill (commonly by some Rivulet or Brooke) into this frequently the Men enter after they have exceedingly heated it with store of wood, laid upon an heape of stones in the middle. When they have taken out the fire, the stones keepe still a great heat: Ten, twelve, twenty more or lesse, enter at once starke naked . . . here doe they sit round these hot stones an houre or more, taking tobacco, discoursing and sweating together; . . . when they come forth . . . I have seen them runne (Summer and Winter) into the brookes to coole them, without the least hurt.

Gyles refers to another form of sweat-lodge, sometimes used by the shamans for their powwows, consisting of a small hut covered with skins or mats. Within was a pile of hot stones over which water was poured.

Gookin says:

The best sort of their houses are covered very neatly, tight, and warm, with the barks of trees, slipped from their bodies at such seasons when the sap is up; and made into great flakes with pressure of weighty timbers when they are green; and so becoming dry they will retain a form suitable for the use they prepare them for.

The bark was fastened to the frame-work so that the upper pieces overlapped the lower. Poles were sometimes laid over the bark to aid in keeping it in place. Lodges thus covered "deny entrance to any drop of raine, though it come both fierce and long, neither can the piercing North winde find a crannie, through which

[133] Kip, *Early Jesuit Missions in North America*, p. 24.

he can conveigh his cooling breath, they be warmer than our English houses."[134]

Portable mats made of flags were also extensively used for lodge coverings. Gookin says that mat covered lodges were "indifferent tight and warm but not so good as those covered with bark."

Another style of mat for lodge coverings, probably not uncommon among the Abnaki, was made of pieces of the outer bark of the white birch sewed together. The pieces forming the mat were usually three or four feet in length (the width of the mat) and of varying width. They were joined by overlapping their longer edges and sewing with split spruce roots. Each end of the mat was finished by placing two narrow and thin strips of wood, one at each side, so as to enclose the edge of the bark between them. These were sewed and bound together with split roots. An additional piece of bark, a foot or more long and four or five inches wide, was caught between these binding strips by one of its longest edges at each end of the mat as a reenforcement. The mat was furnished with tying cords, and when formed into a roll occupied a very small space, being light and portable. It was probably this kind of lodge covering that Father Rasles referred to as bark cloths. In the excursions of the Norridgewock Indians down the Kennebec to the seashore once or twice every season, when camping for the night they would "cover themselves with bark which they carry with them and which they have rolled out until it resembles cloth." These bark mats are still occasionally used as portable lodge coverings from New Brunswick to Lake Winnipeg, and in early historic times were doubtless common to the canoe birch region throughout the Algonquian area.

The poorer wigwams were sometimes covered with a thatch of reeds, grass, or corn-husk, or with boughs of trees.

The walls of the more permanent habitations were lined with embroidered mats, or with mats of rushes "painted" in several colors. For details see chapter on textiles. These mats were also used as bedding and to sit upon. Hearths were often made of small field stones. Sometimes a post reaching to the roof was set up beside the fireplace, the upper end being secured to a cross-piece. At a convenient height a pin was driven into the post, and upon the pin a kettle was hung. At its foot a broad, flat stone was set up to protect the post from the fire.

[134] William Wood. *op. cit.*, p. 99.

Usually a scaffold about two feet high was built over the fireplace by driving four crotched sticks into the ground. Crossbars were laid over the crotches, and over these and at right angles to them were placed sticks, upon which fish and other food was dried and smoked. Small torches made of pitch pine "cloven into little slices" were used as occasion required for lighting the interior of the hut. Fire was produced both by friction and percussion, the latter process being more common.

The people sometimes slept upon mats and skins placed on the ground, but in the better lodges there were rude bedsteads made by setting forked sticks into the earth, which supported poles a foot or eighteen inches from the ground. Over these were laid other poles, or planks. In the large houses the beds were six or eight feet wide, being broad enough to accommodate three or four persons. The bedding consisted of mats and skins.

The following is an excellent description of the wigwams and their furnishings, seen by the Pilgrims at Cape Cod in 1620:

The houses were made with long yong Sapling trees, bended and both ends stucke into the ground; they were made round, like vnto an Arbour, and covered downe to the ground with thicke and well wrought matts, and the doore was not over a yard high, made of a matt to open; the chimney was a wide open hole in the top, for which they had a matt to cover it close when they pleased; one might stand and goe vpright in them, in the midst of them were foure little trunches knockt into the ground, and small stickes laid over, on which they hung their Pots and what they had to seeth; round about the fire they lay on matts, which are their beds. The houses were double matted, for as they were matted without, so were they within, with newer & fairer matts. In the houses we found wooden Boules, Trayes & Dishes, Earthen Pots, Hand baskets made of Crab shells, wrought together; also an English Paile or Bucket, it wanted a bayle, but it had two Iron eares: there was also Baskets of sundry sorts, bigger and some lesser, finer and some courser: some were curiously wrought with blacke and white in pretie workes, and sundry other of their household stuffe: we found also two or three Deeres heads, one whereof had bin newly killed, for it was still fresh; there was also a company of Deeres feete stuck vp in the houses, Harts hornes, and Eagles clawes, and sundry such like things there was: also two or three Baskets full or parched Acornes, peeces of fish, and a peece of broyled Hering. We found also a little silke grasse, and a little Tobacco seed, with some other seeds which wee knew not; without was sundry bundles of Flags, and Sedge, Bullrushes, and other stuffe to make matts.[135]

In addition to utensils of wood, stone, pottery, and other material previously described as intimately associated with the

---

[135] *Journal of the Pilgrims at Plymouth*, Cheever reprint, pp. 39, 40.

daily activities of the Indian household, there were dishes, buckets, and boxes of birch bark used for holding food, carrying water, and storing various objects. It seems probable that these bark containers were more plentiful among the Abnaki and Pennacook than in the southern culture area, although they were doubtless more or less common throughout New England. Josselyn writes:[136]—

"Delicate sweet dishes too they make of *Birch-Bark* sowed with threads drawn from *Spruse* or white *Cedar-Roots*, and garnished on the out-side with flourisht works, and on the brims with glistering quills taken from the *Porcupine*, and dyed, some black, others red, the white are natural, these they make of all sizes from a dram cup to a dish containing a pottle, likewise Buckets to carry water or the like, large Boxes too of the same materials, . . . Kettles of *Birchen-bark*.

Gookin says:

Their pails to fetch their water in, are made of birch barks, artificially doubled up, that it hath four corners and a handle in the midst. Some of these will hold two or three gallons: and they will make one of them in an hours time.

These bark buckets were sometimes used as kettles for boiling, being suspended over the fire at a proper distance from the flame.

The members of each tribe or community were the recognized proprietors of certain hunting, fishing, and agricultural lands, held generally in common. According to Williams they were "very exact and punctuall in the bounds of their Lands belonging to this or that Prince or People (even to a River, Brooke, &c.). And I have knowne them to make bargaine and sale amongst themselves for a small piece or quantity of Ground." Good agricultural lands were necessary for the well-being of every community. The high, rocky shores of the central and eastern portion of Maine were not suitable for agriculture, but the fertile river valleys of the interior of this state, and throughout New England generally, had their well cultivated gardens wherein were grown corn, beans, pumpkins, squashes, artichokes, and tobacco. Roger Williams tells us that

The women of a family will commonly raise two or three heaps [of corn] of twelve, fifteene or twentie bushells a heap, which they drie in round broad heaps; and if she have helpe of her children or friends, much more.

Gookin says the Indian fields at Wabquissit (a village near Woodstock, Conn.) yielded forty bushels of corn to the acre.

[136] John Josselyn, *Two Voyages to New England* Veazie reprint, p. 111.

The Indians taught our forefathers their method of gardening — how to "cull out the finest seede, to observe fittest season, to keep distance for holes and fit measure for hills, to worme it and weed it; to prune it, and dress it, as occasion shall require." Wood also says they exceeded the English in the care of their fields, not allowing a weed to "advance his audacious head above their infant corn, or an undermining worm to spoile his spurnes."

Each family had one or more gardens. Sometimes they were a mile or more apart, and when the work of one field was over they would remove their cabin to another.

When the leaves of the white oak were as large as a mouse's ear it was time to plant the fields. The weeds and stubble were burnt and the ground dug over with planting sticks of hard wood shaped like a spade. The hills were about three feet apart, placed irregularly, not in straight rows as in the later fields of the colonists. In each were placed two or three herring or other fish as a fertilizer, and about four kernels of corn and as many beans. Squash and pumpkin seeds were also placed in the hills, and the earth heaped over them with the shell of the horseshoe crab or some similar implement. Hoes of wood and clamshell are also recorded, and Williams says stone hoes were formerly used (see figure 96). The Stockbridge Indians used the shoulder blade of a bear, moose, or deer fastened to a wooden handle for this purpose.

There were several varieties of Indian corn (Zea mays) grown in these old gardens, the colors being red, blue, yellow, and white. The bean (Phaseolus vulgaris) was also of different colors and varieties. Josselyn writes "They are variegated much, some being bigger a great deal than others, some white, black, red, yellow, blew, spotted." This is our common field and garden bean. Champlain found the artichoke (Helianthus tuberosus) cultivated on Cape Cod in 1605 and at Gloucester in 1606. Tobacco was a small hardy variety (Nicotiana rustica), and was usually the only plant cultivated by men. It was raised in New England as far north as the Kennebec Valley.[137]

The corn was harvested by women and dried on mats. It was stored in caches, in baskets, and in wooden receptacles made by cutting hollow logs into sections. Morton writes:

"Their barnes are holes made in the earth, that will hold a Hogshead of corne a peece in them. In these (when their corne is out

[137] Strachey, *History of Travel into Virginia*, Coll. Maine Hist. Soc., vol. iii, p. 306.

of the huske and well dried they lay their store in greate baskets which they make of Sparke) with mats under about the sides, and on the top; and putting it into the place made for it, they cover it with earth."

Champlain saw "trenches in the sand on the slope of the hills, some five or six feet deep more or less. Putting their corn and other grains into large grass sacks they throw them into these trenches and cover them with sand three or four feet above the surface of the earth, taking it out as their needs require."

Soon after landing at Cape Cod in 1620, the Pilgrims found a heap of sand such as noted in the above quotation. They opened it and found therein "a little old Basket full of faire Indian Corne, and digged further & found a fine great new Basket full of very faire corne of this yeare, with some 36 goodly eares of corne, some yellow and some red, and others mixt with blew which was a very goodly sight; the Basket was round, and narrow at the top, it held about three or four Bushels, which was as much as two of us could lift up from the ground, and was very handsomely and cunningly made."

These old cache holes are often found where the ground has remained undisturbed. I have counted more than thirty-five in an area of less than half an acre on the side of a sand hill in the Kennebec Valley.

The food of the New England Indians varied according to season. From late summer until harvest green corn and other garden products furnished the principal food. Soon after harvest the hunting season opened and lasted until the snow became too deep. During winter the Indians subsisted upon their stores of corn, beans, acorns, nuts, dried berries, dried meat and fish, and upon what fresh game, fish, and clams they could procure. When the lakes and streams opened in the spring fish formed the principal food. Migratory water-fowl were also sought at this season. After planting their gardens the people within reach of the seashore visited the clam beds or oyster banks where they remained for some time living upon various shellfish and drying them for winter consumption. Berries, roots of various kinds, and nuts were gathered in summer and autumn for immediate consumption and for drying. Green corn was a favorite food, and for the purpose of procuring this for as long a season as possible there was a second planting. It was usually prepared by roasting or boiling. If the corn was not ripe when harvested, it was boiled on the ear, shelled, and carefully dried on mats or bark. Thus prepared it would keep indefinitely. The crop of ripe corn was husked and also dried before storing. An idea of the amount of corn stored for winter consumption may be gained from the fact that the Pilgrims in 1622, being short of provisions, obtained from the Indians along the coast of Cape Cod Bay and northward 26 to 28 hogsheads of corn and beans.

There were various preparations from maize. Nokake, one of the most valued, consisted of kernels parched in hot ashes and ground. This was especially useful in traveling. Hulled corn and hominy, still prepared in rural New England, are primitive Indian dishes. They were made from whole or cracked corn, the hulls being removed by steeping in lye made from wood ashes. The kernels thus prepared were boiled until soft.

Succotash was a mixture of corn and beans, boiled. A staple dish was a general stew of corn or corn meal, beans, fish or meat of various kinds, either fresh or dried, together with pumpkins, squashes, and various roots, the ingredients varying according to circumstances. In preparing this stew the larger bones were crushed with stone hammers. When the meat became soft the bones would settle to the bottom. These crushed bones are common upon village sites and in shell heaps.

Gookin writes as follows regarding this common dish:

> Their food is generally boiled maize or Indian corn mixed with kidney-beans, or sometimes without. Also they frequently boil with this pottage fish and flesh of all sorts, either taken new or dried, as shads, eels, alewives or a kind of herring, or any other sort of fish. But they dry mostly those sorts before mentioned. These they cut in pieces, bones and all, and boil them in the aforesaid pottage. I have wondered many times that they were not in danger of being choaked with fish bones; but they are so dexterous to separate the bones from the fish in the eating thereof, that they are in no hazard. Also they boil in this furmenty all sorts of flesh, they take in hunting . . . cutting this flesh in small pieces, and boiling it as aforesaid. Also they mix with the said pottage several sorts of roots, and pompions, and squashes, and also several sorts of nuts or masts, as oak acorns, chestnuts, walnuts: these husked and dried, and powdered, they thicken their pottage therewith.

Corn meal dough sometimes mixed with dried berries was made into cakes, wrapped in leaves, and baked in hot ashes. Acorns of the white oak, shelled, ground, and the bitter principle removed by boiling in lye made from rotten maplewood ashes was often used for thickening stews. A clear sweet oil rose to the surface during this process, which was skimmed off and preserved in bladders or other receptacles. This was eaten with meat and also used for annointing. Hickory nuts were crushed, shells and all, and mixed with water, the oil which rose to the surface being preserved. A substitute for mother's milk was sometimes prepared by crushing the meat of walnuts in a little water and adding a small portion of the finest corn meal, and boiling the mixture.

One of the most important wild roots used for food was the groundnut (Apios tuberosa) a climbing perennial plant with fragrant purple-brown flowers, common in moist thickets. It bears upon its thread-like roots many tubers about the size of a hen's egg, though sometimes larger. During the winter of 1623 these groundnuts formed a most welcome addition to the food supply of the Plymouth settlers. Both fresh and dried meat of nearly all the larger mammals was in common use. Wood says

"Their spits are no other than cloven sticks sharped at one end to thrust into the ground; into these cloven sticks they thrust the flesh or fish they would have rosted, behemming a round fire with a dozen spits at a time, turning them as they see occasion."

Meat was preserved by cutting into strips and drying in smoke. Moose tongues were dried by smoking. Fish, the meat of lobsters, oysters, and clams were dried on scaffolds over a slow fire, and thus preserved for winter use.

The Indians were naturally expert hunters, trappers, and fishermen. Deer were taken in snares attached to a spring pole and baited with acorns. Wood says they were "springes made of young trees, and smooth wrought cords; so strong as it will tosse a horse if hee be caught in it." Deer were also taken in organized drives, V-shaped fences were built a mile or two in length with an opening at the point where the two sides approach nearest to each other. During the day hunters would lurk near this opening and shoot the deer as they passed through. During the night snares were set at the opening. Bears and other animals were taken in dead-falls which varied in size according to the bulk and strength of the animal sought. Fish were caught with hook and line, dipnets, seines, spears, and arrows. They were also taken in basket-traps and weirs.

The arrival of English colonists early in the seventeenth century was the signal for the destruction of the last stages of the native cultures which I have endeavored to describe in the foregoing pages. During the life of a single individual the changes brought about by the great migrations of Europeans to these shores had practically blotted out this interesting people. The introduction of small pox, the sale of captives into slavery, the starving of whole communities by the destruction of their corn fields, the burning of villages and the massacre of men, women, and children soon brought about the practical extermination of the tribes. The individuals who survived — the so-called Christianized Indians — were the ancestors of the few now living in New England. These owe their existence to such humanitarians as John Eliot, Daniel Gookin, Thomas Mayhew, Jr., Roger Williams, Fathers Druillettes and Rasle, and a few others.

SUPPLEMENT

THE drawings which accompany this Supplement have a direct bearing on the probable use of certain types of implements described in the foregoing pages, and as they represent objects from regions remote from New England, they are grouped separately to avoid possible confusion.

In figure 143 a–e, are several combined sinkers and lures for fishing lines used by the Alaskan Eskimo: a, c, are of whalebone, the former having a loop-like projection carved upon either side for the attachment of leaders, and the latter is perforated near either end; b, is of stone, with a horizontal groove near its center to receive a cord to which a pair of leaders is attached; d, is an unworked pebble with a shallow natural depression encircling it by means of which it is firmly bound to the line; e, is a pebble unmodified except at the ends, which are notched to prevent the encircling band from working loose. In f, is shown one of twelve stone sinkers attached to a seine belonging to the Hupa Indians of California, six of which are perforated like the one illustrated. The others are notched. Both types occur in New England. The pear shaped stone fish lures represented in g, h, are from the Hawaiian Islands. An account of them by W. T. Brigham, former director of the museum at Honolulu, is given on page 48. The sinker of coral rock, i, is attached to a stout line carrying a hook for taking large fish. It is from the Gilbert Islands, western Pacific. A comparison of the forms of known use in the above illustration with those in figures 24–27 is of special interest.

Figure 144 is introduced to illustrate the method of hafting many of our common New England chipped knives which are often classed as projectile points or spear heads. Many of our smaller chipped forms, and especially those of triangular shape, were undoubtedly for arrows, but it is significant that nearly all the arrows seen by the early writers in this region were pointed with other material than stone, among the materials mentioned being bone, antler, turkey-cock spurs, eagle claws, the tail of the horse-shoe crab, brass, and wood. The flint pointed spear seems not to have been very common, especially among the later Algonquians. One would not expect to find in our New England graves the wooden handles which were undoubtedly attached to many of the blades found in them, for wood soon disintegrates when buried in the ground.

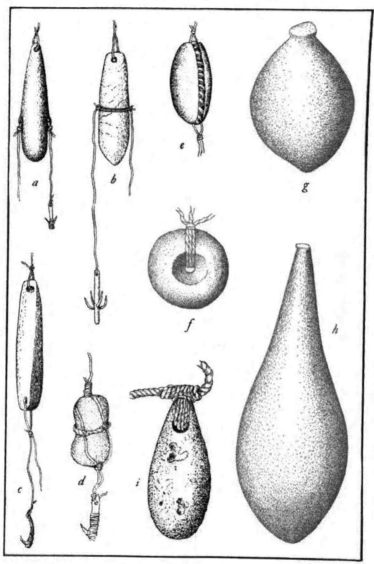

Figure 148. Sinkers and Lures used in Fishing. a–e, Alaskan Eskimo; f, net sinker, Hupa Indians, California; g, h, lures for taking fish with purse net, Hawaiian Islands; i, sinker for hook for taking large fish, Gilbert Islands. For comparison with New England forms. (1/3.)

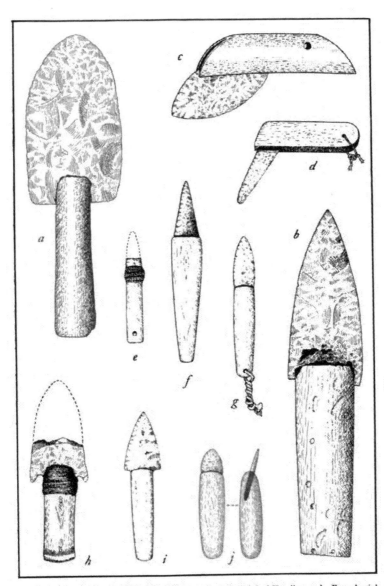

Figure 144. Prehistoric Hafted Flint Knives in their Original Handles. a, b. From burial caves, Coahuila, northern Mexico; c, from ancient hut site, Nebraska; d–j, from burial caves and cliff-houses of the Southwest. a, b, c, h, Peabody Museum. Cambridge; d, e, f, g, i, j, Museum of the University of Pennsylvania, and World's Columbian Exposition, Chicago, 1893. These show the probable methods of hafting similar chipped blades from New England. (1/3.)

The knives shown in this illustration are represented one third natural size, and the blades represent most of the common forms. The two largest, a, b, are from burial caves in Cholula, northern Mexico. The handle of each is of wood, the blade being cemented into the groove with pitch. The handle of c, is made from the rib of a large animal, probably the buffalo. This knife was excavated from an old hut site in Nebraska. All others shown are from

Figure 145. Semilunar Slate Knives, Alaskan Eskimo. The blades are nearly identical with certain New England forms. (About 1/4.)

various cliff-houses and burial caves in the Southwest, and the handles are all of wood. The knives are all prehistoric and the drawings were made from the originals by the present writer.

In figure 145 are shown three semilunar slate knives from the Eskimo of Alaska. This useful implement is found among this people from Point Barrow on the north to Kadiak Island on the

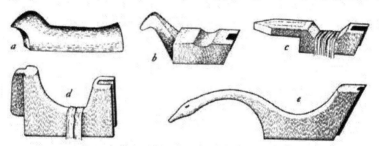

Figure 146. Aperture Slides for Indian Flageolets. Conventionalized bird forms. a, Iroquois; b, Wichita; c, Kiowa; d, Omaha; e, Plains Indians. For comparison with New England bird amulets. (About 1/2.)

south, and was also used by some of the Indians of the Alaskan panhandle. Among the more eastern Eskimo its form has become modified through contact with Europeans, and iron has, in a great measure, taken the place of slate for blades; the shape of the whole implement now frequently resembles that of the common kitchen chopping knife. In Alaska, however, the primitive form has remained unchanged. A blade obtained from the Eskimo of the lower Yukon is shown in a. Although the handle is missing, the incised perforation for its attachment is present. By comparison with figure 44, b, g, i, it will be seen that the New England examples are nearly identical. The handle of the knife shown in b, is cut from a piece of antler, the blade being inserted in a groove and lashed to it, through holes which are drilled instead of incised. Compare figure 43, b. The handle of c, is of ivory and is attached to the blade in the same manner as that of the preceding, through a single incised perforation.

In figure 146 are illustrated several wooden slides for regulating the tone of Indian flageolets. The slide may consist of a plain block or a thin piece of wood, but in the better made older examples they are often conventionalized bird forms, in some instances hardly recognizable as such to the uninitiated. These are bound to the upper side of the instrument, the head of the bird facing its mouthpiece and the grooved tail end resting over or against the whistle opening. There is usually a gasket of birchbark or buckskin between the flageolet and the slide to render the junction air tight. When properly adjusted the slide is firmly bound to the instrument with wrappings of cord, thong, or sinew. In some of the later instruments slides representing various objects are sometimes used which have no connection with the older symbolism. The symbolic connection of this bird form with the bird-like notes of the instrument is obvious. These illustrations are presented for comparison with the bird amulets shown in figure 55. The possible connection of the two groups has already been referred to.

To those not already familiar with the distribution of the types of artifacts described in a preceding section under the heading "The Old Algonquian Group" it may be acceptable to give a few references to some of the more important publications dealing with explorations and the study of implements and cognate objects from graves and mounds in the area shown in figure 2. The central portion of this area was occupied by the highly developed mound-building people of southern Ohio; and from their burial mounds have been taken the remarkable objects which illustrate the culmination of the native art and craftsmanship of this extensive area, and which also indicate the extent of the commercial activities of the people.

Upon the first arrival of the Whites in the Ohio valley these great mound settlements had been abandoned for many generations and the remnants of the descendants of the people who made them may be looked for among the outlying Algonquian tribes, especially those of the Atlantic seaboard to the east. There is a considerable amount of skeletal material from various groups of these mounds in our larger institutions, but the study of these remains has been much neglected. Dr. Hooton's report on the small series from the Turner group is a noticeable exception. This study indicates relationship to the eastern Algonquians. Perhaps the most important evidence regarding the affinity of the ancient people of Ohio with the Algonquians appears in the harmony between certain phases of the symbolism of the mound people and the mythology of the later tribes. It seems evident that the Hopewell Mound settlement, probably the most highly developed cultural and commercial unit of the mound groups of this northern section was under the patronage of priests personifying Michabo, the Great Hare, the well known Algonquian culture hero. (See my article in "American Anthropologist," vol. 37, pp. 280–286.)

An isolated outpost of this Hopewell culture occurs not far from Marksville in eastern central Louisiana, [138] which may have answered the purpose of a trading post, and it helps to explain the occurrence of material from the Gulf region found with burials, especially in the graves of the Hopewell Group. The greatest number of burial mounds of this old culture occurs in southern Ohio, but they are found in decreasing quantity in most of the adjacent states, and the types of stone artifacts peculiar to this culture occur not only in the mounds, but in graves and as surface finds beyond the limits of this central mound-building area. There seem to have been no burial mounds nor stone lined graves east of central New York, but characteristic mound types of stone implements are found with burials in eastern New York and over a considerable part of New England.

To those who care to pursue the subject further, a perusal of certain fundamental records is essential, notably those of the Ohio State Archaeological and Historical Society, at Columbus, which deal with explorations of some of the principal mound groups.[139]

[138] F. M. Setzler, Proceedings of the United States National Museum, vol. 82, article 22, pp. 1–21.

[139] Certain Mounds and Village Sites in Ohio: *Exploration of the Edward Harness Mound*, vol. 1, part 4, by W. C. Mills; *Exploration of the Tremper Mound*, vol. 2, part 3, by W. C. Mills; *Exploration of the Mound City Group*, vol. 3, part 4, by W. C. Mills; *Exploration of the Hopewell Group*, vol. 4, part 4, by H. C. Shetrone.

To these accounts should be added that of Moorehead's exploration of the Hopewell Group in 1891;[140] and the explorations by Dr. Metz of the Turner Group of Hamilton County, Ohio.[141] Among the objects illustrated in these reports will be found nearly all of the types described as old Algonquian in the preceding pages.

Some of these Ohio forms are much elaborated, notably many of the platform pipes, and the "boat-stones" or hollow amulets, the former frequently having a bowl in the form of a bird or animal instead of the usual cylinder, and the latter taking the shape of a bird or quadruped, the flat underside being hollowed as in the simpler forms. Outside this central area the less elaborate types, like those also from the mounds and from New England, persist in mounds or burial places or as surface finds throughout the region specified. This will be apparent in examining the publications relating to the archaeology of the various sections. Below are given the titles of a few of the more helpful articles treating of the subject in general.[142]

There are numerous other publications which will materially aid the student in working out this problem.

In both public and private collections the implements designated as old Algonquian usually occur mixed indiscriminately with those of various periods, and it may be well to emphasize the fact that the basis of classification in the foregoing pages is almost wholly material from graves, supplemented to some extent by objects of corresponding types from various sources, but largely obtained from fields during their cultivation.

[140] W. K. Moorehead, Field Museum of Natural History, Chicago, publication 211, *The Hopewell Group of Mounds of Ohio*.

[141] C. C. Willoughby, Papers of the Peabody Museum, Cambridge, vol. VIII, no. 3, *The Turner Group of Earthworks*. (Notes on the Skeletal Remains, by E. A. Hooton.)

[142] Bulletins of the Public Museum of the City of Milwaukee: *Tobacco Pipes and Smoking Customs of the American Indians*, vol. XVII, by G. A. West; *Copper, Its Mining and Use by the Aborigines of the Lake Superior Region*, vol. X, no. 1, by G. A. West.

The Stone Age in North America, two volumes, by W. K. Moorehead.

Stone Ornaments, by W. K. Moorehead. The Andover Press, Andover, Mass.

Bulletins of the New York State Museum, Albany: *The Archaeological History of New York*, part 1, by A. C. Parker; *Polished Stone Articles used by the New York Aborigines*, by W.M. Beauchamp.

Annual Archaeological Reports, published under the auspices of the Minister of Education of Ontario, Toronto, Ontario.

INDEX

Abnaki group, 228.

Abrading stones, 172–174

Adze blades, animal heads at top, 37, 40; beveled sides, 41; described and figured, 31–41; experiment in cutting log, 39, 40; hafting of double edged blades, 40; Nelson's account of use by Eskimo, 37; typical Algonquian forms, 144; use in Slave and Dogrib region, 37

Agriculture, see Gardens

Agriculture introduced by the old Algonquians, 88

Algonquian group in general, 119

Algonquian group, old, 81

American Academy of Arts and Sciences, 188–189

American Museum of Natural History, vii, 95, 102, 115

Amherst College Museum, vii, 74, 117, 188

Amulets, hollow, see Hollow amulets

Andover Archaeological Museum, vii, 36, 115, 222, 273

Antler artifacts, see Bone and Antler Implements, 213

Archaeological groups in New England, 2

Armouchiquois, 161

Arrowmakers' stones, 111, 112

Arrowmaking, Catlin's account, 222; account by S. T. Pope, 222

Arrowpoints, 131–134; antler flakers for chipping, 222; bone and antler, 220–222; copper and brass, 232, 233, 235, 237; method of chipping stone points, 222–224; triangular form, 131–132, 233; white quartz, 131

Artichoke cultivated in Indian gardens, 296

Artifacts from Ohio mounds like many in New England, 82

Artifacts, principal types, from pre-Algonquian graves in New England, 29

Axes, grooved, 136–141; distribution, 136; methods of hafting, 137, 140

Axes, grooveless, unknown to pre-Algonquians, 141; method of hafting, 141

Bags, see Textiles

Banner stones, see Pre-Algonquian Ceremonials

Bark dishes, buckets, and boxes, 295

Baskets, see Textiles

Bates, Arlo, collection from Maine shellheaps, 48, 100; account of Golden Cove heap, Vinalhaven, 204–205; examined and mapped seventy-seven heaps in Maine, 204; terracotta pipe from shellheap, 100; mentioned, 202, 204, 214, 224

Bates, Oric, 213

Beads, glass, 274–275; made by Indians, of European sheet copper and brass, 233–240; native copper, 83–84; seeds of Cornus 239; shell, 264–274

Beans raised in Indian gardens, 296

Beaver tooth chisels and knives, 224–226

Beothuk of Newfoundland, probably related to pre-Algonquian New England tribes, 11; canoes, 13; cooking vessels 13; emblems of mythology, 65; grave houses and burial places, 14, 15; habitations and store houses, 11, 13; physical appearance and clothing, 11; symbols, whale's tail, and others, 65–66; red ocher, 15

Bird amulets, 106–110; distribution, 106; effigies of similar form as aperture slides, 110, 305; principal types, 108; theories as to use, 108–110

Blodget, George, 18

Boat stones, see Hollow amulets

Bolton, R. P., 188

Bolus for taking waterfowl probably not used in New England, 47

Bone and antler artifacts, 213–227

Bone pins, 224, 227

Bowls of wood, 258–264

Bows, 133

Brass and copper (European), see Copper and brass

Brazier of bronze from grave at Ipswich, 232

Bucksport burial place, 16, 17

Bull, Norris L., vii, 68, 69, 86, 87, 206, 216

Burial places (Algonquian), at Beverly, 87; at East Windsor, 86; at Indian Ridge, Ipswich, 231–232; at Manchester, Mass., 241; at Orwell, 85; at Sandy Point, Penobscot R., 234; at Swanton, 85; at Vassalboro, 234. See also under Graves

Burial places (pre-Algonquian), at Bucksport, 16–20; at Ellsworth, 22–26; at Orland, 20–22; many others mentioned

312

Made in the USA
Middletown, DE
17 October 2023

40978395R00181